DOWN HOME GRIZZARD

DOWN HOME GRIZZARD

Three Bestselling Works
Complete in One Volume

DON'T FORGET TO CALL YOUR MAMA . . .
DOES A WILD BEAR CHIP IN THE WOODS?
SOUTHERN BY THE GRACE OF GOD

Lewis Grizzard

GALAHAD BOOKS
NEW YORK

First Galahad Books edition published in 1998.

Galahad Books
A division of BBS Publishing Corporation
386 Park Avenue South
New York, NY 10016

Galahad Books is a registered trademark of
BBS Publishing Corporation.

Published by arrangement with Longstreet Press, Inc.,
a subsidiary of Cox Newspapers, a division of Cox Enterprises, Inc.

Library of Congress Catalog Card Number: 98–72377

ISBN: 1-57866-038-6

Printed in the United States of America.

CONTENTS

DON'T FORGET TO CALL YOUR MAMA...
I WISH I COULD CALL MINE

To my precious aunts,
Una and Jessie, my other mamas

INTRODUCTION

MY MOTHER WAS the third child of Charles Bunyon and Willie Word of Carroll County, Georgia. They named her Christine.

Her two sisters, Una and Jessie, called her "Cricket." Her two brothers, Johnny and Dorsey, called her "Teenie." Nearly three decades of first graders she taught knew her as "Miss Christine."

I called her Mama.

I have no earthly reason why. I could have called her Mother, of course. Ma and Mom were also available. I knew a kid who went with Mommy. He was a sissy.

Mama just came out of my mouth one day and stuck for the nearly forty-three years she and I had together. Mama died October 1, 1989, two days short of her seventy-seventh birthday.

The primary cause of her death was a disease called scleroderma, Latin for "dead skin." It is a rare disease for which there is no known cure. Mama suffered with it for more than twenty-five years.

It attacked her esophagus, causing it to lose some of its ability to move food down to the stomach. Mama's first symptoms were heart-burn and indigestion. Then came frightening choking episodes.

Later her esophagus closed almost completely. Twice a month she had to undergo the torturous experience of swallowing a tube to reopen the passage.

What else happened was that Mama developed an eating disorder. She became *afraid* to eat. Food burned her insides. Food caused her to choke. Food became her enemy.

In the initial stage of her disease and subsequent disorder—when she was still able to work and do the cooking for her husband, my stepfather H.B.—she simply put food on the table for him and then took a plate for herself into the living room to eat alone.

She had to take small amounts and chew thoroughly. It could take her as long as forty-five minutes to finish one plate. She didn't want anybody else to see her eating. She was embarrassed by the effort it took.

Slowly she began to reject food altogether. She stopped cooking. She didn't want to see food, much less eat it. My stepfather began to cook for himself. Mama wouldn't even go into the kitchen anymore.

She lost weight. She lost her strength. The family went on a crusade to get food down her. We begged her to eat. We pleaded. Mama's favorite food had al-

4

ways been fried shrimp. I brought loads of it from Atlanta restaurants home to little Moreland, Georgia, forty miles to the southwest where Mama lived near her sisters and brother.

She wouldn't eat the fried shrimp. I tried strawberry ice cream. That had been her favorite flavor. She refused that, too.

Her eating became birdlike. A spoonful of this. A little soup. H.B. bought a blender. Her diet became all liquids.

And Mama went to bed in the back bedroom. She took a disability retirement from teaching. H.B. had to quit his job. She had become his full-time responsibility.

Mama became, for all practical purposes, a recluse. When I visited her, I had to go into that back bedroom and pull a chair next to her bed.

H.B. would walk in and ask, "Will you eat some dinner for me?"

"I'm not hungry," she would reply.

"Mama, you've got to eat," I would say.

"I can't, son, I just can't," was always her response to me.

H.B. never gave up. He'd bring a plate to her anyway. A little helping of mashed potatoes run through the blender. Maybe some applesauce. Meat was out of the question.

One evening I sat next to her bed, coaxing her to eat. H.B. had put her pitiful little plate on a tray. I got an idea.

"Mama, do you remember what you used to do when I was a little boy and you fed me?" I asked her.

She didn't recall.

"Well, I do," I said. "I can remember like it was

yesterday. You used to put me in your lap and take a spoonful of food and pretend the spoon was an airplane. You would fly the spoon around my head and make a noise like the plane's engine.

"Then you'd say, 'Okay, the plane is about to land. Open your mouth.' And then you would fly the spoon into my mouth. Do you remember that?"

She forced a little laugh and said, "Well, I guess I do."

"Okay, then," I continued. "Now, it's your turn."

I took a spoonful of food off her plate. I flew it around her. I made the sound of an airplane engine. The child, now the adult. The adult, now the child.

"Okay," I said, "the plane is about to land. Open your mouth."

She opened it slightly. I put the spoon between her lips. She took the food.

I got three or four more spoonfuls down her. Then she said, "Son, I'm tired of this game. Let's quit."

Eventually Mama became non-ambulatory. She wouldn't eat and wouldn't get up out of that bed anymore. The last fifteen years of her life, the only times she left that bed and that house were to go to Humana Hospital in the county seat of Newnan, six miles north of Moreland.

The hospitalizations became more frequent and became lengthy. Her malnutrition and that bed began to cause painful and serious side effects. She developed circulation problems and bedsores. She would become dehydrated. So, off to the hospital for fluids. Maybe a week or two weeks.

Then back home and back to that bed again until another trip to the hospital was necessary. The last fifteen years of Mama's life, she was hospitalized at

6

least a hundred times. The tops of her hands were permanently blue because of the number of IV's she had to endure.

Her limbs began to atrophy. Her feet became swollen and drawn. She developed painful arthritis in both her hands. They became swollen to twice their normal size.

At one point, Mama was brought to Atlanta and hospitalized. Doctors there examined her. Nothing could be done for the scleroderma. A psychiatrist was called in to see if he could help in getting her to eat. He failed.

So the vicious cycle continued. Month after month, year after year.

I saw her waste away. The robust, energetic mother who had raised me became a pitiful picture of agony and suffering.

H.B. never left her side. He administered her medicine. He bathed her. He clothed her. He came up with the best idea anybody, including the doctors, had during mother's last years.

He got her out of that back bedroom. He didn't get her out of bed, but he got her out of that dark place in the back and into the living room. He bought a hospital bed, moved the chair and table and lamp on one side of the living room, and put Mama's bed in that spot.

I think it kept her alive longer. Visitors used to go one at a time to that foreboding back bedroom. But in the living room, she could be around all her visitors at once. There was more of an opportunity to include her in conversations and family discussions.

The doctors think the scleroderma did reach Mama's brain in the last years of her life. She suf-

7

fered periods of disorientation. Her memory suffered.

Occasionally she would speak out and ask, "Where is my mama?"

Someone would answer, "Your mama's dead. She's been gone a long time."

That would send her into a long period of silence. Once, after having her question answered, she cried. A few minutes later, she said, "I sure did love my mama."

But I think the living room and the opportunity to be back in the family circle certainly gave her more periods of lucidity.

There were times she would laugh. There were times she actually would initiate conversations. These are precious memories.

My mother's legacy has so many parts to it. There is the sadness and pain and suffering. But there is also a lesson in survival.

Despite Mama's self-enforced period of reclusion, despite the hospitalizations and agonies I could not conceive, she fought for her life.

"She has an incredible will to live," one of her doctors told me. "She has fought harder than any patient I have ever had."

Once, during a visit to her hospital bed, when she was listed in serious condition with all sorts of problems and complications, I stood above her as she slept.

Suddenly she opened her eyes and looked at me and said, "Lord, I hate to die."

But she came back that time and she kept coming back, and who can know just how many times she turned back an insistent death.

Mama. She walked into a headwind most of her life. But she survived. She endured. She overcame. Her accomplishments were against odds that would have brought so many of the rest of us to our knees.

Mama. I loved her so. She loved me more.

Mama. This is my tribute to her.

1

MAMA MARRIED DADDY in 1942, and soon afterwards he was shipped out to Europe and World War
II.

He came back in 1945, and I was born in October,
1946, in Fort Benning, Georgia, where he was stationed. The army soon had us living in Tallahassee,
and then on to Camp Chafee, Arkansas, and to Fort
Myer, Virginia, Daddy's last stop before Korea.

Daddy survived a near massacre of his company
by the Chinese. He hid under the stacks of dead who
were his comrades and spent six weeks trying to get
back to the U.S. lines. He was listed as missing in
action for those six weeks.

Captain Lewis M. Grizzard, Sr., was a good soldier.
He had landed at Normandy on D-Day. He had

fought through France and on into Germany. He had won a Bronze Star for valor, a battlefield commission, and a Purple Heart.

But war can kill a man in more ways than one. Daddy couldn't handle much of anything after Korea. Alcohol. The Army. Money. He and my mother stopped sharing a bedroom a few months after he came home.

He drank too much. He cried all the time. He ran up huge telephone bills, calling drunk into the night. He ran away from the Army. He ran away from us. And one day Mama found herself in a house in Columbus, Georgia, her man gone for good, with bills she could never pay and with a little boy wondering what sort of demon had taken his daddy away and left his mother in tears.

The only place she knew to go was back to her parents. Charles Bunyon and Willie Word had moved to Moreland in Coweta County from the homeplace in Carroll County when he couldn't keep the farm going anymore. Their oldest daughter, Jessie, and her husband, Grover, had moved earlier from Carroll County to Moreland to work in the village knitting mill.

Mama Willie got a job in the hospital in Newnan taking care of new-borns. Daddy Bun helped out at the Atlanta and West Point Railroad station, became the janitor at the elementary school, and ran a little fruit stand on Highway 29 that went through Moreland.

He also was able to buy twelve acres of land in Moreland. He built Mama Willie a little white frame house on the land, which was across a dirt road called Camp Street from the Baptist Church.

Jessie and Grover then built a house next to Daddy Bun's and Mama Willie's on one portion of the land. Later, their youngest son, Dorsey, built his family a house on the same land.

On what was left of the plot, Daddy Bun planted corn, potatoes, okra, and tomatoes, and spring onions. Dorsey and Jessie's son, Scooter, helped with the planting and the plowing and the harvesting.

We moved to Moreland in the summer of 1953. There were four rooms and a bath in my grandparents house—a kitchen, a living room and two small bedrooms. The house was heated by a kerosene stove in the living room. There was an open back porch with two chairs and a swing for two on it.

Daddy Bun built himself a little shed to the back of the house. He kept his tools there. He stored his corn there. He planted strawberries and scuppernong vines behind the shed. He also planted fruit trees—apples, pears, plums, pomegranates and figs.

We also had a few chickens who produced fresh eggs every morning. Daddy Bun bought a little Briggs and Stratton garden tractor one year. Before he had plowed with a borrowed mule.

My grandmother and Aunt Jessie both loved flowers. Their yards were showplaces in the springtime. Between the house and my grandfather's shed was a weeping willow tree. On Sunday afternoons, the family would gather under the tree to make homemade ice cream or cut a watermelon.

I had lived in cities and on large army bases the first six years of my life. I'd never seen a mule. I'd never reached up and plucked a piece of fruit from a tree. I'd never been around that many country folk, and some of their ways were foreign to me at the outset of my life with my grandparents.

I didn't know some people still didn't have indoor toilet facilities. Several of the children I joined in the second grade at Moreland School still went to outhouses and bathed in water heated in a pot on the stove.

Some of the children in the second grade at Moreland came to school barefoot until Christmas, when they received shoes as gifts.

Some were out of school when cotton picking time came. I met sons and daughters of sawmillers, sharecroppers, dirt farmers, and mill hands.

By following my grandfather around, I learned new, amazing facts about things like guano, post hole diggers, garden snakes, .22 rifles, and how to put snuff on a yellow jacket sting to ease the pain and remove the stinger.

I learned what cotton poison smelled like, how to pour sorghum syrup onto your plate and then sop it up with a biscuit, and the number of each train that came up and down the A&WP tracks through Moreland.

I missed my Daddy and would never stop missing him. But Daddy Bun did his best to fill in.

Mama Willie read to me from the Bible, cooked three grand meals a day, and gave me my first responsibility. I was in charge of emptying the slop bucket. The slop bucket sat in the kitchen. There was no garbage disposal, of course, so every disposable thing left over in the kitchen went into the slop bucket. Egg shells. Coffee grounds. Chicken bones. Peelings. *Slop.*

I had to take the bucket out twice a day and pour

the slop into a hole that had been dug near my grandfather's shed. I emptied the slop and then covered it up with dirt to keep down the smell.

Mama got a job teaching first grade in Senoia, Georgia, a few miles out of Moreland, in the fall of 1953. She was paid $120 a month. She bought a used 1948 Chevrolet to go back and forth to school.

I'd had my own bedroom in our house in Columbus. In Moreland, there were only two beds. My grandparents slept in one. My mother and I slept in the other, which brings up my mother's hair.

Mama's hair, before it turned gray, was black. In pictures I saw of her as a young woman, she wore it cut short with curls to the left and right of her forehead.

My mother's hair nearly killed her in 1948. When we were living in Arkansas—I was two and retell this from later conversations—Mama began to lose her hair. She became quite alarmed, of course (she was in her mid-thirties at the time), and finally sought medical advice.

Doctors found she had an infection on her scalp. More of her hair fell out and the infection grew worse. Treatments were not working.

When local doctors felt they had no other solutions, they recommended that mother be sent to Walter Reed Hospital in Washington. It was her first trip aboard an airplane and she often talked of the fear she felt.

"They had me strapped down in a bed," she recalled. "There was no way to see out of the plane. I knew when we landed and I knew when we took off again. We must have made ten stops between Arkansas and Washington.

15

"I was sick and frightened out of my mind. I told God if he would get me down out of that thing, I'd never fly again."

Mama's plane landed safely. She never flew again.

My father and I took a train to Washington a week later when doctors reported her situation was worsening. Nobody could ascertain what had caused the scalp infection, and it raged on. I can vaguely remember my father taking me to visit Mama in Walter Reed. I can still see her completely bald, her scalp covered with ravaged flesh.

Mother's sister, Una, had come to Washington to take care of me during the crisis. She said I often told playmates that I had two mothers.

"I didn't think Cricket was going to make it," Una would tell me later.

And my mother told this story of a dream she had in the hospital.

"I dreamed I was standing at a beautiful lake," she began. "You were playing down near the water. There were many flowers and birds. Suddenly, I looked across the lake and I saw your daddy's mother, Miss Genie.

"She called to me and said, 'Don't come across. Your little boy is going to need you.'"

Mama, said the doctors, made a miracle recovery.

Daddy got a transfer to Fort Myer, and mother came home to the married officers' barracks. She wore bandages on her head for weeks.

Some of her hair eventually came back, but she had a permanent bald spot on the back of her head. As hair from other parts of her head grew longer, she was able to comb it back to cover the bald spot. But

Mama never got over the sensitivity she felt about her hair. She constantly complained about it.

"Una," she would say to her sister, "I just can't go out with my hair like this."

No trip to the beauty parlor ever satisfied her.

"Now, that looks nice, Cricket," Una would say to her after she returned.

"That woman just ruined my hair," Mama would reply.

Mama's hair became my prime symbol of security. I was a frightened little boy. If my Daddy could go away, why couldn't my mother?

The kerosene stove in the living room at my grandparents' barely heated the kitchen and the living room during the winter. So the bedrooms and the adjoining bath were closed off. Hitting those sheets at bedtime was like diving into a cold pond. Some nights, Mama even heated bricks on the kerosene stove and put them at the foot of our bed to warm us under the piles of homemade quilts.

I began holding my mother's hair when we slept together in my grandparents' home. I would cling to it all night. As long as I had her hair in my hand, she could not leave me.

I clutched her hair. I twirled it in my fingers. I pulled at it. I must have kept her awake many nights, but she never complained.

A few years ago, I received a letter from a female reader who said she had a problem. How familiar it sounded. She said she was divorced and worked days and went to school nights. She said she had a five-year-old boy who slept with her.

"He just won't keep his hands out of my hair at night," she explained. "I know he's frightened, but it's gotten to the point I can't sleep. I need to sleep to be able to get through the long day ahead of me. When I take his hand from my hair, he starts crying and won't stop until I let him put it back. I've tried to get him to sleep in a bed by himself, but he just won't do it. What can I do?"

I understood the woman's problem, but I also understood her son's. I wrote a column about the letter and told the woman, "One night all too soon, you will be lying in your bed, wishing you still had that little boy next to you, out of harm's way, with his hand in your hair. Enjoy it while you still can."

Mama married my stepfather, H.B. Atkinson, when I was ten. The ceremony was at the Moreland Methodist Church.

My grandfather was a deeply religious man, a hardshell Baptist. He believed in the practice of washing feet, which had been standard in his home church. He did not believe in a minister having notes. He thought the word should come from above, directly to the man behind the pulpit. Daddy Bun quit going to church in Moreland because they didn't wash feet and the preachers had been to seminaries.

"You don't learn to preach in no school," he said.

When he refused to enter the church for the marriage, I was drafted. I gave the bride away.

H.B. and I had a rough time of it in the first years of his marriage to Mama. The primary reason was that he took my place in Mama's bed, and I was banished to the couch in the living room. No more hair to hold onto.

I cried, pouted, held my breath, saw faces in the

window, banged on Mama's bedroom door, pitched various fits, and cursed the day Mama brought that man home to live.

That lasted until I was about twelve and H.B. and Mama built a house between Dorsey's and Jessie's, not far from Daddy Bun's and Mama Willie's in a spot cleared out from a portion of the cornfield.

I got my own bedroom and a radio from Sears Roebuck. After that, I spent my nights searching for clear channel sports broadcasts and was weaned off Mama's hair.

I picked up the practice again when I married. All three of my ex-wives have awakened many mornings with their hair in tangled knots. Currently I am living with a dog. He won't sleep with me.

2

MAMA COULD HAVE solved the current federal deficit problem. All the government would have had to do was hand over all its money to her and say, "We're spending more than we're taking in. Could you help us?"

Indeed, she could have. She would have cut the government's needs down to a bare minimum. No new interstate construction for awhile. She would have cut out all that $63 for a screwdriver business by the defense department and figured out a way to get a volume deal with a hardware store at $1.50 a screwdriver. Lawmakers, bureaucrats, and others on the federal payroll would have had to make do on less.

"We don't need anymore rocket ships to outer

21

space," Mama would have told NASA officials. "They've already messed up the weather as it is."

My mother's frugality knew no bounds. There were several reasons for that.

First, she had been raised by parents of modest means who believed that spending unwisely was as big a sin as working on Sunday and drinking.

Second, she lived through the Depression. It had made a remarkable impression on her.

"We made it because we grew our own food, and the family worked daylight to dark, and not a penny earned ever left for anything we could do without, and you'd be surprised at all the things people think they can't live without but can."

She mentioned, as items that fell into that category, a great many things that I thought were necessary for any semblance of a full life. There was candy, and milk shakes at Lee King's drug store in Newnan, and a new baseball, and money for movies and Cokes and popcorn.

As I got older, that list changed a bit. Replacements included a motor scooter, madras shirts, money to buy my girlfriend an ensemble of Evening in Paris perfume and powder for her birthday, a trip to Daytona Beach with older friends during the summer, and the Great Gold Cup Socks Controversy, which needs to be explained further and is the source of why, even today, I avoid socks whenever possible.

The dress for a pre-teen boy in the early fifties was quite simple: a white T-shirt, blue jeans, tennis shoes (which cost around five bucks, instead of what it costs to buy a Buick as it does today) and white socks.

22

Mama bought my socks at Judson Smith's warehouse south of Moreland. Judson sold cut-rate clothes, better known as "seconds," at a very cheap price.

Mama bought my white socks in a bundle, six pairs for less than a dollar. To be sure, Judson's socks were a little thin and tended to lose some of their elasticity at some point during their first wearing, but who could argue with six pairs of socks, of any description, for less than a dollar. I was quite happy with my socks.

Then my cousin Jimmy came to visit. Jimmy was the son of my Uncle Johnny, Mama's oldest brother. Uncle Johnny was a doctor. Jimmy took one look at my socks and laughed.

"Where did you get those stupid looking socks?" he asked.

"What's wrong with my socks?" I asked him back.

"They're too thin," he explained. "You need athletic socks like I'm wearing."

Cousin Jimmy showed me his socks. They were white, like mine, but they were, indeed, much thicker and made of an obvious better grade of material.

"How long have you had those socks?" I asked him.

"A year," he said. And their elasticity seemed completely intact.

"What do socks like that cost?" was my next question.

"Dollar a pair," he said.

I was astounded. *A dollar a pair.* It cost a dime to go to the Alamo Theatre in Newnan. A Big Orange belly washer, as they were called, was only a nickel.

23

After Jimmy left, I told Mama that my Judson's socks wouldn't do anymore. I needed athletic socks.

"What do they cost?" Mama asked me.

"Dollar a pair," I answered.

After being revived, she said, "I've never heard of such a thing."

The following Christmas, there was a pair of white athletic socks in my stocking. I wore them to school five days a week, to the envy of my friends, and then Mama washed them on the weekend.

After the eighth grade, Moreland children were bused six miles to Newnan High School. Newnan was a prosperous community. Cotton money. Old money. Doctors. Lawyers. Bankers. The Newnan boys laughed at my white socks.

"You don't wear those anymore," they said. "You need to get some Gold Cups."

Gold Cup socks, it turned out, came in different colors. The idea was to match your Gold Cups with your shirt.

"How much are Gold Cups?" I asked a Newnan classmate.

"Two dollars a pair," he answered.

Same story. Mama's eyes rolled back in her head and she lost consciousness temporarily. But for Christmas, there were two pairs of Gold Cups in my stocking—a light blue pair to go with my blue shirt and a yellow pair to go with my yellow shirt.

I made it all the way through high school on those two pairs of socks. Then I went off to the University of Georgia.

My freshman roommate, George Cobb, Jr., from the great metropolis of Greenville, South Carolina, saw my Gold Cups and laughed at them.

"You don't wear socks like that in college," he explained. "You need dark, over-the-calf socks."

Third verse: "How much do they cost?"

"Four dollars a pair."

That was it. I loved my mother, and I wasn't about to put her through the sock shock again. So in the autumn of 1964, I simply quit wearing socks. Sure, my feet got cold during the winter, but I endured the pain and actually started a trend that continues today.

Many Southern males no longer wear socks. Check them out the next time you're at a cocktail party at any Southern country club. Even Guccis with no socks. I've actually made a career of not wearing socks. Albert Einstein didn't wear socks, either, you can look it up.

Mama's frugality stemmed from two other sources. When Daddy left, she basically was penniless. I think of her in that Scarlett O'Hara scene where she says something like, "I'll never go hungry again." Mama would never again be caught in such a financial emergency. She would do without, scrimp and save, and an emergency would never find her empty of pocket again.

The main reason Mama was so frugal with money, however, was that she had determined that, no matter what, her child would get a college education.

I was an original Baby-Boomer, the first crop in '46. The catch phrase for Baby Boomer parents was, "I want you to have it better than I did."

"When the time comes for college," Mama would say, "I'll have the money."

Lord, the ends to which she went.

When the old '48 Chevy quit, Mama had to buy another car. She had fretted about it for months. Such a major financial commitment to buy another car. She drove the '48 until it just lay down one day, turned over on its roof and died, belching smoke and spitting oil.

Somebody told Mama she could get a great deal on a new '55 Chevy south of Moreland in Manchester, Georgia. So we went there in Uncle Dorsey's truck, and Mama haggled with the salesman until he was willing to make any sort of deal just to get her off the lot.

Mama bought a new 1955 Chevy. It was green. A rather God-awful shade, I might add. And we are speaking generic car here. Mama didn't want any chrome. Mama didn't want any whitewall tires. If Mama could have gotten by without a manifold, she'd have done it.

When the salesman asked, "Would you like for us to put in a radio?" Mama was adamant.

"Radio?" she asked incredulously. "What on earth do I need a radio in a car for?"

I don't think Mama bought one stitch of new clothes for herself while I was in high school. As much as she fretted over her hair, she might have made one visit to the beauty parlor a year.

Additionally, she was perhaps the greatest bargain shopper in history. She never bought a morsel of food without making certain it wasn't being sold cheaper at another grocery store.

She bought cut-rate ice "milk" instead of ice cream, and only about one carton of that a month. She got a deal on day-old bread at a local bakery. I never saw a bar of soap with writing on it until I was nearly grown. Mama always bought some plain off-brand, and until it had become almost microscopic due to repeated washing, she wouldn't buy another bar.

To squeeze a tube of the cheapest toothpaste anywhere other than the very bottom was an offense punishable by a severe tongue-lashing. Then there was the deal about toilet paper.

I will attempt to be as careful as I can here not to overstep the bounds of good taste by being overly descriptive, but the toilet-paper deal was a large part of my life as a child. Even as a small boy, I liked to use a lot of toilet paper. I had a special thing about toilet paper. I suppose it stemmed from all those stories older relatives told about the days when corn cobs were the forerunners of Charmin.

Also, I had visited homes of some of our rural relatives who still had outhouses, with a lot of wasps flying around, and the only available material for the final stage of a bowel movement was pages from an old Sears Roebuck catalog, which were quite harsh and lacked absorbent qualities.

I hated such situations and always tried to find a page without human forms pictured upon it out of respect. I normally searched for pages advertising garden hoses or kitchen appliances.

So when I was at home, I relished the fact that we had indoor plumbing and toilet paper, so gentle. I tended to use it in abundance. Consequently, we often violated Mama's one-roll-a-week rule, despite the fact that there were four of us living in my grandparents' house and three after she married H.B. and we moved into our own house.

"You're using too much toilet paper, young man," Mama would say to me.

I didn't want to talk about such a sensitive subject, even with my own mother. I would mutter or babble incoherently.

I might have avoided notice of my inability to use toilet paper in moderation, but I tended to use so much that I often clogged the toilet, which would send mother into a rage as well.

Mama put me on a strict toilet paper budget. "I just can't afford your toilet paper habit," she said.

I was allowed to roll off four individual toilet paper sheets twice. That was it. My own mother even demonstrated to me how to use one side of the paper ration, then turn it over to the other side and use it again.

Perhaps part of Mama's concern with the toilet paper usage had to do not only with saving money but also with her plan to instill in me the desire for higher education. Often she spoke about the fact that I could not expect to be a financial success in life unless I earned a college degree.

As I folded my little handful of toilet paper over to the other side to save money for my education, I often said to myself, "If I ever do get out of college and become a financial success, I'll use all the damn toilet paper I want."

I did get out of college and I did become somewhat of a financial success, and I have used so much toilet paper at various sittings that I have single-handedly kept several plumbing concerns in business.

Despite Mama's careful watch over the money, there were a few financial crises that came about.

H.B. was laid off from his job with a local gas company for a time, and we went on the highest state of alert during that period. I ate a lot of bologna sandwiches.

Still, Mama managed to save. She kept pennies and dimes in a jar. She kept shoe boxes of small bills in the far reaches of closets. She quit smoking. Not for her health, but because she could save if she dropped her quarter-a-day habit.

All for me. All for my education.

I was a good student in high school. To have made poor grades and risked college rejection would have hurt Mama more than if I had joined a gang that stole hubcaps and wore greasy, ducktail haircuts.

The day my acceptance from the University of Georgia came, Mama cried. The day I left home for Athens, she cried again.

After my freshman year, I began to work full-time at an Athens newspaper. I later won a scholarship. I was able to pay a lot of my college expenses on my own. But even then, Mama always worried if I had enough money.

"Have enough for books?" she would ask when I called home.

"You sure you can pay this quarter's tuition?" she would ask another time.

I worked in college mainly because I loved my chosen profession and figured out early that practical experience was the best teacher of the skills I sought. But Mama paid for my start, and if I had not chosen to work, she would have paid for it all.

In some ways, I think she even felt disappointed that I provided some of my own college costs.

I married at nineteen. It was a year later before my

29

bride and I were able to take a honeymoon. Mama paid for our four-day cruise to the Bahamas. She insisted. I still felt guilty. All that going without and now she was sending me to the Bahamas.

Mama gave me the down payment on our first house. She insisted again. Mama said, "Whatever I got, son, it's yours."

"Spend something on yourself," I would often tell her before she became bed-ridden and could have splurged a little on her own pleasures.

But she never did. And when I got into a position to begin giving back, it was too late.

3

I WANTED TO give Mama a lot of things. I felt I owed her for what she had done to get me educated and out into the world making a few dollars. And I loved her, too. And when I was a child, buying Mama a gift was the way I used to get out of trouble.

Until I was about ten, Mama tied my shoelaces each morning. I've never been very good with my hands, and I simply couldn't get the hang of tying my laces. (I was also a failure as a Boy Scout, but that's another story.)

So Mama tied my laces, but I was hard to please. I wanted them tied tightly, but not too tight, and anything short of perfect usually resulted in what was known as "pitching a fit," which basically consisted of crying and whining and stomping.

Whenever I would do something like that, say the morning of a school day, Mama would say, "Young man, I don't have time to deal with you now, but I'm going to wear the filling out of you this afternoon."

What a horrible thing. I had to sit in school all day worrying about getting my filling worn out when I got home.

So I devised a plan. I got a quarter a week allowance. I usually had at least fifteen cents in my pocket at any given time. On my way home to my thrashing, I would stop by Cureton and Cole's store near Moreland School and buy myself a Coke and a bar of candy, which came to a dime. Then I'd buy Mama a nickel's worth of something like fig newtons.

When Mama came home from school, I would run and jump into her arms and say, "Mama, I love you so much. Look at what I bought you out of my allowance." This naturally would put her in a forgiving mood, and I wouldn't get my punishment. Not only that, I'd also usually get to eat the fig newtons.

Once Mama got sick, it became harder and harder to buy her anything. She wanted a larger television in the living room because she couldn't see the old one. So I bought her a larger television.

Mama wouldn't let me put an air conditioner in the house, but she would take a ceiling fan in the living room.

I bought her a portable phone to make it easier for her to talk to callers from her living room bed.

Her circulation became very poor. She suffered from arthritis. I had the bright idea to rebuild the little bathroom of her house and put in a Jacuzzi. I thought it might help her circulation and ease some of her pain.

That suggestion went like this:

"How about a Jacuzzi?"

"A what?"

"You'd love it. A Jacuzzi is a big tub, and you fill it with hot water and there are all these jets shooting out water and you sit in there and it's very relaxing. It would be great for your arthritis."

"I never heard of such a thing."

"What we could do is knock out a wall and extend the bathroom."

"I don't want a bunch of carpenters sawing and hammering and tracking mud into the house. Don't get me a bacuzzi."

"Jacuzzi."

"However you say it, I don't want one."

So what else can you do for your invalid mother? I'd have given her a trip anywhere in the world. Obviously that wasn't possible. Even if Mama had been healthy, she wouldn't have flown. I would have built her a new house, but she would have said, "There's nothing wrong with the house I'm in."

What I did was buy Mama a lot of gowns. I bought silk ones and cotton ones. I bought them plain. I bought them in bright colors. I bought them with floral patterns.

"Oh, son," she would reply when I opened a box and pulled out a new gown and handed it to her in her bed, "this sure is a pretty gown, but you didn't need to spend the money on me."

We had only one real Christmas together, my mother, my father and I. Only one Christmas when we were actually in our own house with coffee and cake left out for Santa, with an excited five-year-old awakening to a pair of plastic cowboy pistols, a straw hat, and an autographed picture of Hopalong Cassidy.

My first Christmas I was only a couple of months old, and that doesn't count. Then we were traveling around for a couple of years. The Army does that to you. Then there was Korea. And then we had that one Christmas together before whatever demons my father brought back from Korea sent him to roaming for good.

That one and only Christmas together, my father had duty until noon on Christmas eve. I waited for him at the screen door, sitting and staring until that blue Hudson—"The Blue Goose," as my father called it—pulled into the driveway. I ran out and jumped into his arms.

"Ready for Santa?" he asked.

"I've been ready since August," I shouted.

But before we could settle in for our Christmas, my father had to take care of a problem. He had found this family—the man out of work, in need of a shave and a haircut, and his wife crying because her babies were hungry. My father, whatever else he was, was a giving man. He couldn't stand to have when others didn't.

"They're flat on their butts and it's Christmas," I remember him saying to my mother. "Nobody deserves that."

So he somehow found a barber willing to leave home on Christmas eve, and he took the old man in for a shave and a haircut. Then he bought the family groceries. Sacks and sacks of groceries. He bought toys for the kids, of which there was a house full. The poor are often fruitful.

We didn't leave them until dusk. The old man and the woman thanked us, and the kids watched us with wondering eyes.

As we drove away in "The Blue Goose," my father broke down and cried. My mother cried, too. I cried because they were crying.

We all slept together that night and cried ourselves to sleep. Next morning, I had my pistols and my hat and my picture of Hopalong Cassidy.

Maybe the three of us had only one real Christmas together—my father had left by the time the next one rolled around—but it was a Christmas a man can carry around for a lifetime.

Each year at Christmas, with my father long since in his grave, I thank God that one is mine to remember.

Mama was never big on Christmas after that. I think she liked Christmas okay, but even before she got sick, she tried to keep our Christmas celebrations with H.B. in Moreland to a minimum.

That usually started with an early-December pronouncement that went, "I don't think we'll have a big tree this year."

We *never* had a big tree. We started with a small tree and worked down, and finally Mama bought an artificial Christmas tree that sat on the living room coffee table. It was more of a Christmas plant than a tree.

One Christmas, H.B. decided that since all we had was a table tree, he would string lights across the front of the house.

Mama was against that idea from the start. "I don't know why you'd waste money on lights," she told H.B. "We're so far off the road nobody is going to see them in the first place, and we've already got a tree."

H.B. would not be denied, and I was in his camp. There was no opportunity for me to throw tinsel on a tree, spray it with that snowy-looking substance that came in an aerosol can, or get on a chair to put the star on top of the tree. So stringing lights across the front of the house seemed a grand yule adventure to me.

We went out there one cold December evening and carefully tacked several strings of Christmas lights onto the front of the house. Mama remained inside worrying about how much the lights had cost.

The big moment came. The lights were up. H.B. sent me into the house to turn on the juice for the lights. I flicked the switch. There was a hideous popping sound. Not only did the Christmas lights not come on, but every light inside the house went off in a massive blowing of fuses.

We had to eat by candlelight. The next morning, H.B. went out and took the lights down from the front of the house.

The following year, he suggested we put lights on a tree in the front yard. Mama said, "Don't you go near that tree with Christmas lights."

Mama's first-graders gave her a poinsettia that year. We made do with that and the toy tree she brought out from the back of some distant closet from the Christmas before.

This is not to say we didn't have happy Christmases. We just didn't fall victim to any excesses. And most years, my Christmas wishes came true.

I got an air rifle when I was ten, despite the eternal parental fear that any child with an air rifle would shoot out at least one eye within an hour of taking possession of it.

When I asked for an air rifle, Mama said, "Didn't you hear about the little boy in Hogansville? He got an air rifle and he was running with it and fell down and the rifle went off and shot out one of his eyes."

It was the old "little boy in Hogansville" trick. Mama saw me running through the yard with a sharp stick once. She said, "Don't run with that stick. A little boy in Hogansville was running with a stick and he fell down and put out one of his eyes."

Another time, I was going swimming with some friends at a local farm pond. "You be careful," Mama said. "A little boy in Hogansville was swimming in a pond and he stepped off into a deep hole and drowned."

No wonder. The kid was blind.

Still, Mama got me the air rifle and I managed not to shoot out an eye. I did shoot a bird once, however. I think it was a sparrow. The bird fell out of the tree and writhed in agony on the ground. It proceeded to die right in front of my eyes.

I was just playing around with my air rifle. I didn't actually mean to kill the bird. I picked up the dead bird, got a shovel from Daddy Bun's shed and dug a hole near the scuppernong vines and buried it.

I was heartbroken and sick and scared. Later, I told Mama what I had done and asked her, "Do you think I can still get into heaven?"

"God forgives," she assured me.

I sort of lost interest in my air rifle after that incident. The following year I wanted a radio. Mama ordered me one from Sears Roebuck. Another year, I asked for a bat, a ball and a glove. I got those as well.

There were only two Christmases I failed to get what was at the top of my list.

When I was twelve, I wanted a Flexy Racer. A Flexy Racer, the fore-runner of the skateboard, was a wondrous instrument.

What you did was lie down stomach first on a Flexy Racer, which had four sets of wheels underneath it. There was a handle on each side you could turn in order to move right or left. You got on your Flexy Racer in front of the Methodist Church on the Moreland square and aimed it toward the railroad tracks, located down the paved hill.

My friend John Cureton had a Flexy Racer. He allowed me a turn or two down the hill. I was the wind.

When I asked Mama for a Flexy Racer for Christmas, she had me describe it to her. I mentioned the part about being the wind, soaring down the hill from the church towards the railroad tracks. I shouldn't have done that.

"What if you couldn't stop and a train was coming?" she asked.

"This hasn't got anything to do with a little boy from Hogansville, does it?" I asked Mama. I didn't get a Flexy Racer.

When I was fourteen, I asked for a motor scooter. Dudley Stamps, my friend, had a motor scooter. I wanted my own desperately.

"You're not getting a motor scooter," Mama said.

"Why?" I asked.

"They're too dangerous," she answered.

"But Dudley's got one," I countered.

"And Dudley will probably fall off that thing and put out one of his eyes, too," she said.

I got a desk for my bedroom and some underwear and pajamas that year.

When Mama became sick, I think she actually dreaded Christmas. She couldn't get out of the house to shop for presents for the family, and that made her feel guilty. Sometime around Thanksgiving, she would look up from her bed and say to me, "Son, don't get me anything for Christmas this year. I can't get to town to get you anything."

"I don't expect that, Mama," I would reply, "but I want to get you something."

"I just don't want to be any trouble, son."

"It's no trouble, Mama. I want to get you something. What do you need?"

"I can't think of a thing."

"What about some new gowns?"

"I'll never wear the ones you've already given me."

"Need any warm house shoes? I know your feet get cold."

"I've already got some."

"How about a warm sweater?"

"You gave me one for my birthday. Why don't you take the money and buy yourself something. Do you have a warm coat?"

"Three of them."

"What about a hat?"

"I don't wear hats, Mama."

"Well, how do you keep your head warm?"

"My head doesn't get cold."

"Have you got enough cover for your bed?"

"Plenty, Mama. What if I just surprise you with something?"

"If that's what you want to do. I just don't want to put you to any trouble."

"No trouble."

One year I gave her a down blanket with ducks on it. She liked the ducks.

Another Christmas I gave her a cassette player and some gospel and country tapes, Mama's kind of music. And the last Christmas she was alive, I couldn't think of anything else to buy her, so I bought another gown, a pretty blue one.

"That's the prettiest gown I've ever seen," Mama had said. Nine months later, we buried her in it.

Rarely does anyone give up a parent or a mate or a brother or sister or a friend without regret. I have my own when it comes to Mama.

I am ashamed of it but will tell of it. Perhaps others can avoid the same mistake.

What Mama always wanted most, what cost the least and meant the most, was a simple phone call. I didn't call Mama enough. I called her, but not enough. I tried to remember to call at least twice a week, but I'd be travelling or get caught up in some project, and I'd just plain forget.

It was difficult talking to Mama on the phone the last several years of her life. Once I said, "Mama, how are you?" and she answered, "I guess I'm doing *pretty* good." It was hard to get any lengthy dialogue going after that.

There were times I even felt like it was hard on Mama to get a telephone call. She had lost some of her hearing and had to ask me to repeat most everything I said. She often would put the receiver at her mouth and would complain to H.B., "I can't hear Lewis."

He would turn it around for her. What she always

40

was interested to hear was when I was coming to visit her.

"Mama," I'd say, "I'll be down to see you a week from Monday."

"A week from when, son?"

"Monday, Mama. Anything you need me to bring you?"

"I can't think of a thing."

"Anything you need to talk to me about?"

"Well, I guess not."

"I love you, Mama."

"I love you, too, Sugar."

"Let me talk to H.B. before I go."

"Okay."

"Bye, Mama."

"Bye, son."

That was about it for the last years of her life.

Still, when I would visit Mama, she would always tell me as I left, "Don't forget to call me. I just like hearing your voice."

H.B. chastised me at times when I'd go a week or two without calling. "She always seems to sleep better after she hears from you," he said.

Yeah, I regret not calling her more. There's some guilt that will probably remain with me. It's such a simple little thing to do. Call your Mama. Even if you talk for just thirty seconds, she enjoys it. She might even *live* for it.

A true story:

I was at Point Clear, Alabama, speaking to a group of South Central Bell executives. At dinner, some of us were swapping stories about the Bear. Alabama's late, great football coach, Bear Bryant.

A gentleman who handled the advertising account

41

for South Central Bell was recalling when Bryant was hired to do commercials for his South Central Bell account.

"What the Bear was supposed to say at the end of the commercial was, 'Call yo' Mama,' as only he could say it.

"But we were shooting, and he just ad-libbed a line. He said, 'Call yo' mama.' And then he added, 'I wish I could call mine.'

"We never would have asked him to do something like that, but it worked out perfectly."

Another of the Bell executives carried the story further.

"Soon after the commercial began running," he said, "my secretary came in and said there was a customer on the line that just had to talk to me. I was pretty busy, but I figured if she was being that persistent, I should talk to her.

"When I got her on the phone, she asked, 'Are you the one responsible for the Bear Bryant commercial on television?'

"I sort of wanted to ask her how she liked it before I took responsibility for it. But I said, 'Is there any problem?'

"She said, 'Gracious, no. But I just wanted to tell you a story: My husband and I were sitting watching television the other night, and we saw that commercial for the first time. We were very moved when Coach Bryant said, "I wish I could call mine."

" 'I got right up and called my own mother, and we chatted for a few minutes. I forget to call her sometimes, and she gets worried about me.

" 'My husband's mother is still alive, too. I asked him why didn't he call his mother, and he went straight to the phone and called her. They must have talked for forty-five minutes. I'd never known him to stay on the line with anybody forty-five minutes, much less his mother.

" 'They talked about old times, and he told her how much he loved her.'

"I said to the woman," the executive continued, "that her story was really heartwarming and I appreciated her passing it on.

"She said, 'You haven't heard all the story yet. Less than an hour after my husband hung up from talking to his mother, she died. He never would have had that conversation with his mother if it hadn't been for Coach Bryant's commercial.' "

I don't have to hit you over the head with the message, do I?

4

I NEVER HAD Mama as a teacher. I missed her by two years. I attended first grade at Rosemont Elementary School in Columbus. Daddy was stationed at nearby Fort Benning.

I was in Moreland School for the second grade. What I recall most vividly about my first day at Moreland was that a couple of ruffians, the brothers Garfield, made a small bomb out of gunpowder and set it off on a window ledge in the second grade room as our teacher, Mrs. Bowers, was welcoming us to her class.

The bomb blew out several windows, sent Mrs. Bowers screaming to the principal's office, and I, along with several other students, wet my pants.

One of the Garfields was ten, having failed first

grade twice, and the other one was nine. It took him only two years to get out of first grade.

The principal suspended the Garfields from school for a week, which is what they wanted and why they set off the bomb in the first place. More about the Garfields and their terroristic activities later.

Mama's first job teaching after Daddy split was the first grade position at Senoia School, ten miles west of Moreland.

The following year, however, the first grade job came open in Moreland and Mama filled it. The school was in walking distance of my grandparents' house. That was a lot easier on Mama. She would teach first grade there for two more decades.

Having your own mother as a member of your school's faculty had a couple of advantages. One, I could go by her room on my way home each afternoon and ask for a few coins to spend on treats at Cureton and Cole's store.

A Coke was a nickel. So was a Zagnut candy bar. There were two benches outside the store. My friends and I would drink our Cokes and eat our candy and speak of the day's affairs and hope we could finish both before one of the Garfield brothers showed up and took them away from us.

Another advantage had to do with recess. We took one in the morning and one in the afternoon. Each class would take part in some sort of physical activity, accompanied by their teacher. The fact that my mother was on the playground made it less likely that one of the Garfields, or any other number of boys who could beat me up, would do so. I even had a distinct advantage in a boys' playground game called Squirrel. Whoever invented Squirrel was a sick person. And simple-minded. You ran up and grabbed somebody in the gonads, squeezed and said, "Squirrel! Grab the nuts and run!"

The problem with Squirrel was that you couldn't simply say, "Thanks, but I'd rather not play today." If a Squirrel game broke out on the playground, you were in it.

One day, somebody started Squirrel. I had managed to avoid a few earlier attempts at my crotch with some artful dodging and even showed several flashes of flanker speed. It's amazing how much faster you can run if you're fleeing an individual who wants to inflict serious pain by squeezing your testicles.

I was never, ever a pursuer in a Squirrel game. First, I thought the game was a little odd. Even then I knew there was something, well, not exactly right about grabbing at another boy's crotch. I wasn't even aware of the possibilities as they applied to girls at that point.

Also, I didn't want to introduce the revenge element in the game. So I get somebody at Squirrel. It would make them just that more determined to get me back.

On this particular day, I was fairly sure the recess bell would save me from any direct hits, what with my speed and footwork. But then two of my classmates came at me. Could I avoid them both?

Then I heard one of them say, "Aw, leave him alone. He'll go over to where the first graders are and cry to his Mama and she'll send us to the principal."

I was happily saved from the horrid fate that likely had awaited me, but that also brings up one of the disadvantages of having your mother teach at your school.

I sort of got a reputation as a "Mama's boy" amongst some of the older boys, a horrid fate in its own right.

First, there was the business about the fact that my father wasn't around. Divorce was a rare thing in those days.

"Where's your daddy?" was a question I got often.

Mama had said to tell them that he had been a good soldier but that he was sick.

Then the word got out that I was still sleeping with my mother, and then somebody else leaked the fact that I was eight years old and my mother was still tying my shoes. (Hey, I did finally learn when I was nine. I never could do much with mechanical things.)

"Mama's boys" were supposed to be weak, easily frightened, and spoiled. The fact is that I was all three and still am to a degree. But I wasn't what else was supposed to go along with being a Mama's boy— a sissy.

I was no sissy. The quickest way to figure out whether or not a boy was a sissy was to watch him throw a baseball. If he threw it with too much wrist and not enough extension of the arm, that was all you needed. The child was a sissy. Other sissy characteristics were wearing rubber overshoes on a rainy day, not wearing blue jeans and white T-shirt or white socks with tennis shoes, not belonging to the Boy Scouts, and failing to know the participants in the last World Series.

Well, none of that applied to me. I had a wicked curve ball by the time I was ten. I once struck out all eighteen batters in a six-inning church-sponsored boys baseball league. By the time I was twelve, I had learned to scuff the ball so it would curve even more and how to grab my own crotch on occasion and spit through my teeth like Reggie Jackson.

I never wore rubber overshoes. I didn't even own a pair. I wore the uniform, and I can still tell you the starting lineup of the 1956 Brooklyn Dodgers, the victims of Yankee pitcher Don Larsen's perfect game in the World Series that year.

But we were talking about having your mother teaching in your school. The teachers expected more of you, of course. They figured any child of a teacher was naturally smarter than any child of, say, a welder or a truck driver. That's not always true, but it was accepted as fact.

I got a lot of, "Your mother certainly wouldn't be happy if she knew you turned in such sloppy work."

There was also the matter of classroom conduct. Alice McTavish, the biggest girl in my class and one of the biggest in five counties, sat behind me in the third grade. Alice was an aggressive child. She could also beat up most of the boys her age, including me.

One morning during arithmetic class, she began thumping my ears from behind. At first I decided not to retaliate and risk angering Alice, who would then proceed to thrash me, mother on the playground at recess or not.

But the ear thumping got to me after a while, so I turned around in my desk and tried to bonk Alice on the head with my fist.

Unfortunately, the teacher, who hadn't seen the provoking ear thumping episodes, saw my swing, which had missed, by the way. Alice caught it with a forearm.

"I cannot believe you, the son of a teacher," she admonished me, "would attempt to hit a girl right in the middle of class."

I tried to explain, but the teacher wouldn't listen.

"I'm going to talk this over with your mother at faculty meeting this afternoon," she went on.

Great.

At the dinner table that evening, Mama said to me, "I've never been so embarrassed in my entire life as I was when your teacher told the entire faculty what you did in class today."

"Mama," I began, "Alice isn't like other girls. She's bigger than this house."

"Probably just a gland disorder," Mama said, "and you had no business trying to hit her."

I tried to get in a few more words regarding how my swing, which never had a chance of landing, was provoked. Mama wouldn't hear of it and said that if she ever heard of me doing anything like that again, my punishment would be swift and harsh.

A few weeks later, however, Alice broke Alvin Bates' nose when he asked her if she had won any prizes at the hog show at the county fair, and Mama said, "I guess Alice is a rather stout girl for her age."

Having a mother around to protect you on the playground certainly is a benefit, but there was one occasion when I had to beg her not to report a rather painful incident to the principal.

I had managed to stay unmarked by the Garfield Brothers, other than a few punches to my arms and the day the elder, Frankie, got me in a headlock and rammed my head into the tether-ball pole, but

Frankie had been just kidding around. When Frankie was serious about hurting someone, he did not let them go until they were bleeding, exhibiting large knots and bruises, and groveling around on the ground screaming pitifully for mercy.

In the fifth grade, I finally got mine. I had ridden my bike to school. Afterward, I was riding down the path that led away from the school on my way to Cureton and Cole's store.

It was a very narrow path, and at the end of it was a deep ditch that forced a hard left turn. A seventh grader named Billy Gaines was in front of me, walking quite slowly. There wasn't room to pass him on my bike, and besides, something like that might be deemed a lack of respect for somebody two years older than me and Billy Gaines might have taken offense and belted me.

The problem arose when Frankie Garfield walked up behind me and my bicycle. "Get that damn bicycle out of my way. I'm in a hurry," Frankie demanded.

I wanted to get my damn bicycle out of his way, but Billy Gaines was in my way.

I decided if Billy Gaines beat me up for passing him, it would be better than Frankie Garfield beating me up for not getting out of his damn way.

So I took Billy on his left and began pedaling as fast as I could. Unfortunately, I apparently had not acted as quickly as Frankie had wanted me to.

He ran behind me and my bicycle. When I got to the end of the path and the deep ditch in front of it, I had to slow down to make the hard left-hand turn.

The moment I slowed, Frankie lifted up the back of

my bicycle and flipped it, with me astride it, into the deep ditch.

At mid-flip, I came off my bicycle seat and landed nose first in the ditch. My bicycle then landed on top of me. Frankie walked into the ditch after me, but after seeing my nose bleeding and my face scratched and a giant knot on my forehead, he figured the job was done and proceeded on to the store to forcibly detach other children from their Cokes and candy bars.

My bicycle wasn't damaged nearly as much as I was. Except for a small dent in the front fender, it came out of the experience quite well. I rode my bike home as fast as I could.

My mother wasn't home from school yet, my grandmother was working in her flowers, and my grandfather was plowing.

I went into the bathroom and took a survey of the damage to my face and head. I looked like I'd been in an ax fight and finished fourth.

I tried to wash away as much mud and blood as I could. I even tried to press the knot on my head flat. That didn't work.

My fear was this: Mama sees me in this condition and wants to know under what circumstances I had received such ghastly wounds.

I rarely lied to Mama. Actually, I always lied when I thought telling the truth wasn't a good idea. But Mama usually unveiled the truth eventually.

She finally would force it out of me that I had fallen victim to a Garfield, and the following day at school she would tell the principal. The principal would then call Frankie into his office. He would ask the other male on the faculty to come into the office, too. Even a grown man didn't want to have to deal with even just one Garfield alone.

He would then suspend Frankie from school for a week. That would delight Frankie, but he would also be angry that I had ratted on him to my mother, so the first opportunity he got, he would pummel me further. On top of that, he would probably tell his brother, David (a.k.a. "Killer"), and he would also take his turn at bruising my person.

I went outside and avoided Mama until dinner time.

"What happened to your face?" she asked. "And that knot. How did you get that knot on your head?"

"Bicycle accident," I said.

"You weren't trying to ride and not hold to the handle bars were you? A little boy in Hogansville was doing that, fell off his bike and a stick stuck in his eye and now he's half-blind."

"I was riding down the path after school and I thought I was farther away from the ditch than I really was, and so I went too far before I tried to turn left and I rode my bike into the ditch and I fell on my nose and head."

Not bad.

"It was one of those Garfields, wasn't it?" Mother said.

How does she always know these things?

Still, I stuck to my story.

"It wasn't a Garfield, Mama," I said.

"Are you sure?"

"Sure I'm sure."

What gave me away when I lied to Mama? Did I do something funny with my mouth? Was I unable to look her directly in the eyes when I answered one of her interrogatives?

"Did one of those boys hit you?" she asked.

"No ma'am," I said. Well, he didn't *hit* me. At that point, I was hoping she didn't use the verbs "flip" or "push" or "shove" next.

"You've been down that path hundreds of times," she went on. "I just don't think you'd drive your bicycle directly into that ditch. Now, you tell me what really happened this instant."

I told her.

"I'll see Frankie Garfield in the principal's office in the morning," she said. "I'm tired of those boys bullying you children around. They're too old to be with you kids anyway."

Just as I thought.

"Mama," I started, "please don't tell Mr. Killingsworth (our principal). He'll call Frankie in and then Frankie will beat me up again, this time worse."

"I have to report something like this to the principal. You're hurt badly. He could have broken some bones."

"He will if you tell the principal," I said.

Mama turned thoughtful.

"Okay," she said, "I won't tell the principal, but I'm going to have a talk with Frankie myself."

"He'll still kill me," I said.

Mama wasn't to be denied. She took me into the bathroom and put something that burned terribly on the cuts on my face, and she put a cold washcloth on my knot and suggested it would be gone by morning.

"I'll have four more by tomorrow afternoon," I said.

"No, you won't," she said.

The fact that I was still alive by the time school ended surprised me greatly. I figured I'd be dead by lunchtime anyway. I had spent the morning daydreaming about what my funeral would be like. There would be lots of crying, of course, and they'd probably sing "Precious Memories." It was a terrible thing to think about, dying. I wondered if there would be baseball in heaven. I was certain that's where I would go. The only Commandment I'd breached at that point in my life, besides killing that bird with my air rifle, was that I had coveted the electric train Bobby Entrekin had received for Christmas. It blew real smoke. Mine didn't.

That didn't seem like much of a sin, really, when you considered that Bobby Entrekin also had his own football helmet and I didn't. I figured God probably would even overlook that one little transgression as he flipped through my list of good deeds, like dutifully taking out the slop bucket and actually making an attempt on cutting back on the toilet paper I used.

When school was over, I didn't even ride my bicycle down the path. I passed up the afternoon trip to the store, too. I took another route home and went into the bedroom and got under the bed. If the Garfields came looking for me at home, maybe they wouldn't think to look under the bed.

Forty-five minutes after I got home, I heard Mama come in the door. She walked in the bedroom and asked for me.

"I'm under the bed, Mama," I said.

"Well, come out from under there," she said. "Frankie Garfield isn't going to hurt you."

Mama called the sheriff. That's what had to have

happened. She had called the sheriff and he had come to get Frankie, as well as his brother, and had taken them to jail. I would be safe until they were released. I began to wonder how long a sentence you got for throwing somebody and his bicycle into a ditch.

Mama said to come into the living room and sit down. She had something to tell me.

"Before I talked to Frankie," she said, "I pulled his records. Do you know he doesn't live with his daddy or his mama?"

I didn't know that.

"His aunt is raising both those children alone. His daddy is dead and they don't know where his mama is. I talked to the other teachers, and they said before his mama left, she used to beat those boys. They simply haven't known much love in their lives, and that's why they have turned out the way they have.

"They haven't had any spending money for Cokes and candy like you have. They haven't been taken to Sunday School or church. I doubt they've even been in a picture show in their entire lives. All they know is that they have to fight for everything they get. I really feel sorry for them."

This wasn't exactly what I had expected.

"Do you know what I did?" Mama asked.

I had the feeling that whatever she did hadn't involved the sheriff.

"I had Frankie come down to my room during recess, and I asked him if he would help me put up the children's blocks and crayons and clay from the morning. I told him if he did, I'd give him a quarter and he and his brother could go to the store after school and spend it on whatever they wanted.

"He was as nice and co-operative as he could be. So I told him if he would come back and help me tomorrow, I'd take him and his brother and you to the show in Newnan Saturday. I'd never seen a boy smile quite that much. He ran and got his brother and brought him back to the room.

" 'Miss Christine says she's going to take us to the picture show Saturday. Tell him, Miss Christine. Tell him.'

"I said, 'I told Frankie if he would help me in the room tomorrow, I'd take you both and Lewis to the show in Newnan. Do you like that?'

"He said, just as polite as he could, 'Yes ma'am.' Those were the two happiest boys I've ever seen leave that room."

Obviously, the ditch incident of the previous day had damaged my hearing. Me going to the picture show in Newnan with the Garfields? Me, alone with the Garfields, in a darkened theatre sitting through a Flash Gordon serial, a cartoon and a Randolph Scott feature? I wouldn't make it to the first horse chase scene.

I protested. "I'm not going," I said.

"Yes, you are," Mama said. "The Bible tells us, 'Love thy enemies.' "

"The Bible also says, 'Thou shalt not kill.' "

"Those boys just need some love and attention," Mama replied.

Saturday morning, we drove to where the Garfield brothers lived to pick them up. Where they lived was what had formerly been a house. At this point, it might have been classified as a shelter but obviously not a very good one. There were windows broken out on one side. One Garfield brother probably had thrown the other through the window. Or they had been practicing at home for bombing the school window.

Mama honked the horn on the '55 Chevy. A woman appeared on the front porch of the house. She was in a tattered house coat. Her hair was multi-directional.

"Won't you come in, Miss Christine?" the woman said to Mama. "I'm Frankie and David's aunt, Pearl."

Mama got out of her car. I stayed put. As Mama approached the porch, Frankie and David came out of the house. They seemed to be uncharacteristically well-scrubbed.

I heard the Garfield's Aunt Pearl say to Mama, "I shore do appreciate you doin' this for the boys. I ain't got no car to take 'em no where."

Mama said, "Frankie worked real hard for me last week at school, and I know David will help me, too. Little boys like to go to the picture show."

Frankie and David got into the back seat of Mama's car. They were wearing old clothes, but they were clean and fairly wrinkle-free. Both had their hair combed. I'd never seen anything like that on a Garfield before. Even I could sense their anticipation of the adventure to Newnan and the picture show.

As we drove away from the house, Mama said, "Son, Frankie's got something he wants to say to you."

I turned around. Frankie turned his eyes downward. I also sensed a certain embarrassment on his part, almost a shyness. Was this the same Frankie Garfield, the Mengele of the playground? Frankie mumbled something I couldn't understand.

"Speak up," Mama said to him.

Still unable to meet my eyes, he said, "I'm sorry I threw you and your bicycle in the ditch."

I couldn't believe what I was hearing. Frankie Garfield apologizing to me? He hadn't even used the modifier "damn" when he referred to my bicycle.

"And what else Frankie?" Mama asked.

"I promise not to hurt anybody at school again," he said.

My God. A miracle. Dillinger goes straight. Attila the Hun agrees to stop raping and pillaging.

"What do you say, son?" Mama asked me.

What I wanted to say was, "Hitler promised a lot of stuff, too." But I didn't. As a matter of fact, I was too stunned to say anything.

Mama finally said, "Tell Frankie you appreciate his apology."

"I appreciate your apology," I said to the front window. I was afraid to turn around and look at Frankie. I was afraid I would see him with his tongue stuck out at me, or see him doing the old slit-the-throat sign. I would believe all this when the Garfields could go an entire week without inflicting physical harm.

"You're not going to be rough on the boys at school either, are you, David?" Mama asked.

"Yes ma'am." said David. "I mean, no ma'am."

We rode on to Newnan in silence. What if this were nothing more than a clever ruse? What if the Garfields, once they got into the movie, decided to do something to me? Like hit me and take away my popcorn and Coke. What if they decided to attack the entire audience? What if they had brought a gunpowder bomb with them?

Mama stopped the car in front of the Alamo theatre. She gave each of us a quarter. It cost a dime to get into the movie. That left fifteen cents for a nickel Coke, nickel bag of popcorn, and some nickel candy. I looked at Mama. My eyes said to her, "Don't make me get out of this car."

"Go ahead," she said. "Everything will be okay."

What the Garfields did was ignore me. They were so mesmerized by the fact that they actually were at the picture show with a Coke, popcorn, and candy in their hands that they were not interested in killing or maiming anyone.

Flash Gordon ray-gunned half the universe in the serial. There was a Woody Woodpecker cartoon. Randolph Scott saved the ranch again in the feature.

Mama was parked on the curb when the three of us walked out. Frankie and David immediately began to recount the celluloid adventures they had seen on the screen.

When we pulled into their driveway back in Moreland, they got out of the car. David walked into the house. Frankie came to Mama's side of the car and said, "Miss Christine, do you need me to help you Monday?"

"I'll see you at school and let you know," she said. "Now, go tell your Aunt Pearl about the show."

He turned and ran toward his house. Mama watched until he disappeared into the shack. She smiled and then we drove away.

As far as I know, the Garfields never bothered anybody very much after that. And the three of us went back to the picture show a few more times.

The Garfields and I never became good buddies or anything like that. But Mama's kindness toward them obviously had had a profound effect. They always were at Miss Christine's beck and call when she needed them in the first grade room. They cleaned her blackboard and took the erasers out and dusted them. They watered the plants she had in her room and found a special pleasure in feeding the fish Mama had in a small aquarium.

After the eighth grade, we were all bussed to Newnan High School. David was sixteen his freshman year, so he quit school and somebody said he joined the Navy. I never saw him again.

Frankie didn't come back to school after his sophomore year. His Aunt Pearl died and he got a job at a welding plant in Newnan. I came home one weekend from college and Mama said Frankie had been killed in an auto accident. He and a friend had been drinking and they ran head-on into a freight truck.

"I didn't hear about it until a week after it happened," Mama said. "The county had to bury him."

Mama had that thing some teachers develop, the idea that her students were her children, too. Often when I visited her in the hospital, a nurse would come into her room and introduce herself to me and say, "Your Mama taught me in the first grade."

I must admit that I did have an educational advantage because my mother was a teacher, especially when it came to grammar. My mother was on constant grammar patrol at home.

Ain't was forbidden. So were double negatives. Put the two together and it was hell to pay, as in, "I ain't got no more homework to do."

"You *have* no more homework to do," Mama would correct me.

"That's what I said," I once replied.

Mama made me go out in the yard and pull weeds out of her flowers.

Words like *his'n* (his) and *her'n* (hers) I picked up at school. Also *are* (over *are*, instead of *there*), *cher* (here), *rat* (as in *rat cher*), not to mention the usage of a personal pronoun when it wasn't needed, as in "Mama, *she* went to town last night."

Those were all forbidden to me. So was, "Mama, where's the milk at?"

Her response was, "Behind that 'at.' "

"What do you mean, Mama?" I'd ask.

"Never end a sentence with a preposition," she would explain. "It's simply, 'Where is the milk?' "

I thought I had it.

"Tell me again the rule on prepositions," Mama said.

"Never use a preposition to end a sentence with," I replied.

Back to the weeds.

I have no idea how many first graders Mama taught during her career. Over the years, however, I've received a great many letters that began, "Your mother, Miss Christine, taught me in the first grade. . . ."

A nurse who was with Mama when she was pronounced dead at the hospital had been a student of hers.

I've often thought about first grade teachers. Most of us don't have the patience to teach children that young. Mama often said she spent the first six weeks of each year teaching half her class to ask permission to go to the bathroom instead of wetting their pants.

First grade teachers, I've come to believe, may be

the most important teacher a person will have in his or her educational experience.

Reading and writing are the basis of all learning. First grade teachers teach that. Imagine being able to take a six-year-old mind and teach it to write words and sentences and give it the precious ability to read.

As for me, Mama taught me that an education was necessary for a fuller life. She taught me an appreciation of the language. She taught a love of words, of how they should be used and how they can fill a creative soul with a passion and lead it to a life's work.

I'm proud of my Mama, my teacher. On her tombstone we put "Miss Christine."

5

I WAS MARRIED and out of college when Mama's condition made it impossible for her to cook anymore. It was the greatest of ironies that a woman who loved good food and was so accomplished at preparing it would suffer a disease that made food her enemy. But I had seventeen years of full-time eating at her table, for which I will be eternally grateful.

One of the greatest compliments I can give to her cooking is that my mother never—not once—opened a can of those make-believe biscuits. Jerry Clower, one of my heroes, has always referred to those horrid things as "whomp biscuits," that coming from the fact that to open a can, the instructions say to hit it against the side of a table. "Whomp!"

"One of the saddest things," Jerry once said, "is the sound of them whomp biscuits being opened in more and more houses these days. Whomp! Another poor man is being denied homemade biscuits. No wonder the divorce rate is so high."

Mama made her biscuits from scratch, the same as her mother had done. They were soft as angel hair. When Mama and Daddy were living together, he called Mama's biscuits "cathead biscuits," as in, "Great God, Christine, what mahvelous cathead biscuits."

I asked him one day, "Daddy, why do you call 'em cathead biscuits?"

"Just look at one of these things," he said, holding up a biscuit. "They're as big as a cat's head."

There are a lot of things you can do with a good, homemade biscuit. The simplest maneuver is simply to slip a pat of butter into a piping hot biscuit, give it a second or two to melt, and then bite, chew and swallow a piece of culinary heaven.

I picked up this from my grandmother: Slice open the biscuit, put in the butter and then add a little brown sugar. The result is a sweet buttery, delight.

You can also put syrup on a biscuit. And then there's gravy, which further enhances the taste of a homemade biscuit.

Basically, there are two kinds of gravies that go so well with biscuits, and my mother made both of them.

There's milk gravy. I have no idea how Mama made it, but it was brown and thick. I have also heard this called "sawmill" gravy, but I know not of its origin.

Then there's "red-eye" gravy, which normally is

made from the grease left in the pan after frying country ham. It's thinner than milk gravy and has a reddish tint, but it can pull a biscuit up a notch itself.

I cannot discuss Mama's biscuits without also discussing her eggs and the fine art of the sop.

First, allow me to admit openly and without shame that my mother spoiled me in many ways, especially when it came to feeding me, a fact that worked its way into helping dissolve a couple of subsequent marriages.

There was the way Mama fried an egg. When Mama fried an egg, and you broke the yellow with your knife or fork, it did not run willy-nilly across your plate. As a matter of fact, Mama's yellow didn't run at all. It *crawled.*

Mama fried her eggs *over medium well.* Over easy or over medium makes the yellow too runny, and I could never stand a bunch of thin, runny yellow stuff on my plate.

Over well, of course, turns the yellow into a solid mass, quite disturbing to one who seeks perfection in his fried eggs.

But *over medium well* is a masterpiece, and rarely in my adulthood have I been able to get my eggs cooked the way Mama cooked them.

And to "sopping" for a moment. Mama usually cooked me two fried eggs. After I had finished the solid parts, some crawling yellow would be left on my plate.

I'd reach for another biscuit. I'd pull apart a chunk and run it through the yellow left on my plate. That was "sopping." You can sop syrup as well as gravy off your plate with a biscuit. The only humorous line

I know about sopping is I heard a man say once, "I'm so broke I couldn't afford syrup if it went to a penny a sop."

Mama, of course, had other specialties besides biscuits and eggs. Let us begin with her fried chicken.

It was our normal after-church Sunday fare. Fried chicken with rice, gravy and fresh vegetables from the family garden. Green beans (cooked for an hour with a little ham thrown in for flavor), fresh tomatoes, boiled new potatoes, creamed corn (that wasn't sweet like every damn serving of creamed corn I get today), squash, and maybe some spring onions from my grandfather's onion patch near the Baptist church cemetery. Mama would cook biscuits or some of her equally-as-impressive corn bread with that. Sometimes she'd even cook both.

But back to her chicken. I don't like runny eggs and I don't like fried chicken that has been fried to a serious crisp.

Mama fried her chicken in a big black skillet on top of her stove. And when it was served, it was, by-God, *done.* Don't give me no chicken, if you will pardon the grammatical license, that's got any juices left. Fried chicken is not supposed to be juicy, like they often serve it in a restaurant.

Mama's crust was perfectly browned, but the meat inside was dry. I can eat a steak with a little juice, but if you've ever smelled live, wet chicken, you would know why a cooked dead one should be void of anything that will flow downhill.

I liked white meat. Mama always saved the breast for me. H.B. never complained, but I often wondered if he were muttering to himself, "Why does he get the breast everytime and here I am with a wing and a back?"

Mama cooked dinner six nights a week. She took Sunday night off. But that was never a problem. She always cooked enough chicken for Sunday lunch that there would be several pieces left over for Sunday night.

Here's something else about chicken as well as biscuits: They're both pretty good cold. Around seven on Sunday nights (when "The Ed Sullivan Show" started off slowly with an opera singer or seals doing tricks), I'd go to the kitchen and search out the leftover chicken and biscuits. I would have eaten all the white meat for lunch, but there is absolutely nothing wrong with a good leg and a cold biscuit.

Mama's country fried steak took my breath for years. She also could do wonders with a baked hen and dressing or with a roast or a ham.

But I must tell of my favorite meal Mama served me during my childhood and adolescence.

She would buy canned corned beef. It came in a squatty little can and was very inexpensive. Mama would open the corned beef, put it in her pan, toss in a little butter, and then fry it, also to a crisp.

With that she would serve white beans. (These are also known as "northern beans," but nothing that good can be northern, so I do not hold with that name.)

Also she would serve me French fries. Not French fries out of some box. Not *frozen* French fries, but French fries she had carved from a couple of potatoes with her very own hands.

Mama's French fries always had a nice outside

crust but remained a little gooshey (if that is a word) on the inside.

I would get hot, buttered corn bread with that, along with some green onions and lots of her ice tea. It was a glorious concoction. I had a name for it— corned beef á la Christine.

I mentioned earlier about Mama's spoiling me and the effect it had on my subsequent married lives, currently standing at three.

My first wife was also from Moreland and thought nothing of frying me up some corned beef and adding the aforementioned side dishes. My second wife came from rural South Carolina. She was not quite the cook my first wife was, but this can be explained by the fact that she was much younger than my first wife and didn't like country music.

But my third wife, Kathy—the one who wrote a book about me and later told the *New York Times* that I was basically a "doo-doo pot"—grew up in Atlanta. She came from a wealthy family. They had servants and maids. Besides all that, Kathy was a runner. She even ran the Boston Marathon. So she was into a health thing and had an aversion to anything fried.

It wasn't that Kathy was a bad cook. Quite the opposite. She could prepare the best tenderloin I ever ate. She also made great spaghetti. And I had begun eating my eggs scrambled by that time anyway, having finally realized that no other person on earth could prepare my eggs like Mama did.

We'd been married about a month when my wife asked me, "What would you like for dinner?"

I said, "How about some fried corned beef, white beans, hand-cut French fries, and corn bread?"

70

"Fried what?" she asked

"Corned beef," I said. "It comes in a squat little can at the grocery store. You take it out of the can and put it in a frying pan and add a little butter."

"My God," she said.

"What's the matter?" I asked.

"I've married a man who eats Spam."

"It's not Spam," I said. "It's corned beef that just happens to come in a can."

"I'm not cooking any Spam in this house," she replied.

I continued to argue, but I never got my fried corned beef and we got a divorce two years later.

Kathy was further perplexed because I preferred white bread over wheat, ordered my steak well done, refused to eat anything that even resembled broccoli and once tried to order a cheeseburger at Maxim's in Paris.

My mother's cooking, then, has had an effect on my adult life, and in more ways than causing me marital strife.

There's the ice tea problem. Mama's tea was sweetened, but she used saccharine. I have no idea why. I got used to Mama's tea, of course, but when I left her home I was confronted with tea I had to sweeten myself out of a jar of sugar.

I could never again recreate the taste of my mother's tea. So I quit drinking sweet tea altogether and, although I still drink ice tea by gallons, I am very partial to unsweetened. As a matter of fact, I avoid eating with friends who serve sweetened tea. Once I ordered tea in a restaurant and a man came out with tea in a can. I barely avoided throwing up on his shoes.

71

My mother's cooking was pure down-home Southern. I took her table for granted as a boy, but now I
am on a constant search for food of that sort.

I despise fancy food. I've been to restaurants
where they served the green beans damn near raw
and cooked the tomatoes. I don't like sauces; I like
gravy. And as a man said to his wife in a movie I saw
once, "Don't serve me any 'ini' food." I'm like that. I
don't want any linguini, and I especially don't want
any zucchini.

I despise any kind of chicken that isn't fried—it's
an insult to my heritage—and I've tasted corn bread
that was sweet and suggested a pox upon the heretic
who cooked it.

I used to eat a little Chinese food until a guy told
me the Chinese sometimes cook cats. I can abide
Mexican food once a month. I don't eat anything
French, except fries, and I ordered something off a
German menu once and they brought me a weenie
that was a yard long stuck in the middle of a little
hard roll. The only thing I like Italian is a soup they
serve in Italian restaurants. They call it *pasta
rigomortisini* or something like that, but it's basically
a bunch of beans cooked with ham hock.

I went to Greece once and they tried to serve me
squid and octopus. Remember in one of those old
movies based on Jules Verne books when that giant
squid or octopus swallowed an entire ship? I don't
eat anything with tentacles that tries to eat a ship.

English food is rarely fit to eat. I was in Russia
once for two weeks and I lost twenty pounds. I have
no idea what Scandinavian food tastes like and
never will, because I don't want to visit any place
that's cold. I actually have seen restaurants featur-

ing the cuisine of Thailand, India, Ethiopia, Viet-Nam, Korea, Peru, and places like that. Not for me.

I almost forgot Japanese food. I went into one of those Japanese restaurants where the guy chops up the food and fries it in front of you. The guy doing the cooking at my table made some little remark about Pearl Harbor, which I haven't forgiven the Yellow Peril for, so I left and vowed never to eat Japanese food again. Besides, those people brought raw fish to these shores. I don't eat bait.

I want my food simple and I want it Southern. Luckily, I have found a few down-home restaurants in Atlanta and around the South, so I can still get good home-cooked food occasionally.

Once I was watching my Mama prepare her biscuits. She was rolling the dough. I said, "Mama, you make the best biscuits I ever ate. What do you put in to make 'em taste that good?"

She kept rolling and then looked at me and said, "It's the love, son. That makes anything better."

I'll drink a glass of unsweetened tea to that.

It was also my mother who first introduced me to barbecue. I can even remember the first barbecue pork-pig sandwich I ever ate.

Mama had driven us to Newnan in the '48 Chevy on a Saturday for her weekly grocery shopping trip.

Afterward, she drove us to Sprayberry's Barbecue. My life was changed forever.

We parked under the curb service shed. For those who may be too young to know what curb service is all about, it worked like this:

You pulled your car into the parking lot of the restaurant. You blew your horn. A person would respond by coming to your car and taking your order.

73

It would be delivered to you on a tray that attached to the window on the driver's side.

You sat right there in your car and enjoyed your meal. No standing in line. No making your own salad. No going to a fast-food place, driving through the drive-in lane and talking to a machine that asks, "Would you like some French fries with that?" and the fries are frozen in the first place.

I didn't know there was such a thing as beef barbecue until I was nearly grown and met somebody from Texas. Georgia barbecue is pork. They will sell you some barbecued beef in the South, but ordering it is frowned upon, like passing gas in church.

I would never get over my first pork barbecue sandwich at Sprayberry's. Mama ordered it for me sliced, in contrast to chopped. I still prefer sliced. Chopped isn't bad, but sliced is state-of-the-art barbecue as far as I am concerned.

I have continued to eat Sprayberry's barbecue throughout my life. It calls to me at least twice a month, and I get into my car and drive southwest forty miles from Atlanta and gorge myself. I lose all sense of time, space, and reality at Sprayberry's. I always order two sliced pork sandwiches. (One would fill a good-sized elephant.) I also order Sprayberry's marvelous Brunswick stew, served with white bread as God intended (it's in the Bible somewhere), the delicious homemade onion rings, and then I top that off with Sprayberry's magnificent homemade lemon ice-box pie. And after all these years, Sprayberry's continues to offer curb service.

I always order from the curb. After I eat, I can immediately lie down in the backseat for a few minutes before attempting to drive back to Atlanta. Someone who has just eaten at Sprayberry's should not attempt to operate a motorized vehicle until he or she has taken a little rest.

In fact, there is now a bill before the Georgia Legislature making driving under the influence of Sprayberry's barbecue a misdemeanor, as in, "Lewis Grizzard was charged with driving under the influence of Sprayberry's Barbecue. His blood test revealed a 1.3 level of porcine tendencies."

Houston Sprayberry, who founded the restaurant in 1926, died in early 1991. When I first began eating there, the staff was made up of him, his wife, and their two sons. Shortly before he died, a third generation of Sprayberrys were cooking and serving the food.

Houston Sprayberry was a man of few words. At the funeral, the preacher said of him, "He was what he did."

It was Houston Sprayberry who always collected the money at the cash register. A man came in and ate one day and as he paid his bill, he said, "Mr. Sprayberry, I've been eating your barbecue since I was in the Army back in the forties. It's got to be the best in the world. I've talked about it all over the country and there's no telling how many customers I've sent you."

Mr. Sprayberry punched his cash register and replied, "That'll be eleven forty-five."

I became a barbecue expert over the years, thanks to my mother's introduction to it. I have standards by which I judge all barbecue joints. Here are a few:

• The more the people working in a barbecue restaurant look alike, the better the barbecue will be.

Family places, like Sprayberry's, tend to be more mindful of quality. There's usually the head of the family in charge of the restaurant, and that individual will see to it that nobody goofs around or gets sloppy. There are very few divorces or problems in a family that cooks and sells barbecue. A family that barbecues together stays together.

• If a barbecue restaurant specializes in anything but barbecue, it's risky. In other words, if you look on a menu in a barbecue restaurant and it also features veal marsala or broiled fish, the barbecue likely will suffer due to neglect.

• The more religious posters there are on the walls, the better the barbecue. Deeply religious people think it's a sin to serve sorry barbecue. My favorite religious poster appeared on a wonderful barbecue place in Atlanta called Harold's. The poster said, "Get Hold of Jesus Before He Gets Hold of You."

• If the floor of a barbecue place is nothing but sawdust, you're in for a taste extravaganza.

• Don't dare eat at a barbecue chain restaurant. Too many bean counters figuring out a way to cut corners.

• Never eat at a barbecue place that appears to be less than five years old. It takes some time to get it right.

• Never eat barbecue in North Carolina. They put coleslaw on barbecue in North Carolina, which is also forbidden in the Bible somewhere: "Thou Shalt Not Eat Barbecue with Coleslaw on It." North Carolina ignored that directive and God sent them Jesse Helms as punishment.

• The barbecue won't be any good if it is served in a bun with seeds on it. Harold's serves its barbecue sandwiches on white, toasted bread, which enriches the taste of the meat.

• If the restaurant in which you are eating puts English peas in the Brunswick stew, be careful.

• If the word "pig" appears anywhere in the name of the restaurant, you're probably in good shape. Some examples are "Pig 'N Whistle," "Pig Palace," "The Greasy Pig," "The Hungry Pig," "Pig Out's," and "Mr. Pig," and one I made up, "Pig O' My Heart."

• Never order barbecue north of the Mason-Dixon line. They don't understand it up there.

Beer and barbecue sort of go together, too, which is another story about Mama. She enjoyed an occasional cold one. I never saw Mama ripped, or anything like that, but she would drink a beer. Two were usually her limit.

They sold beer on the curb at Sprayberry's. Mama would always order one, a Pabst Blue Ribbon, with her sandwiches. And she would tell the curb boy, "Can you please bring my beer in a brown paper bag?"

We are talking early- to mid-fifties, Baptist-infested Deep South. Mama, as a teacher, certainly didn't want anybody to know of her fondness for the brew.

When her PBR came, she would keep it in the brown bag and put it on the floorboard of the car.

Each time she took a sip, she would lower her head beneath the window level. I thought it amusing. I thought adults could do anything they wanted to. Later I learned more about Baptists.

Mama did allow me a couple of sips off her Sprayberry beers. Not every time we went. On occasion, however, I would beg, "Let me have a taste," and she would give in.

I took to beer right away. During my high school years, I had a few here and there as well. You could bribe a curb boy, especially at Steve Smith's truck stop in Moreland. And down at Lucille's beer joint in Grantville, you actually could sit and enjoy one at the counter. Lucille didn't see or hear very well, so if you had thirty-five cents, you could count on having a beer from Lucille.

I never had a beer at home, however, until I was out of high school. Mama likely knew I was tipping a few during those days, but she never said anything about it. I was careful not to do something stupid like drink a case and try to drive home, or worse, drink a case and start a fight and come home missing teeth.

On visits home from college, however, Mama didn't mind if I had a few sitting in the living room with her and H.B. She no longer drank beer in any volume at that point. Practically everything that went into her mouth caused her indigestion and a sour stomach.

My first marriage took place at the Moreland Methodist Church after my sophomore year at Georgia. I had asked several friends from college to be in the wedding. They would be over at the house after the rehearsal. I knew they would want some beer. I told Mama.

"How much do you think I should get?" she asked.

"At least a couple of cases," I said. "Pabst Blue Ribbon." I got that from Mama, too.

She bought the beer and H.B. iced it down, of all places in Mama's washing machine.

The party started about eight o'clock. H.B. had joined us, and he had a fondness for beer as well. By 9:30, we were running terribly short.

Mama had gone to the back bedroom, but she must have heard us speaking of the worrisome shortage. She called me to her bed and handed me a twenty-dollar bill for more beer.

"I guess if you're going to get married," she said, "you're old enough to have a few more beers the night before."

There was only one thing Mama ever prepared for me to eat that I absolutely detested. Liver. I didn't like liver. As a matter of fact, I knew I wasn't going to like it even before I tasted it.

"What's this meat?" I asked Mama the first time she served it to me. I knew it wasn't chicken, pork chops, or roast.

"It's liver," Mama said. "Eat it. It's good for you."

That, of course, was my first clue. She had said the same thing when she pried open my mouth and poured milk of magnesia down it.

"I don't want this," I said.

"Why not?"

"It won't taste good."

(Heard this one before from your own mother?) "But how do you know it doesn't taste good until you try it?"

"I'll tell you how I know," I replied. "First, it doesn't look good. Second, it doesn't smell good. Third, you've never given me anything that's supposed to be good for me that tasted good."

"Young man," Mama said, her voice giving away her increasing displeasure with my attitude toward liver, "you're not leaving this table until you try that liver."

I had plans for the rest of my life, so I realized I would, indeed, have to try liver. I cut off a small piece and lifted it to my mouth. I closed my eyes and bit down on it.

I knew then that would be the last liver I ever tasted. I had some mud once when I was three. It tasted better than liver. I ate a piece of chalk in the first grade. It tasted better than liver.

I spit the liver back onto my plate and made a face like Jimmy Swaggart makes when he confesses he has committed sins of the flesh (fooling around with a hooker who's uglier than bowling shoes in a cheap motel room).

"Okay," I said, "I tasted it and it was just as bad as I thought it would be."

Mama shook her head in disgust. Then she went to the pantry and took down a can of corned beef.

6

MAMA WARNED ME often about getting married too young.

"I just hate to see young people get married," she would say. "They've got all the time in the world to get married. But they go and do it young and first thing you know, they've got two screaming children, living in a house trailer, and living day to day."

I got the message early on. Mama, who didn't marry until she was thirty-five, had the same in mind for me.

But I developed a certain fancy for girlpersons early. My first girlfriend was Sally. She was in my first grade class in Columbus. We often shared the same modeling clay, and I gave her half the chocolate rabbit I found at an Easter egg hunt. That's love.

I moved away, however, and have no idea whatever happened to Sally. Perhaps she became a sculptress or a Playboy bunny.

I got a new girlfriend in the second grade. Elaine was her name. When we got to the third grade, I went on my first official date. Mama drove Elaine and me to the Alamo Theatre in Newnan for a movie date. It was Frank Sinatra in "Young at Heart." I don't know how I remember that, but I do.

I also remember, even at that age, being a little embarrassed because my mother had to drive me on a date.

In the sixth grade, I dumped Elaine for Shirley Ann. That's because a friend of mine said he'd seen Shirley Ann and her mother at the Belk's store in Newnan on Saturday and they'd been shopping for a training bra for Shirley Ann.

I anxiously awaited the next day of school to see if, and how, her appearance had changed. I broke into an immediate cold sweat and my heart began to pound when she walked into the classroom wearing a sweater that featured two small yet distinct points that certainly had not been there the last time she had worn that, or any other, sweater.

I never actually got to touch Shirley Ann's trainees with my hands, but the first time I closed my eyes and drew her close to me for a slow dance, I did feel something pushing into my chest, and I was filled with ecstasy. What I felt, however, turned out to be her nose. Shirley Ann was quite short, even for a seventh grader.

Our love affair grew steadily. I tried to make her aware of my affection in a myriad of ways, not the least of which was changing my dog's name from

Duke—in honor of my favorite baseball player, Duke Snider of the Dodgers—to Shirley Ann.

My girlfriend was quite flattered by this, but my dog growled at me everytime I called him after that, as if to say, "Don't call me Shirley Ann, or I'll bite off your toes."

I also bought her popsicles after school—or, because I was not exactly well-off financially at the time, I would buy one popsicle, break it apart, and give her one stick and keep the other. After licking away at a stick of popsicle, Shirley Ann was a vision of loveliness with grape all over her gums and tongue.

As much as I dearly loved her, and as much as she seemed to enjoy my companionship, I could sense our days were numbered when we entered the eighth grade and we both turned thirteen.

When girls turn thirteen, they are suddenly open game for boys in high school. When boys turn thirteen, it means absolutely nothing, except they're too old for Little League and still three years away from obtaining their driver's license.

As long as a girl isn't thirteen yet, it is possible to hold her attention with walks back and forth to school, a little smoochie-woochie on the way home from MYF, an occasional movie where your mother drops you off and then picks you up again, and popsicle-sharing and dog-renaming in her honor.

Afterwards, however, girls turn their attention away from such timid activities and begin to think about all the possibilities a boy old enough to drive an automobile could provide them.

From thirteen until sixteen is probably the toughest period of a male's life. He is certainly old enough to want to graduate from what few romantic opportunities the preteen years provide, but he is not yet old enough to do anything about it. It isn't really true that girls mature faster than boys, it's just that they are able to discover the back seat of a 1957 Chevrolet long before boys their same age have the same opportunity.

Willard Haines, who had just turned sixteen and who had been given not a 1957 Chevrolet but a 1948 Ford for his birthday, began to show an increasing amount of interest in Shirley Ann at Sunday School.

Shirley Ann's sweaters were growing more and more interesting with every day that passed, and the pangs of jealousy I had felt when my mother first began dating my stepfather came rushing back with a fierce intensity.

Willard did what every other sixteen year old with his first car was obliged to do. He put taps on the bottom of his shoes, started smoking Luckies and rolled them up in the left sleeve of his T-shirt, hung a pair of foam rubber dice on the rear-view mirror of his car, and installed loud mufflers that sounded like the start of the Darlington 500 every time he cranked his engine. He also developed the ability every new male driver must have in order to compete with his peers—the talent to peel a wheel whenever more than two were gathered to watch him drive away. How could half of a stupid grape popsicle compete with that?

I lost my darling Shirley Ann in the blink of an eye, the beat of a heart, the sudden lurch of a '48 Ford, and the screech of two soon-to-be-worn Armstrong tires.

Many were the nights I would lie in my bed and

hear Willard Haines' car roaring down the blacktop road near my house, knowing full well that with the changing of every gear and with the subsequent squalling of his tires, my first love was getting farther and farther away. Willard Haines had my girlfriend, and all I had was a dog who hated me for making him the laughingstock of the canine community.

Well, that's not all I had. I had my mother, of course, and I went to her with my fractured heart.

"Have you tried talking to Shirley Ann and telling her how much you care for her?" my mother asked me, tenderly.

"I even offered to let her have the entire popsicle next time," I said.

"I know how it hurts, son," my mother continued, "but just remember that no matter what happens to you or how much you are hurt, your mother will always love you."

For the first time in my life, I realized there was an occasion now, and there would be occasions in the future, when that wouldn't be enough.

Paula had entered Moreland School when we were in the sixth grade, but I didn't consider her overly attractive. She was a gangly child and had not blossomed as early as the lovely Shirley Ann.

By the time we entered high school, however, a lot had changed. From gangly, Paula went to blonde and willowy, and her sweaters also had changed dramatically.

We went on a church hayride one autumn night when we were both thirteen and I enjoyed my first real kiss on the mouth with her.

Six years later, I decided to marry her.

I was in school at Georgia. Paula was in Atlanta, going to modeling school and working in a bank.

Nothing I had seen on campus had compared with her. Each weekend, I would drive to Atlanta and stay with her in her apartment. I would leave early Monday morning for the sixty-mile trip back to an eight o'clock class.

The driving back and forth had become a nuisance. Then some yo-yo at the bank, in his thirties, had asked Paula to go on a weekend trip. She didn't accept, but I took it as a threat. If I had Paula with me at all times, something like that couldn't happen.

So I asked her to marry me, and she accepted. We planned a summer wedding after my sophomore year at Georgia. We were both nineteen. Mama was the only hurdle.

I was home for a weekend. My mother was in the kitchen cooking.

"I've got something to tell you," I said.

Mothers know. Somehow, they just know. There was no reason for her to speak. I could see in her face and in her eyes that she was anticipating a momentous, and perhaps dreaded, announcement from me.

She walked to the kitchen table and sat down. Perspiration was running off her forehead from standing over the heat of the stove. I sat across the table from her.

"Paula and I want to get married," I said.

Our eyes were locked together. I thought I read her clearly. She had known this was coming, she was saying to herself. She realized the impatience of youth, but if only they really knew what they were doing, if only there were some way she could tell me, tell us both, that we had so much time yet to go; if only she could make us aware of the dangers and the risk; if only there were something she could say to make us change our minds.

I had dreaded this, and I had already played the scene over in my mind a thousand times.

"You promised me you wouldn't rush into anything like this," she would say.

"I know," I would reply, "but I miss Paula so much, and this turkey asked her to go to Gatlinburg with him, and I just can't wait any longer."

"But what about school?" she would ask.

"I'll finish," would be my answer. "I've got a job, and Paula will get a job, and I'll stay in school."

"She's not pregnant, is she?"

"Of course she's not pregnant. We just love each other very much, and we want to be together."

"You're sure?"

"I'm sure."

"But you're both so young."

"We're nineteen."

"You're making a horrible mistake, son," my mother would continue, beginning to sob. I would feel awful about breaking my promise to her, about disappointing her. I wondered if she would come to the wedding.

The scene, however, was nothing like that at all. My mother and I had both grown out of the protective role she had played in our relationship before. She had given generously, and I had taken, a great deal of independence. We had remained close, but she had not fought against her emptied nest.

As a matter of fact, she had begun to prepare me for life out from under her most comforting wing long before I first took flight. She had allowed me the freedom to make a certain amount of my own decisions. She had, more than anything else, given me her trust. I had abused it at times, but never so much as to cause her to take it away. It was because I knew of that trust, and cherished it so much and appreciated it so much, that I had guarded myself against any intense violation of it. Simply put, the primary reason I never stole a hubcap in my life was because I knew it would have broken my mother's heart.

Now I sat before her, having made the most important decision of my young life, and I had underestimated that precious trust. I had not acknowledged the fact that this woman, my mother, was also my friend, and that her love for me would not allow her to come down hard on me for any decision I made. To have done so would have violated that relationship we had grown to—one of mutual respect, one of understanding. I had no way of knowing it at the time, but to have reached that peak of comfortable interaction with my mother was a monumental happenstance, one that few are ever able to achieve with any other person, much less with a parent.

I sat before her, the result of her raising. She would only bless my decision. The little boy who had bound himself so closely to her, when all around him had seemed so unsettled and temporary, had found himself another attachment. She let him go without the slightest resistance.

We talked about when and where the wedding would take place. We talked about who we would invite. We talked about some old times.

"How did you and Daddy decide to get married?" I asked her.

"I thought he would never ask me," she said.

"Were you happy when he did?"

"I didn't sleep for a week."

"You must have loved each other a lot."

"We did. He was always laughing, and your daddy was a handsome man. He had that black, curly hair."

"Do you ever still miss him?"

"When you really love somebody, it never really goes away, even if they do. You have to learn to accept it."

"I'll never leave Paula."

"Don't, son," said my mother.

Things change. Especially when you're nineteen. No reason to go back into a lot of details.

Three years after our marriage, I told Mama that Paula and I were getting a divorce. I wasn't sure how she would take that news, either.

She surprised me. Maybe because of the fact I had finished college and hadn't wound up with two babies in a trailer.

She asked simply, "Are you sure there's nothing that can be done?"

"No," I said. "I made some mistakes Paula says she can never forgive me for."

"Is there anything I can do?" she asked.

"Put your arms around me," I said. I cried on her shoulder. Regrets.

"I'll squeeze you some fresh orange juice," Mama said. "You'll feel a lot better."

Not a lot better, but a little better. I still had Mama.

I would marry Kay. I would marry Kitty. They both were kind and loving to Mama. I would be with Jo Beth. I took her to Moreland to meet the folks. I had twenty years on her.

I introduced her to Mama as she lay in the living room bed.

"It's nice to meet you," Mama said. And then she added, "How old are you?"

And then there was Christel. The first time I got married, she was still in her crib. But we had found something to bridge the age gap, and no woman in my life was sweeter to Mama than she was. One of the last pieces of advice Mama gave me was, "Son, Christel sure is a nice girl. Don't you think it's time you settled down and had some children?"

I didn't take the advice, and I currently sleep alone.

I wrote earlier of the fact it was difficult to find appropriate gifts for Mama. It finally occurred to me after she was gone what would have been the best gift I could ever have given her. A grandchild.

What can I say? It just never happened. It's better that it didn't, of course. I will always have certain emotional scars left by Mama and Daddy's parting. What of a child of my own who had to deal with the same trauma?

Still, I would have liked to have seen Mama with her grandchild. I would have liked to have seen the pride and love in her eyes when I put a baby in her arms as she lay in her pain in that bed. I would have eased some of her suffering. I know that.

To this day, I fantasize about such an occurrence. And I have made a pact with myself.

I'm forty-four. There's still time. And if it ever happens, Christopher will be the boy's name. Christine will be the girl's. And I will tell him or her stories about their grandparents. I'll tell them how brave a man was their grandfather. I will show them his Bronze Star and his Purple Heart I have framed on a wall.

And I will tell them their grandmother was an angel who would have loved and cherished them. And I will take them to her grave and tell them they stand on hallowed ground. Christopher or Christine.

"Your grandmother was a special lady," I will tell them.

And I will see her in them, and there will be peace in that.

I'm forty-four. There's still time.

7

I HELD MY daddy's hand as he died in 1970. I'd never seen anybody die before. It was a peaceful thing. He was in his hospital bed, lying unconscious. First there had been a stroke. Then pneumonia.

He was struggling to breathe. He took a hard-fought breath. Then another. And another. Then he stopped. Seconds passed. Minutes. He simply stopped breathing and that was that.

I would have liked to have been with Mama when she died, too. But they told me she went like Daddy. It was Sunday, October 1, 1989. Two days before her seventy-seventh birthday.

Mama's two sisters, Una and Jessie, and my step-father, H.B., were with her in the living room of the house where I grew up. On the day she died, Una and Jessie both agreed, Mama laughed more than she had in a long time.

"She was really jolly, Lewis," Una told me. "I couldn't remember the last time I saw her so pert."

They said Mama just went to sleep with the three of them sitting in the room with her. H.B., who'd been by her side for all those years, who'd nursed her and fed her and bathed her, had the keenest sense of her. He noticed she wasn't breathing.

"Call an ambulance," he said to his sisters-in-law. "I think she's going."

The ambulance was there in ten minutes. The attendants rolled her out of the house and into the ambulance parked in the driveway behind H.B.'s Pontiac.

There's some sort of law that requires paramedics to start CPR on such a patient and not stop until a doctor has pronounced the patient dead. Mama was pronounced dead on arrival at the emergency room at Humana Hospital in Newnan.

I was in my bathroom shaving when the call came. It was late afternoon. I had dinner plans with Christel. We were sharing each other's lives at the time.

There had been other calls over the years. Usually, they were something like H.B. saying, "I had to put your Mama in the hospital again. She's having trouble breathing." But Mama always got as well as she could get and she'd go back home until another hospitalization would be necessary.

My cousin Gerrie, Jessie's daughter, lives in Moreland, too. She had driven over to see her mother as Mama was being put into the ambulance.

Christel answered the phone. "It's your cousin," she said as she handed it to me.

Gerrie said, "They've put Christine in the ambulance. I think she's gone." And with that, Gerrie hung up in the midst of the anguish and excitement.

I called back. She answered again.

"Are you sure?" I asked.

"They're driving her to the hospital now," she said.

"Call me back as soon as you hear anything," I said.

I was forty miles away in Atlanta. It would take me an hour to get to Moreland. I didn't want to be in my car driving home, not knowing for certain. H.B. called me from the hospital fifteen minutes later.

"Your Mama didn't make it this time," he said.

I sat down on the side of my bed. Stunned. Empty. My mother had been dying for twenty years. I had said to friends, "Every day she lives is a bonus."

Southerners have set words and phrases for the event of death. I rolled out mine, burned indelibly into me after losing a father, grandparents and uncles and aunts. "She's better off," I thought to myself. From pulpit after pulpit rising above casket after casket, I'd heard, "She's (He's) in a far better place."

Christel sat down on the bed beside me. I turned my thoughts aloud. "But you're never ready," I said to her. "Doesn't matter how much you think you're prepared for the inevitable, when they go, you're just never ready."

The thing that hit me first, when I walked through the carport door two hours after I'd first gotten the word, was that Mama's bed was already gone. She'd only been dead for two hours, but the bed was no

95

longer there. Just a chair and a table with a lamp on it where my mother had been for ten years.

First it puzzled me. Then it angered me. How dare somebody move that bed this quickly? Two hours and already there's no trace of her tiny universe.

I half-heartedly embraced the mourners—my stepfather, Aunt Una, Aunt Jessie, cousin Gerrie.

"Where's the bed?" I asked H.B.

"I put it in your old bedroom," he answered. "There'll be a lot of people coming in, so I had to make room."

It made sense. But as I sat on the couch looking toward where Mama had spent the last years of her life, the void left by losing her felt even greater. Not a trace of her was left in the room.

I was sitting next to Una, Mama's baby sister. Una has some of Mama's features. Their voices were similar, too. She took my hand, squeezed it and said, "She was my best friend."

At that moment, I swear I felt Mama's presence. I felt it in my heart. Never before had I experienced any linkage between the living and the dead. But at that moment, a ray of light shone from behind the curtain. It soothed me. Perhaps some bonds, mother and son in this case, were so strong that even death could not break them completely.

The last time I saw Mama alive, she had said something to me I hadn't paid much attention to. I was standing over her bed. She looked up and asked me, "Son, do you love Jesus?"

"Yes, Mama," I answered. "Why did you ask me that?"

"Because if you don't go to heaven, I'll never see you again."

"You'll see me again before heaven," I said to her in a joking manner. "I'll be back to see you in no time."

She closed her eyes and took a nap. She was still sleeping when I left. She knew. She must have known. And she believed the bond between us could go beyond death. Maybe this moment had been our first contact.

The death rituals in the small-town rural South have undergone very few changes in my lifetime. The only one that hasn't endured is the practice of bringing the body back to the house before moving it to the church for the funeral and burial.

They brought Mama's father, Daddy Bun, back home after he died in 1960. People came in, signed the visitation book, then took their look inside the casket. The phrase most used upon gazing at a corpse was, "Lord, they sure did a good job on him (her), didn't they?" "They" was the funeral home.

I have no idea what changed the practice of a body lying in the home. Perhaps it had to do with too many mourners in too small spaces. Whatever, there was no thought of bringing Mama back home before her funeral.

She had been taken to McKoon Funeral Home after her death. Monday morning, H.B., Aunt Jessie, Aunt Una, her husband, Uncle John, and I would go there to make the final arrangements.

One distinct rite of death that hadn't fallen into history is that of the community making certain the survivors have plenty to eat. I hadn't been home thirty minutes when H.B. said, "If you're hungry, there's plenty of food in the kitchen."

Enough to feed half the state of Georgia, it seemed.

There was fried chicken, vegetables, corn bread, biscuits, and pies and cakes, from neighbors. A couple of friends of mine from high school days who still lived in Newnan soon came by with a heaping plate of barbecue and a vat of Brunswick stew from Sprayberry's, the Newnan barbecue mecca. Somebody knocked on the door and came in with a roast. Somebody else dropped off a casserole.

I'd been an urbanite for twenty-five years. I had forgotten the love a small town can show at such a time. I was touched by it. I ate some chicken and topped it off with a barbecue sandwich. I recall feeling somewhat guilty for enjoying my food so early into the mourning process. But Mama would have said, "Son, you've still got to eat."

That's what she had said after my dog was run over by a car and I had gone to my room to cry. Mama had come to my bed and said, as she stroked my head, "Dinner's ready."

"I'm not hungry," I sobbed.

"I know it's hard, son," she replied, "but you've still got to eat."

Life goes on and all that.

There are vocal rituals as well, questions that are always asked, statements that are made.

"If y'all need anything, please call me," which means, "There's nothing I can do to help you through this, but it makes me feel better to offer."

And "Do y'all have enough room for everybody? Me and Doris got an extra bedroom." Moreland still hadn't got used to the fact there was a Holiday Inn a few miles north where the interstate came through.

Arrangements were made for incoming relatives to stay with family friends.

I drove back to Atlanta late Sunday evening. H.B. thought it was senseless. "Why don't you just stay here?" he had asked.

But I resisted. I didn't think I could sleep in that house that night. There were too many memories and too many regrets. I would be safer from them in my own home.

And there were no more decisions that needed to be made at that hour. The funeral would be Tuesday afternoon at the Moreland Methodist Church. Mama would be buried in the family plot in the Methodist cemetery. The local Methodist minister, who had taken great care to visit Mama both at home and at least once in each of her many hospitalizations, would officiate.

Another minister, whom Mama had grown up with and who had also given her much comfort in her sickness, would also speak. And H.B. asked me, "Is there anything you'd like to say?"

"No," I had answered him. I tried a eulogy at a friend's funeral once. I had choked on my own words. I didn't want that experience again.

Vodka helped me get some rest Sunday night. But Monday morning came anyway. My first thought upon awakening was, Could it have been a dream? But a heart beat or two later, reality came in all of its jolting starkness. The first full day in my life without my mother began with a momentary denial. I suppose that's normal. But more reality awaited. The mourning, the comforting, the dream-like state of initial shock must give way to the business end of dying.

* * *

Christel and I met H.B., my aunts and my Uncle John at the funeral home Monday morning. A man said to us, "If you need to talk a few things over, you can have the room to the left."

We went inside the room. The man from the funeral home closed the door.

I said, "I want you all to know that I'm paying for all the costs. It's something I had always planned to do."

"Well," said my Aunt Una, "we sure appreciate it."

My family certainly isn't poverty-stricken, but they must rely on the pensions and benefits they acquired before retirements. It was my place to pay. I would have insisted in any instance.

That settled, I said, "This is the last thing we can do for Mama. Let's do it right."

We told the man from the funeral home we were ready. He sat down in a chair in the parlor. "Before we can go any further," he said, "I've got some things I must explain to you. It's federal law."

The man read from a handbook for at least ten minutes. He had to show us all price levels, he said. There could be no hidden charges, he said. We should ask any questions that came to mind, he said. What he was really saying is that funeral homes make a lot of money on mourners determined to give their beloved the best, more as a balm for themselves than anything else. And in that state, they could be led in any direction by the funeral home. Sometimes the government does smart things.

When the man stopped reading, Una said, "We've picked out a blue gown for Christine," indicating, I suppose, that we were shopping with color coordination involved.

We were led to the room with the caskets. I was slightly spooked. We saw the brass. We saw the wood. We heard the price of each. Una found a casket with a light blue lining. Silk, I think the man said. But Jessie and H.B. didn't like it.

"It just doesn't look like Christine," Jessie said. We looked some more. The figure came mostly in fours.

I saw the casket first. The others were looking elsewhere and I saw this casket. It was shining metallic gray. The lining was blue. A heavier shade than the first we saw.

It was the inside of the casket lid that marked it as, well, distinctive. Against the same blue as the casket lining were what appeared to be four seagulls. Three of the seagulls were flying one way in formation. But a fourth had turned away from the others. There was writing underneath the birds. The words said, "Going Home."

Not this casket. They wouldn't pick this casket, would they? Isn't it a little tacky? Would Mama want to buried in a casket with a message on it?

Una saw it next. She walked over next to me and said, "This is really close to the blue in Christine's gown." She called the others over. I stood back out of the way. I had told them it was their decision to make and I meant it. But seagulls?

"What do you think, Lewis?" Aunt Jessie asked me.

"Do you like the birds?" I asked her.

"Not particularly," she answered, "but I do like the blue."

I knew then we would send Mama to rest in that

101

casket. There were her relatives standing in formation before the casket, and she was going away. Going home. I looked at the birds again. I never gave them another thought.

Next we had to pick out a vault. The man said "waterproof" a lot, and one vault was guaranteed to protect the casket inside it for fifty years. It was more expensive than the one with the twenty-five-year-guarantee. I thought, "How in hell would we know if the thing doesn't stand up to its guarantee?"

We took the fifty-year vault.

Then the man said I needed to give him a check for a hundred dollars to pay the man who dug the graves. The total cost of the funeral was four figures, as I had expected. We left the funeral home and went back to Moreland.

The flowers began coming in. Even friends I considered as casual had sent flowers. One of my ex-wives, my childhood sweetheart from Moreland, sent flowers. There were flowers from people I'd never heard of.

And food was still pouring in. The house was crowded with family. I had to ask what child belonged to which adult. There were second and third cousins coming in and out of the house, slamming the door to the carport behind them. Plenty of time for them to know the solemn nature of death, I thought.

I saw my mother's body that evening. The man at the funeral home led the family into the room where she lay. I thought of that old gospel song that went, "Mama's Not Gone, She's Just A-Sleepin'."

Una said, "They sure did a good job on her, didn't

they?" There was specific mention of her hair. The man from the funeral home said, "The only thing we had trouble with was her lips. We couldn't get them perfectly matched." I looked at my mother's lips. They seemed perfectly matched to me.

There she was. In the blue gown. In the blue lining of the casket. With the birds. The stillness of the dead amongst the living is always so pronounced.

Dead. Mama.

I leaned over the casket and kissed her forehead, as I always did when I greeted her or said goodbye. The coldness against my lips stunned me. I cried for the first time. Why hadn't I cried before, I wondered to myself. Because there had been no physical manifestation that Mama was gone. Now, I had it. There she was.

We buried Mama on her seventy-seventh birthday, October 3, 1989. The women of the church served us our lunch in the old Sunday School room where I rarely missed a Sunday for the ten years I lived in Moreland.

Then we drove back to Newnan and the funeral home. The drill is specific. The friends gather, too. They look in the casket a last time and give out their condolences. Mama's preacher friend from childhood said to my aunts, "She's better off." He said it again. "She's better off."

Then the visitors are asked to leave the room to the family. The funeral director ushers everyone out and says to the family, "There's a few minutes left until we leave for the church. This is your time."

I don't remember who was in the room besides H.B., my aunts, and Uncle John, and dear Christel, who had always been so kind to Mama. Even when she was mad at me. Maybe there was a cousin or two. A few minutes were left. Then the casket would be closed. It would not be opened at the church.

We all cried. We all hugged. We wound up in a semicircle next to the casket. I had one last thing to say.

"If it weren't for Mama . . . If it hadn't been for her saving every dollar to give me an education . . . If she hadn't shown me the necessity of an education and hadn't instilled in me a thirst for knowledge, I have no idea what would have become of me. But she did all that, and I have known success beyond my wildest dreams because of it. I want to put something in the casket that was a direct result of Mama's guidance."

I had brought with me a hardcover copy of my first book, *Kathy Sue Loudermilk, I Love You*. I had dedicated it to Mama and H.B. It was a collection of columns. Several were about her.

I walked to the casket and put the book near her right arm. I looked at her again, for the last time. I kissed her forehead again, for the last time. H.B. walked over next to me. I put an arm around him. He was crying.

Suddenly I felt terribly selfish. My thoughts had all been about me. MY memories. MY regrets. MY loss. But I had lived with my mother only seventeen years. He had been with her for over thirty. His life's mate was gone. That big man's heart was breaking. I said something to him I'd never said before. I said, "I love you."

He nodded and continued to stare down into the casket. I walked away with the others. He should be the last to say goodbye.

* * *

It's six miles from Newnan to Moreland. As the procession left the funeral home and entered the town square in Newnan, there was no traffic. The police department had sealed off the road and turned off the traffic lights so we could pass without having to stop.

The officers watching as we passed had taken off their hats and were holding them over their hearts. As we left town and drove down the highway toward Moreland, each car we met pulled off to the side of the road, a show of respect I had forgotten existed.

The little church couldn't hold all the people. As many as had found seats inside had to wait on the outside. I was astounded at the number of people who knew my mother only through my conversations and writings but came to honor her with their presence.

H.B. sat at the end of the right front pew of the church. Christel sat next to him. I sat next to her.

And, yes, I had decided there was something I wanted to say. Only I couldn't say it myself. I wouldn't have gotten through the first sentence. But I had typed my thoughts on a piece of paper and asked Stanley Cauthen, my cousin Mary Ann's husband, to stand and read it. I had known Stanley since our childhoods. Stanley had been my Senior Patrol Leader in the Boy Scouts. I had never lost the respect I had for him for achieving such a lofty position.

H.B. and I had decided on two songs we wanted one of the church ladies to sing. He picked "Precious Memories." I picked "It Is No Secret." Mama had always liked that song.

The lady sang the songs. The two preachers spoke. There was mention of Mama's suffering. The Moreland minister said he'd never known anyone to fight so hard in order to continue living in pain. The other minister said, "I've known Christine all my life. There's never been a more loving, caring person. Heaven has welcomed her with open arms."

Then it was Stanley's turn. He walked to the pulpit and stood Scout-like erect behind it. He then read my words:

> *I asked Stanley to stand in for me because I wasn't sure I could get through it myself. Emotions run unbridled at times like these, and I want this message to get through. Attempting to choke back tears of love and even regret is no way to communicate such thoughts as I have today.*
>
> *As much as I appreciate the comforting words of the ministers and the promise of eternity afforded by the scriptures, I wanted this eulogy to be read because at too many such occasions not enough is said about the life and times of the one to whom we are saying goodbye.*
>
> *My mother lived a very difficult life. It seemed every time something went right it was followed by something that went terribly wrong.*
>
> *She met her love and married him and then had to send him off to war not knowing if she would ever see him alive again. But he did return safely and their reunion produced a child. And there were some happy years that followed.*
>
> *But then she had to send her man off to war again. He came back changed and broken, and she lost him forever.*
>
> *Imagine my mother's predicament; she would have been content to have continued as wife and mother, for those were simpler times. But suddenly she was faced*

with supporting herself and her child in a world that had not yet seen fit to give women easy access to financial security.

But her determination overcame all obstacles. I remember so well the summers she spent at West Georgia College attempting to gain her certificate to teach. Then there were years of night school. This was a woman already in her forties. I remember distinctly the first year she taught in the Coweta County School System; she was paid $120 a month.

And then she met my stepfather, H.B., and they were married. They built a house and order was restored to her life. How I wish that would have been the end of her troubles, but we know it certainly wasn't.

My mother was ravaged by disease the last twenty-five years of her life. I don't remember the last time I saw her standing. We are saying today, "She's better off now." With all my heart, I hope so, because her suffering was long and hard.

But let us also remember this about my mother as well. She was an inspiration to so many. She had a wonderful sense of humor, even through the bad times, and her laugh was infectious. I can remember a time when there was a twinkle in her eye, a lilt in her voice and a spring in her step. That is a favorite memory.

Practically every value I have, she instilled in me. It was her love of the language and her guardianship of the grammar while I grew up that had a great deal to do with my choosing the profession I did.

And how many children did she introduce to first grade? And how many of them had better lives for it?

We all admired her courage. She fought a fight with such tenacity, we should all think of her when the little problems of life get to us. Compared to her, most of us will never know the real definition of pain.

Personally, I would like to thank the Moreland Community for the love it showed my mother during her illness. "Miss Christine" was special, and you all seem to know it.

I would like to thank my stepfather, H.B. I lived with my mother for seventeen years. He lived with her for over thirty, and he was there. Always! A rock. His loss is the greatest of all. We lost a friend, and aunt, a sister, a cousin, and a mother. He lost his life's companion. Remember him in your prayers, too.

Goodbye, Mama. And Happy Birthday.

I had been fine throughout the rest of the service. In the middle of Stanley's reading, I broke down and sobbed. Christel held me.

We put Mama next to her mother and father in the plot where her younger brother, Dorsey, was buried. Each headstone was etched with the name that the dead had been called by the rest of the family.

My grandmother was "Mama Willie." My grandfather was "Daddy Bun." Uncle Dorsey's children called him "Pop." We had decided to put "Miss Christine" on Mama's headstone. That's what her legion of first graders called her.

It was over so quickly at the grave site. A few words. Another prayer. Then the funeral people ushered the family away. To spare them from the covering of the grave, I suppose.

I greeted friends. My first ex-wife came up to me. We embraced. I recalled the feel of her in an instant.

We went back to the house. I told Una and Jessie to keep an eye on H.B. "This is going to be a rough night for him," I said. "The first night alone without her."

I wasn't planning to stay that night, either. Home was where Mama was, and she wasn't there anymore. I said my goodbyes. Christel and I got into my car. I said, "Let's ride over to the cemetery before we start home."

There were still a lot of flowers. The red clay over Mama's grave was moist. A man I didn't know drove up in a truck. He was an older man. He wore overalls.

"I'm the one what dug the grave," he said to me. "I had to figure out a way not to dig up any of your boxwoods in your plot. I just came back to see the pretty flowers."

The grave digger. I was talking to Mama's grave digger, and the man had gone to extra trouble for a family he really didn't know. I thanked him. Only in a small town.

We drove away. Moreland was behind me in a matter of minutes. I began to hum "It Is No Secret."

Christel touched my shoulder. Mama touched my soul.

8

A MOTHER'S LOVE is the purest of all. It holds steadfast against any occurrence. It is unconditional. I think of words and phrases from street and song:

— ". . . a face only a mother could love." I'm ugly, but my Mama thinks I'm beautiful. Or, even Hitler had a mother.

— "The hand that rocks the cradle rules the world." From a country song. Isn't that the truth? What I am is my mother's child. She yet has a part in every decision I make, every step I take. Her influence will go with me to my grave.

— "I turned twenty-one in prison/doing life without parole/but there's only me to blame/'cause

Mama tried."—Merle Haggard. Mama tried to tell me, "Son, don't ever have that first cigarette." There's only me to blame.

— "Mama knows. . . ." From another country song. You can't put no shuck (pardon the double negative) on your Mama. She's like Santa Claus. She knows when you've been bad or good. She knows what you're thinking and she knows when you've been drinkin'. There's another country song waiting to be written in that sentence.

— "Mamas, don't let your babies grow up to be cowboys. . . ."—Willie Nelson. That reminds me of another line which I think came from the late Brother Dave Gardner: "Mama said, 'Son, you could make a million dollars as a preacher.' I said, 'I know that, Mama, but what the heck would I spend it on?'"

— "Mama, he's crazy. . . ."—The Judds, mother and daughter country duet. Mama had to quit the act because she's sick. I'm familiar with the drill.

— "Yo' mama." The deepest insult of them all. I was in the eleventh grade. There was a crowd of us, and we'd all been drinking beer.
A boy walked up and I said, "How are you doing, you old son of a bitch?" It's a time-honored phrase. I certainly meant no disrespect. But the boy didn't take it that way.
He said, "Nobody calls my Mama a bitch," and hit me in the stomach.

— "Lord, I Sound Just Like Mama"—a book title. The older you get, the more Mama comes out in you. I did a high school commencement address. I told the kids, "Don't get married until you're thirty-five, and don't ever smoke that first cigarette."

I am my mother's child. And I have one untold story that says it as no other can:

I was fifteen. I was on a boys baseball team that was entering a statewide tournament. The coach said, "You've all got to have a physical that says you're okay to play."

No problem.

Mama said, "There's a new doctor in Grantville. We'll go see him."

Grantville was four miles south of Moreland and twice its size. Grantville had a stop light, a swimming pool and six hundred residents.

The doctor, whose name escapes me, had set up his first practice. I'd had a physical before. I used to worry that I had leukemia. Mama had said, "A little boy in Hogansville went to the doctor and they found out he had leukemia. He died." I also worried about the genital check.

I went to Boy Scout camp when I was nine. You had to get a physical first. An older boy said, "The doctor's going to check your balls."

"Check my balls?" I asked. "Why?"

"To see if they're okay," he explained. "The doctor puts his finger on each of your balls and pushes them up and tells you to cough. If you can't cough, there's something wrong with your balls and you may have to have them cut out."

Cut out my balls? I went into the bathroom and pushed up my balls and coughed. But could I do it for the doctor?

No Camel smoker ever hacked as deeply and as long as I did when the doctor gave me the order.

The doctor in Grantville looked down my throat and into my ears and up my nose and administered the cough test, and I managed to leave there with my balls still intact.

But he also listened to my heart. He walked out of the examining room and asked Mama, "Are you aware that your son has a heart murmur?"

Mama said, "No." I thought to myself, "A what?"

The doctor explained. "A lot of children have heart murmurs. Sometimes, it's nothing, and it goes away with age. But it can mean a valve isn't closing properly."

Now I was thinking, "Can I still play ball?"

The doctor said, "I don't think there's any reason that Lewis can't play ball, but you might want to keep a check on this thing."

Mama had turned white.

"What could have caused this?" she asked the doctor.

"I think it's congenital," he answered. "Or it could be from rheumatic fever. Any history of that?"

Mama said "No" again. Then she told the doctor something I'd never been told myself. "He was six weeks premature."

I was premature?

"He didn't weigh but just a little over five pounds. Could it have been something I did?"

The doctor assured Mama there was no reason to blame herself. But she would never be certain.

I played in the baseball tournament. I played baseball and basketball in high school with no problems. The doctors continued to say, "It's just a heart murmur. It will probably go away with age."

The summer between my high school graduation and the start of college, I worked for a bank in Atlanta. My second day at work, the bank sent me to a doctor for a physical.

The doctor also okayed my balls, but he asked following my examination, "Have you ever been told of a problem with a valve in your heart?"

"Yes," I said. "I've got a heart murmur that will probably go away with age."

"I don't think so," the doctor replied. "I think you have an aortic insufficiency."

"That's not a heart murmur?" I asked.

"From what I hear," he answered, "it sounds like you may have a bicuspid aortic valve. The healthy valve has three leaflets. But you may have just two."

"What's the problem with that?" I asked.

"When a valve is bicuspid, it means it leaks. When the heart pushes the blood out through the bicuspid valve, if it's bicuspid, some of the blood comes back into the heart. The heart has to work harder in that instance."

What is this man telling me? That I'm going to die?

"The problem is the heart is just like any other muscle," the doctor went on. "If it has to work harder, it can enlarge and fail."

"Fail?"

"Cardiac arrest."

"I could die, then?"

"Well," the doctor went on, "I wouldn't be concerned at your age, but keep having it checked."

"So what happens if I keep having it checked and I start to get older?" I asked.

"They are doing valve replacements now," the doctor said.

"You mean heart surgery?"

"They go in and replace the valve with one that is artificial."

"How do they do that?"

"They make an incision in your chest, saw open the sternum and put in a new valve."

An incision in my chest? Saw through my sternum?

"But at least my balls are okay, aren't they?" I asked the doctor.

"They're just fine," he said.

I walked out of the doctor's office. I was afraid, especially in my stomach. When I was afraid, I always went to Mama. She had saved me from lightning and thunder and bee stings. From stubbed toes, skinned knees and darkness. From growling dogs and my granddaddy's rooster that was bad to peck.

She would save me now. I went to a pay phone and called her.

"Mama," I said. "I've just been to the doctor. He said I don't have no heart murmur. It's worse than that. It's an aortic insufficiency."

" 'I don't have a heart murmur,' " she corrected me. "You do not need to use the 'no.' "

I think she was stalling.

I explained what the doctor had said to me and told her about the possibility of surgery.

"I want you to come home as soon as you can," she said. "We'll get a doctor to look at you here."

Nobody in Moreland trusted anything that had to do with Atlanta. They sold liquor in Atlanta in places where you could dance.

Mama took me to her doctor in Newnan. She was in the early stages of her scleroderma.

"You've never had a problem with shortness of breath or fatigue, have you?" Mama's doctor asked me. "I remember seeing you play ball when you were in high school."

I assured him I wasn't aware of any such symptoms.

"Do you think I'll have to have surgery?"

"It's hard to say," the doctor answered. "Hard to say" meant to me, "Hand me the scalpel, nurse."

The doctor went over my condition with Mama. He said to her basically what the doctor in Atlanta had said to me.

She was quiet on the drive home to Moreland. A couple of miles out of town, she said to me, "Lord, son, I hope I didn't do something wrong when I was carrying you."

Mama's guilt never left her after that day. She would say, "I dropped you once when you were two. I hope that wasn't what caused your heart not to be right."

And she would say, "I was worried when you came prematurely. You know you didn't weight but just over five pounds."

"It's not your fault, Mama," I would say. I wanted to tell her of my perfectly healthy balls, but I decided against it.

Vietnam was raging when I left Georgia in 1968. That's when Mama found a bright side to the fact there was a malfunction in my heart.

"I don't want to see you go to war," she said to me. "Your daddy did enough. Maybe your heart will keep you out of the Army."

It did. A few weeks before leaving school, I went to

the campus doctor and asked him to listen to my heart.

He listened. Then he told me to jump up and down a couple of times. I did. He said, "There's no way the Army will take you with an aortic insufficiency."

He wrote my condition on a piece of paper and signed his name. I mailed the piece of paper to the draft board in Newnan.

I previously had been classified 2-S, the prized notice that I was a full-time student and was not draftable.

I received a new notice from the draft board in Newnan a few weeks after mailing in the doctor's report. I had been re-classified as 1-Y, a step above 4-F. I figured I would be called into duty only when the Gooks reached the outskirts of Atlanta.

I've carried some guilt about the fact that I was able to skirt Vietnam. I was no peacenik, no hippie. My daddy had been a soldier. He'd been in two wars. And here I was, physically unable to serve. Daddy died two years later, in 1970. I never told him about my heart, and he never asked me about any military service.

But I've always wondered about myself. I've wondered if Daddy passed along any guts that would have kept me in position in combat, or would I have run? Reaction in combat must be the ultimate gut check. The recent war in the Gulf brought it all back again. What would I have said to a son of my own if I had had to send him to the Gulf?

I thought of only one thing: "You'll do fine, son. You've got your granddaddy's blood."

* * *

January, 1982. I was married to Kitty. I went to
my doctor for a routine physical. He of course, was
aware of my valve problem, and he also had told me
of the possibility of surgery one day.

But I was in splendid condition. Kitty was a runner. Sometimes I ran a few miles with her. I had
stopped smoking. I had taken up tennis ten years
earlier, and it had changed my life. I played every
day. Every day. When it was cold or raining, I had
access to indoor courts. I was thin and swift. Woe be
it to an opponent who would hit to my backhand. My
forehand side was weakest, but what opponent
would think of such a rarity?

That January day I had a five o'clock singles
match scheduled. My doctor's appointment was at
two. I never made the match.

After my examination, which included a chest
x-ray, my doctor asked me to step into his office. Big
trouble. I knew it. I sensed it.

He showed me the chest x-ray that had just been
taken. He compared it to a chest x-ray taken a year
earlier.

"You can see the heart has begun to enlarge," he
said. And then he went on, "Blah, blah, blah, blah,
blah . . . surgery."

"Can I still play tennis?" was my first question.

"Not until the surgery," the doctor answered.
"We'll have to see after that."

I walked out his door and headed to my car. That
same fear I felt leaving the doctor in Atlanta eighteen
years earlier was camped again in my stomach.

"Mama," I said to myself. "Don't let them do this to
me."

Mama had saved me from so many previous ill

119

fates, and this was the mother of all ill fates, to steal a phrase from the Gulf war.

But what am I saying? I was a grown man. You can't go running to your mother if you're a grown man.

I told Kitty. She cried. I told friends. They wished me the best.

But I held off telling Mama. She already was so fragile. I would wait until shortly before the surgery so as to spare her as much worry, and guilt, as I could.

I went through three months of testing. Finally my surgery was scheduled for late March. They would replace my valve with a prosthesis, a tissue valve that once belonged to a hog.

I sat there on the couch at Mama's house. I had told H.B. of the impending surgery, and he had agreed that we not tell Mama until as late as possible.

H.B. was in his chair. Mama was in the living room bed by then, frail but still lucid. I went over the whole thing. Mama listened intently.

"Mama," I said, "we've known about this since you took me to Grantville to get my physical so I could play ball. Do you remember that?"

"I remember," she answered.

"Well," I went on, "the time has come to get all that repaired. I'm going to have the surgery next week. I don't want you to worry. The doctors are sure I'll do just fine."

She was crying then.

I got up off the couch and went to her. I kissed her on her forehead.

"I don't want you to worry, Mama," I said.

But the guilt that was still in her came pouring out.

"I tried to be a good Mama to you, son," she said. "I hope I didn't do anything wrong."

Once again, I assured her she hadn't.

Leaving her that day was more difficult than it had ever been before. I could die. My youthful sense of immortality had left long before. I think it happened when Paula left me and took the stereo with her.

So what if I did die? Perhaps I had my most unselfish thought ever, at that point. I worried what it would do to Mama. I wondered how she would be told. I was so proud of her strength against her illness. I wondered if she would give up if she knew she had lost me.

The night before my surgery, a few friends visited me in my hospital room. H.B. had come. He would spend the night at my house and be with Kitty the next day during my surgery.

He walked out of the room and left me alone with my wife.

This, I kept telling myself, was my combat. I would not go screaming and crying. I would take this with a stoicism that would prove my strength.

So there we were. Man and wife. What to say? What to do?

We said very little. Just before she left, Kitty kissed me on my cheek and said, "I love you."

A month after my surgery, Kitty and I split up. I take all the blame. The truth is, I just never seemed to like being married. I think it was because of the options marriage closed.

We remained friends after we divorced. Kitty once said to me, "I knew that night in your hospital room you weren't going to stay married to me. I thought you would say things to me like, 'If I don't make it, I'll meet you on the other side of the moon.'

"You didn't even ask me to hold you before I left. You were being too strong. It should have been the closest moment we'd ever had before or would ever have again. But you seemed preoccupied."

I had never been consciously aware of what was taking place in my soul and mind that night before my surgery. But after what Kitty told me, I went back. I went back to the few moments I lay alone in the darkness of my hospital room, the few moments before the medication took effect and I went off to sleep.

Mama. Absolutely. That had been it.

Friends, a stepfather, and a wife. They were pretenders. I wasn't going to spill my guts to them. They weren't going to see any fear and weakness in me.

I had been almost empty of any emotion, that night. I was totally within myself.

I thought, Why was I like that? Why didn't I tell Kitty I'd meet her on the other side of the moon?

Because. Because I had *wanted my Mama.*

I wanted her to hold my hand through it all. I wanted her there at my side. I wanted to hear, "Don't worry, son. Mama's here."

I wanted my Mama. I wanted her there more than at any other time in my life. Subconsciously, I likely was angry that she wasn't there. Angry at her. Angry at the fates for making it impossible for her to be there.

I had wanted her touch. Her kiss. Her hands in

mine. Her hands stroking my head. I had wanted to twirl her hair as I went to sleep.

I was thirty-five years old, but it didn't matter. Don't dying men on a battlefield call to their mothers as they cling to their last moments? I recalled an article I had read in a newspaper about an airplane crash. The cockpit recorder had the last words of the pilot as his plane hurdled toward his death. He had said, "This is it. Ma, I love you."

So I had gone back that night. Back to the most solid piece of security I had ever known. Mama. She had been with me through all previous sicknesses, both of body and soul.

And here was the biggest scare ever, a threat to my life. And I was having to face it without the rock I had leaned on so many times before.

Shortly after I left Mama the day I told her about the surgery, she had to be hospitalized again. They said she was dehydrated, but I wondered if worry might have put her there, too.

A few weeks after my surgery, a cousin, Mary Ann, wrote me a letter. She had been with Mama at the hospital during my surgery.

"Your Mama was worried," Mary Ann wrote. "And she kept saying to me, 'I hope I was a good Mama to my little boy.' "

The last words of the letter said, "Your Mama loves you and she's proud of you."

I had a second heart surgery five years later to replace my first artificial valve that had been ravaged by an infection.

And four years later, my doctors informed me that a third would be necessary sometime in the future.

Mama was gone by then. So one day, as I was visiting H.B., I told him of the necessity for another operation at some point.

"I hate to bring up anything like this," he said. "But if anything were to happen to you, what do you want done?"

He was asking me about my funeral.

"There's a place next to your Mama in the cemetery lot," he went on. "Is that where you want to go?"

"Yeah," I answered him with complete assurance. "Put me next to Mama."

DOES A WILD BEAR CHIP IN THE WOODS?

DEDICATION

To all those golfers who hit 'em like they live . . .
low and hard.

CONTENTS

WHAT IT WAS
WAS GOLF

THE REASON I'LL probably never shoot par, nor
dare to shoot under it, is because I come from a
golf-deprived background. (I also come from a yacht-
deprived background, a tell-Charles-to-saddle-my-
horse and a Europe-for-the-summer-deprived background, but this is a golf book, so I won't bore you
with stories about turning over in a boat in Mud
Lake, about my grandfather's mule "Daisy," or
about the fact that the first time I went to Europe, it
was with my third wife.)

I grew up in Moreland, Georgia, a town of three
hundred people about forty miles southwest of Atlanta. There was no such thing as the Moreland
Country Club. We had Steve Smith's Truck Stop
where you could play the pinball machine or go in

the restroom and buy a twenty-five-cent condom, which was an exercise in futility, given the fact nobody had sex in Moreland until the middle seventies.

Not only was there no golf course in Moreland, I also grew up with a negative attitude about golf. That is because my grandfather (I lived with my mother and her parents in my formative years) saw golf as what was wrong with this country between 1952 and 1960.

He was a Roosevelt Democrat who relived the Depression every day. When my grandfather read newspaper accounts or saw television reports of President Eisenhower taking a few days off to golf at Augusta National, it angered him.

"Angered" really isn't the correct word here. It was more like his face would turn red, his blood pressure would go up and his hands would shake and he would say, "That Republican son of a bitch ought to get off the golf course and get back to Washington where he belongs. That's what's wrong with this country."

In addition to my grandfather's dislike for Ike's golfing habits, it seemed disdain for golf and for golfers was universal in the low-income South in those days.

Golf was pasture pool. Golf was a sissy game. Bankers played golf, and everybody hated bankers. Golf was the game of the idle rich, who had all the money and wouldn't give any of it away.

Because of this background, I turned to other sports, such as baseball, a very cheap sport. All you needed was a ball, which could be covered with electrical tape and used for years after its original hide wore off, a bat, and a few gloves to swap around when one team came into the bat and the other went out to the field.

While those who didn't come from a golf-deprived background were out on the practice range at their snobby country clubs learning to keep their heads down and their right elbows in, I was swinging at a ball of black tape with a baseball bat while wearing a pair of black, high-top U.S. Keds, the poor, distant cousin to the Foot-joy.

I firmly believe that, with very few exceptions, you can never be a low handicap golfer if you were out playing baseball when you were a kid and didn't get a chance to learn the proper golf swing and how to sign a club ticket. The problem was that I didn't know all that at the time, and when the opportunity did arise for me to take up golf, I didn't know it probably was too late, and I would never really know how not to "come over the top," a golf term meaning hitting the ball left into a swamp, or "blocking out," a golf term for hitting the ball right into a condominium.

But, at sixteen, when I took my first official rip at the golf ball, I didn't know a lot of other things, either, such as there are no answers in the bottom of a glass, never take the Denver Broncos in a Super Bowl no matter how many points they are getting, and just because a woman says, "I love you," it doesn't mean she won't take your car, your house and your stereo when she runs off with some blond stud on the mini-tour.

Three things happened to get me started in golf when I was sixteen:

(1) My grandfather died. I don't think he would have ever forgiven me if I had taken up golf during his lifetime, and I loved that old man.

(2) I got my driver's license when I was sixteen. I was suddenly mobile.

(3) Mr. Brown opened a golf course four miles from my house.

Actually Mr. Brown didn't open a golf course at all. He opened what he *called* a golf course, the Brown Bell Golf Course in scenic Turin, Georgia. (Turin is near Senoia, which is an old Indian word for "triple bogey.")

Mr. Brown had some land. There was an old house and a barn on the land. He dug nine small holes (I presume with a post-hole digger, which you need when you are building a fence or burying a small dog), put poles with flags in the holes and had instant golf course.

The old house became the clubhouse. You teed off on the first hole down near the barn.

It cost seventy-five cents to play nine holes, $1.25 to play eighteen. That included a pull cart. If you wanted to ride, you could rent Mr. Brown's John Deere tractor for a slightly higher fee.

When I heard about Mr. Brown's golf course, I immediately decided to take up golf. I drove to the hardware store in the county seat of Newnan. (Newnan had a country club. Nobody from the country could afford to join, however.)

I purchased a set of Chandler Harper golf clubs. In case you don't remember Chandler Harper, he probably doesn't remember you either.

My set included a driver, three-wood, a three-,

five-, seven- and nine-irons, a pitching wedge and a putter. The set cost me $29.95, which is what a sleeve of Slazenger Belata balls costs today. I didn't have a bag. What did I need bag for? I carried my clubs on my shoulder.

The very next day, I drove over to Mr. Brown's golf course, paid my seventy-five cents for nine holes, bought three used Club Special golf balls for a quarter each, walked down to the barn, teed up one of my Club Specials, and my golf career began right there.

I had seen some golf on television. First, you put the head of the club down near the ball and just stood there. The ball wasn't going anywhere until you hit it, so if you wanted to stand there a half an hour, you could. I stood there about three minutes, thinking, "Wasn't Chandler Harper Millard Fillmore's vice president?"

What you did after that was take the club back and hit a line drive to centerfield.

The first golf shot I ever made was a foul ball into the seats behind first base. Strike one.

My second shot was a swing and a miss. This guy had a helluva curve ball. My third shot was a dribbler to the mound.

The good thing about golf, I reasoned at that point, was even if you hit a dribbler to the mound, you were still at bat.

I probably made a fourteen on my first hole of golf. I've seen high-handicap women golfers reach the green in twenty-six and plumb-bob their putts. At least I didn't plumb-bob my putts on my first golf hole ever. That's because I didn't know what plumb-bobbing was, and I still don't understand it. Whenever I try to plumb-bob a putt, all I see is the non-conforming grip on my putter.

I have no idea what I shot on my first nine holes of golf. Three figures, but that's about as close as I can come. I did, however, lash a frozen rope over the third baseman's head on one of the holes. The ball wound up in a ditch. Ground rule double.

I got better at golf the more I played. I even had an eagle on the seventh hole at Brown Bell, the treacherous 180-yard par four. Yes, par four.

One of Mr. Brown's cows' favorite grazing spot was No. 7, which made the hole quite difficult. First, your shot might be going right at the hole and then hit a cow.

God knows where your shot might land after hitting a cow, and what if the cow died because your tee shot hit it in the head? You'd probably have to pay Mr. Brown for his dead cow, and it was such pre-swing thoughts that made the hole so fearsome.

There was also the matter of what cows inevitably will leave in the vicinity of where they have been grazing. Plumb-bob that.

But swinging at the ball and making putts through bovine calling cards was not the most difficult thing I encountered during my early days as a golfer. And neither was stepping in some, which was difficult to get off the tread of a tennis shoe, which is what I wore to play golf before noticing that real golfers wore spikes. After that, I played in my baseball spikes. When I stepped in the aforementioned substance wearing baseball shoes, it was easier to get the substance off since there was no smearing.

The most difficult thing about golf was that I had to locate every ball, no matter where it went or how long it took to find it. The term "lost ball" didn't mean loss of stroke and distance to me. It meant financial disaster. Losing a ball would mean I'd have to fork over another quarter for one of those slightly-used, mud-covered, oft-cut Club Specials. A quarter would buy a gallon of gasoline and a Dairy Queen hamburger in those days. A quarter, in other words, was a by-God quarter.

I searched through woods. I searched through briars that cut my hands and legs. I searched through muddy ditches, up under Mr. Brown's tractor, and, after a particularly nasty slice on the first tee, inside the hayloft in Mr. Brown's yard.

(At this point, some people inevitably will have thoughts regarding the rural sexual ritual known as rolling in the hay. As I mentioned earlier, nobody had sex in my hometown until after the Beatles came and Elvis got fat, so the term is not applicable in this case.

I should explain, however, there was a non-sexual activity that also went on in barns in those days. It was known as rat-killing. Here's how it worked:

A number of farmers, including my friend Mike Murphy's father, Mr. Red, kept their corn in their barns. Rats like corn. They especially like feeding on corn at night. Thus the modern term, "lounge rat."

The idea was to gather a group, all armed with .22 rifles. We would sneak into the barn at night and, at a given signal, a light would be thrown at the corn bin. The rats, quite surprised and temporarily blinded, would begin to run in circles in search of cover. The participants in the event would cut down on them with their .22s.

It was a joyous experience, probably like the one

Indians had when they attacked a wagon train at night and massacred all the pioneers.

I realize none of this has anything to do with golf whatsoever, but when you throw a little sex and violence into a book, studies show sales usually rise as a result. I'm trying to raise enough money to buy a dozen Slazengers, which now run somewhere around what you once could buy a new Buick for.)

I was so diligent in my efforts to find any of my missing Club Specials that I played my entire first year of golf with the same three balls . . . which reminds me of what happened one day at Brown Bell.

I was in the clubhouse when a guy came in bleeding profusely from the head. I said, "What on earth happened to you?"

He said, "I was out on No. 7 with my wife and mother-in-law. My mother-in-law hit her ball in the woods and I was trying to help her find it. I came upon a cow and I noticed something protruding from under its tail. I looked closer and what was protruding was a golf ball.

"My mother-in-law was nearby, so I raised the cow's tail and pointed to the ball and asked, 'Does this look like yours?' and she beat me over the head with her seven-iron."

You and I know, of course, the preceding didn't occur in the clubhouse at Brown Bell but is actually an old joke. I know several hundred other old golf jokes, some of which will be included later in the book. Most of them—no, all of them—are better than the story about the guy and his mother-in-law, but you never serve the dessert first.

During my senior year in high school, I stepped up a notch in golf sophistication. I bought a used bag at

Brown Bell, my mother gave me three new Maxflis for Christmas, and I discovered another golf course.

South of Moreland, in adjoining Troup County, was Hogansville, where most everybody worked in a rubber plant and the girls were supposed to be hot, but I never learned if that were true because the boys were supposed to be mad dogs in Hogansville and had no intention of allowing anybody from outside of town to mess with their women, a phrase people used in the sixties before women had double last names.

Hogansville also had a nine-hole golf course. There were no cows on the Hogansville course, but there were sand greens. (I'm not really sure "sand" greens is correct. You can say "grass" greens because grass is green. But sand isn't green. Or at least I've never seen any green sand. Sand is mostly white or brown. I suppose what would be more correct is to say Hogansville's golf course featured putting surfaces of sand.)

There are some advantages to putting surfaces made of sand. First, you never have to worry about a ball rolling off the putting surface. Balls tend to bury themselves when hit into sand. (The local rule was any time the ball hit on a sand green and disappeared under the sand, it was okay to take out a sand wedge and excavate in order to find it.)

Secondly, you didn't have to worry much about break while putting on a sand green. You simply made full turn with your putter and attempted to blast the ball straight into the hole.

The disadvantage involved in sand putting surfaces is after you walk all over them and dig large holes in them looking for your missing ball, they resemble what the beach probably looked like where they filmed all those Frankie Avalon-Annette Funi-cello movies.

So, after putting out on Hogansville's sand putting surfaces, it was necessary to locate the homemade dragging tool on each hole and smooth out the sand again, which took approximately ten minutes and was a large pain. Failure to drag the sand putting surface was considered the same breach of conduct as wearing purple patent-leather golf shoes at Augusta National while Clifford Roberts was still alive.

Hogansville, I am happy to report, eventually put in grass putting surfaces and expanded its course to eighteen holes. They also constructed a large building near the course and had professional wrestling matches there. One night an elderly woman watching the matches became so incensed at the antics of one of the bad guys that she walked over to the ring and, when he was pinned in a corner, she stuck her nail file into one of the poor man's legs. Hogansville was a tough town.

I continued to play golf after I entered college at the University of Georgia. It was at this point in my career that I discovered the agony involved when a golfer knows there is a great golf course in the area but he or she can't play on it because it's private.

The Athens Country Club course is a marvelous, plush Donald Ross layout. The Georgia golf team played there. The Southeastern Intercollegiate tournament was held there. Arnold Palmer played there when he was at Wake Forest.

I wanted to play there. But, no. I had to be content to play at area public courses, all a beat ahead of Brown Bell in Turin and sand greens, but a driver, three-wood, two-iron and wedge away from Athens Country Club.

What made things worse was as I drove to a public course in nearby Commerce, Georgia, I had to drive past the Athens Country Club. I could see the beautiful, par-four eighteenth and longed for the opportunity to play it. I felt like a hungry man passing Maxim's in Paris on his way to a soup line.

The golf course in Commerce did have some features in common with Brown Bell. It basically was a large pasture, too. The cows, however, were fenced off from the course and one didn't worry about stepping in and putting through what we discussed earlier.

There was the unique problem of Slim, the guy who drove the mower, however. When Slim decided to mow, he mowed. He didn't care if there was a group playing the hole he had decided to mow.

It often was a bit unnerving to be standing over an approach shot, knowing Slim was behind you in the mower. I don't know if Slim ever mowed down a golfer, but the possibility was always in your mind.

What Slim did one day, however, was run over my ball with his mower. I was in a foursome and had hit a marvelous tee shot on a par four.

Before I could get to my ball, however, Slim ran over it and cut it into many pieces.

"What should I do?" I asked one of my opponents.

"Find the biggest piece and hit it," he answered.

I must point out that I did finally get to play the Athens Country Club course. A fiendish friend came up with the idea.

"Look," he said, "there's no starter at the first tee. All we have to do is hide in the bushes near the swimming pool. When there's nobody about to tee off, we simply run out there and hit. When we finish eighteen, we can slip behind the trees near the tennis courts and then run to our car."

"I have just one question," I said.

"What's that?" replied my devious friend.

"Do you think it will be safe to hit a mulligan on the first tee?"

I'm not certain how many times we did sneak on the country club course at Athens, but it was well into double figures by the time we finally got caught.

The club pro happened to be riding around the course one day and saw two young men he didn't recognize walking and carrying their own bags.

"Are you boys guests of a member?" he asked us as we were set to tee off on the par five, sixteenth.

He had us. We knew he had us and he knew he had us, but we did try to talk our way out of a terribly embarrassing situation.

"I'm a landscape architect major," I said, and I was assigned to play the course and do a report. "Didn't my professor phone?"

"No professor called," said the pro.

My friend then gave it a shot.

"I'm leaving town tomorrow to join the Army and go to Vietnam to fight for our country against the fearsome possibility of communism spreading further into the free world. Since I was a small boy, being raised by my poor grandparents after my mom and dad died in a tenement fire, I have always wanted to play this golf course. And since I might not be coming back from war (he choked a little here to signify he was fighting back tears), I decided to slip onto your wonderful golf course. If you love your country," he continued, "you will allow us to finish this round and not press charges against us."

The pro said, "If I ever catch you little turds out here again, I'm calling the police. You have five minutes to be off the property." The man clearly wasn't a patriot.

I continued to play golf after college. I had reached the point where I could actually break ninety on occasion. I had not reached the point, however, where I had enough money to join a private club.

I moved to Atlanta, home of such wonderful, historic tracts as East Lake Country Club, where Bob Jones's locker is still preserved, Peachtree Golf Club, which Jones designed, the grand old Capital City Club course and the new Atlanta Country Club course, home of a new stop on the pro tour.

I never got near those courses, however. I played public courses where the greens often looked like the landscape of the moon, which we actually would see on television in a short period of time.

What caused me to give up golf a few years later was a duck hook. A duck hook is when you hit the ball, it goes out about one hundred yards, then takes a ninety-degree turn to the left into either a lake, the woods, the course maintenance shack, the foursome on the adjoining fairway, or, as my duck hook became even worse, into the adjoining county.

I'm not certain why a duck hook is called that, but when you hit one, your playing partners usually respond by quacking. There is nothing quite so demeaning as hooking a ball into Never Never Land (you'll never make another par as long as you live hitting the ball like that) and having your playing partners begin quacking in unison.

I tried everything to get rid of my duck hook. I teed the ball lower, then I teed it higher. I moved the ball up in my stance; I moved it back. I aimed right. I even thought of having my right hand amputated when somebody said to me, "You're getting too much right hand into your swing. That's why you're hooking the ball."

What I did was quit. One day, I finished a round and had picked up on practically every hole, had lost a dozen golf balls and had set a new world record for swearing.

I said, "This is a stupid game in the first place, and it really isn't a sport because you can smoke while you play it, and God doesn't want me to play it or He would have answered my prayers by now and I wouldn't still have this [an impressive litany of filthy modifiers]duck hook."

I took up tennis. As a matter of fact, I became obsessed with tennis. I played tennis every day for the next sixteen years. When it was cold or raining, I played in an indoor facility I was able to join for a few bucks, not the thousands country clubs wanted. I became a fair tennis player. My doubles partner and I were even once ranked thirteenth in the state in the thirty-five-year-old doubles. He was No. 2 in the South with another guy, but I don't care.

I used to laugh at golfers after I became a tennis player. "Golf's not a sport," I said. "The ball sits still while you try to hit. Try to return a topspin forehand, if you think golf is tough."

Golfers don't get any exercise. It takes all day to play. I never lost a single tennis ball in my sixteen years as a player. My language improved as a tennis player. If I hit a bad shot in tennis, it wasn't fifteen seconds until I was in another point and had completely forgotten about the bad shot. I would brood for days over a missed putt when I played golf.

The change didn't come on suddenly. It came on over a period of years. God didn't intend for people to play tennis every day for sixteen years, either. That's because the longer you play tennis, the more your body tells you it's a sport that can create invalids.

I developed tennis elbow. That's where your elbow always feels like there's a little man with a pitchfork inside it. I developed tennis toe. That's where your big toes swell to twice their regular size. I developed tennis shins. That's from bouncing around on hard tennis courts for years.

The bottoms of my feet turned into two giant calluses that often cracked and bled.

I got bursitis in my right shoulder. I began taking four aspirin a set for the pain.

And one morning in 1984, I awakened and was so crippled I could no longer brush my teeth with my right arm.

So I tried brushing my teeth with my left arm. Impossible. If I didn't stop playing tennis, I reasoned, all my teeth would fall out in a matter of months and I would be in a wheelchair.

Yes, I did seek medical advice. My doctor advised me, "Stop playing tennis."

So I did. And then I took up golf again at the age of thirty-eight, because I certainly couldn't play baseball anymore, I had no interest in getting into automobile racing, bowling is for nerds and you have to wear those ugly shoes and the ball is too heavy, and riding a bicycle all over town in those tight pants seemed to me a sport people who were in the science club in high school would enjoy.

And by this time, I had become financially successful to the point that I could afford the latest golf equipment and I could afford to join a private club.

I ordered a set of Pings (blue dot), bought one of those big Jack Nicklaus putters (which you could kill a rat with), a pair of white Foot-joys, and a golf bag with seven compartments. I also bought a membership in the Ansley Golf Club (founded in 1912) in Atlanta.

This time it was going to be different. I bought some golf shirts and sweaters with the name of my club on them. I bought some of those cute little half-socks like golfers wear, and I decided before I went out to play, I would take my first golf lesson to learn once and for all the proper way to strike a golf ball so as to keep it out of places it had no business going into. If I still had my duck hook, I was certain my PGA golf professional could teach me a way to rid myself of it forever.

We went down to the range, me and my pro. Here's what he told me:

"Put forty percent of your weight on your left foot, sixty percent on your right. Bend your knees slightly, but not too slightly, and do a semi-squat, but not too semi.

"Relax your arms and hands. Pretend you are shaking hands with a lady, say your grandmother. Don't pretend you are shaking hands with a female lawyer because if you don't squeeze her hand in the same manner you would shake hands with one of your male friends, she will become offended and knee you in the groin.

"It is very difficult to swing a golf club after being kneed in the groin.

"Okay. Now, take the club back slowly along the ground after your groin has stopped hurting. Turn your hips and shoulders and lift your left foot, shifting all your weight to your right.

"Bring the club up parallel and hinge your left wrist. Take a deep breath and think about bringing the club down on an inside-out plane. Now, plant your left foot back on the ground and bring the club back down towards the ball. Do not *hit* at the ball. Swing through the ball.

"And I forgot the part about keeping your right arm close to your body and your left arm straight on the takeaway. And did I mention the club dress code? Something else to think about as you bring the club back towards the ball is, 'Do my long shorts have at least a sixteen-inch inseam?'

"Now, begin to shift your weight back towards your left side. Make certain to keep your head down and behind the ball at impact.

"At impact, never ask yourself, 'Where is this ball going to go? Will it go into the water? Out of bounds? Backwards? Into the clubhouse and strike my assistant, who is selling a golf shirt for eighty dollars, on the head, causing him permanent brain damage? And where is that female lawyer who kneed me in the groin? I wonder what she will charge to represent me in the subsequent lawsuit?'

"If you start asking yourself these questions, you will tighten up and not swing through the ball and you might lose all your money, your house, your family and your friends.

"Finish your swing with the upper half of your

body facing the target, and all the weight on your left side. Did I mention pronation? That was back in the thirties when alcohol consumption was made illegal in the United States.

"You may be asking yourself, at some point during your back swing, 'What in the hell does that have to do with golf?'

"Well, how would you like to go out and shoot 108 and not be able to get a drink in the men's grill?

"Just remember the golf swing is very simple, and I'd like to see you swing at one, but a new shipment of eight hundred dollar sweaters is due in the pro shop at any minute, and I'll have to be there to sign for them. The Brinks people are very touchy about that."

So I've been playing golf again now for six years. I've played golf in such exotic places as Hawaii, California, Mexico, Ireland, Scotland and Alabama.

I am as obsessed by golf as I was obsessed by tennis. But my right shoulder hurts only when it rains now, the bleeding calluses are gone from the bottom of my feet, my tennis elbow and shins and toes have all gone away. I do have golf hands now, however.

I play so much golf my right hand is richly tanned. My left hand, where my golf glove goes, is the color of sheetrock. Small children see me off the golf course and ask their mothers, "Mommy, what's wrong with that man's hands?"

I don't duck hook anymore. As a matter of fact, lately I've been orangutan fading the ball. But my game is coming along. I started out with a twenty-two handicap. I have it down to an eleven, which is as low as I ever want to go, because if I get into the single digits, I won't get any shots anymore, I'll be upset if I don't break eighty every time out, and I'll have to buy a bag with my name on it, which is against the Rules of Golf if you don't have a single-digit handicap.

What this book proposes to do is to talk about golf as it has never been talked about before. This book will not improve your golf game. But I hope there are a few yuks along the way.

Just remember while you are reading this book, to keep your head down. Reading is a lot easier that way. But if you can't, after all these years of looking up to see what mischief your golf ball has gotten into as a result of your hitting it, nail the book to the ceiling.

By the way, I stole the title for this book. I saw it printed on a T-shirt in the golf shop at Busch Gardens in Williamsburg, Virginia. If you are a beginning golfer, no, you can't wear a T-shirt when you play golf. If you can't live with that, go bowling. Hey, nice shoes.

The fundamentalist preacher was quick to admonish his congregation for violating the Sabbath, but being an ardent golfer, he himself was often tempted to play golf on sunny Sundays. One spring Sunday morning dawned so glorious that he could not resist the temptation. He sneaked out to the course before anyone else and teed off.

When he was on the third tee, facing a 440-yard par four with a dogleg left, an angel spotted him and reported the transgression to God. "We must punish this sinner, Lord," said the angel.

"I shall," said the Lord.

The preacher hit his drive long and straight, but then a miraculous thing happened: the ball hooked slightly, gained momentum and carried all the way to the green. It hit softly on the front edge, hopped twice, and rolled gently into the cup for an ace.

The angel turned to God and said, "I thought you intended to punish him. But, instead, you just allowed him to hit the shot of a lifetime."

"Oh, but I did punish him," said God. "Who's he going to tell?"

SNICKERS FOR
YOUR KNICKERS

THERE'S AN OLD story about two fellows watching an unattractive woman cross the street.

"Lord, Cordie Mae Poovey is uglier than a train wreck," says one.

"Don't be so rough on her," says the other. "She can't help being ugly."

"Maybe not," says the first, "but at least she could've stayed home."

Within that story, allowing a good bit of room for artistic interpretation, is my philosophy about golf course attire.

The last statistic I saw said that fewer than ten percent of the people who play golf in America can break ninety and that the average score is well over

151

a hundred. That means that nine out of ten of you are never going to be called "good golfers." In fact, it's more likely that your game will be called "possum ugly." But just because you play ugly doesn't mean you have to look ugly. If you do, you might as well stay home.

The truth of the matter is that it's downright hard to look bad on a golf course. Where else, besides New York City and Southern California, can you wear a purple plaid shirt with chartreuse pants and not turn a head?

On a golf course you can dress like a clown and have people ask you where you shop. You can wear baby blue shoes and not even get propositioned. You can wear Bermuda shorts with white socks and still use the men's restroom.

Even polyester, the fabric of choice among used car salesmen and house painters, is haute couture on the golf course. It is used to make, among other things, lime green pants without belt loops, the kind usually worn by insurance salesmen who shop in the portly section of men's stores. Those same pants, in smaller sizes, can be quite fashionable on the links.

Polyester is lightweight and stretches with the wearer, making it an ideal fabric for athletics. It has only three natural enemies—Ralph Lauren, the Junior League and fire.

Some golf courses have become designated non-smoking areas, not because of the cancer risk but because of the fire risk. Polyester is so flammable that a stray ash from a cigarette could ignite you, and the resulting smoke and noxious fumes could leave your playing partners coughing for several holes. It is also not good golf etiquette to barbecue on the course.

Proper golf wear is generally either very cheap or outrageously expensive. K mart has some of the best deals at very low prices. These stunning outfits usually can be found in the sections marked "Dress for Success" or "The Junior Executive." (WARNING: Do not wear these clothes anywhere except on the golf course, unless, of course, you are a used car salesman or house painter.)

If there's not a K mart nearby or if your social standing in the community does not allow you to shop there, then the only place you're likely to find such colorful clothes is in golf pro shops.

Pro shops are like exclusive boutiques—there's usually no one to wait on you, the selections are small, and the prices are outrageous. They take your basic fifteen-dollar polyester and cotton knit shirt, have the name of your club (or somebody else's club) embroidered on the pocket, put it in a plastic bag and charge you forty-five dollars for it.

If you dare to complain about the price or, Heaven forbid, try to haggle the price down, you are treated like Jethro Bodine with herpes. What you see in their eyes but is never spoken is, "If you can afford to be a member of this club, you can afford to pay forty-five dollars for a shirt."

That's precisely why you cannot afford to pay forty-five dollars for the shirt: your club dues are only slightly less than your house payment.

In the pro shop of an exclusive private club, I recently encountered a new high-water (or low intelligence) level: eighty dollars for a knit golf shirt. It didn't even have the name of the club on the pocket, just a little golfer embroidered on the inside of the collar.

"Why on earth does this shirt cost eighty dollars instead of the usual forty-five?" I asked the pro, who acted like I'd just passed gas.

"Because, sir, that embroidered image of Bobby Jones on the collar makes it most exclusive and worth every penny of the price in sheer prestige," he said.

"Bobby Jones?" I said. "I could have sworn that was Orville Moody."

"Certainly not, sir. The Orville Moody version sells for $19.95, but you wouldn't want to be caught dead in it on a private course."

There are, in fact, certain things you wouldn't want to be caught dead in on any respectable golf course, public or private. Following are some of the classic no-nos from *GRIZZARD'S GUIDELINES FOR PROPER GOLF COURSE ATTIRE:*

• Do not wear tennis, basketball or running shoes on the golf course. They make courts, gyms and roads for those. I used to play golf with a man who was a stickler for proper dress and etiquette. "If I owned a golf course," he often said, "I'd have me a trap door right in front of the cash register. When some fool came up wearing tennis shoes and said he wanted to play golf, I'd just pull the switch on the trap door and send him back where he came from." Like I said, the man was a stickler.

• Do not wear golf shoes with little flaps over the laces. Only Yankees and tourists (south of Washington, D.C., they're one and the same) wear those. Likewise, do not wear golf shoes with little loops on the sides for holding tees. Only female Yankees and female tourists wear those.

• Speaking of Yankees and tourists, do not wear dark stretch socks pulled up to the knee with baggy Bermuda shorts. If you wear Bermuda shorts, they should fall approximately three inches above the knee. Save the coaching shorts, running shorts and old bathing suits for the company picnic. Tube socks and tennis socks with fuzzy balls at the heels also are not appropriate for the golf course (or anywhere else, for that matter). Rule No. 214, subsection E, of the USGA Rules of Golf also prohibits the presence of fuzzy dice anywhere on any golf course. (They are, however, required for play on any Mexican course.)

• Do not wear any hat that has fishing lures or advertising for farm machinery or chewing tobacco on it. Also do not wear any hat that has a ♥ on it, as in, "I ♥ my dog . . . and my wife." Also, do not wear hats with supposedly cute sayings, even if the cute saying is, "Save the South. Buy a Yankee a Bus Ticket."

Even proper golf hats can be dangerous. Once I was having a late lunch with a friend after a round of golf. He was wearing a hat with the word PING across the front (it came with his new Ping clubs). A good old boy walked in, spotted the hat, and yelled across the restaurant, "Hey, Ping, whar's Pong?"

• Beware of any golfer whose hat, shirt, pants, socks, shoes and tees are all the same color. If that color happens to be pink, do *not* help him look for his ball in the woods, and be alert whenever you mark your ball.

As a final word on proper golf attire, I must address the issue of knickers—the traditional golf pants that end just below the knees. Knickers look pretty good on Gene Sarazen and Payne Stewart, but most of us look like Mickey Rooney, or Andy, in them.

It is my personal opinion, based on extensive research and on being easily embarrassed, that only golfers with a handicap of ten or less should ever wear knickers, and even then only on private courses. Knickers on a public course will get you cut.

IN SEARCH OF THE LARGER SWEET SPOT

IT USED TO be that when a man or woman went into a store to buy golf clubs, the only question they were asked was, "Right-handed or left-handed?"

Nowadays that answer won't even get you to the cash register, much less to the first tee.

I went shopping for new clubs recently, and here's how it went:

"Hi, I'm interested in buying a new set of golf clubs."

"Fine, sir, just have a seat while we fill out this information sheet. Now, I need to know your height, weight, shoe size, any distinguishing birthmarks or scars, frequency of bowel movement, current handicap—other than your looks, and your annual income."

157

"Hey, I just wanted to buy some golf clubs, not apply for a secret service job."

"Sir, ours is a very scientific business, based on years of research and development for the sole purpose of improving your golf game. But if you don't appreciate all the trouble and expense we've gone to just for you, then I'll have to ask you to leave right now."

"Do you know my ex-wife?"

"No, sir, I'm just here to do my job, thankless as it is. Now, are you interested in wooden woods or metal woods?"

"Isn't *metal wood* an oxymoron?"

"Sir, I'm an expert in golf equipment, not in animal husbandry. I have no idea why your ox isn't smart. Now, if you want real wood woods, we have this set crafted from genuine, aged, hand-selected, U.S. grade-A persimmon."

"Sounds like a beef commercial to me."

"Sir, for the second time, I'm not into animals. Now, if you prefer metal woods, we have this new model which features a lightweight steel shaft with a graphite and kevlar compound interwoven and baked onto the butt of the club."

"The Jim Bakker model?"

"Excuse me, sir?"

"Never mind."

"This particular club also comes in jumbo size that is forty percent larger than a conventional driver. The larger size provides a bigger sweet spot that is far more forgiving."

"If only I could find a woman like that."

"It comes standard with a ten-degree loft, and we

also have it in a graphite head reinforced with boron."

"Isn't graphite what they use in pencils? Will I
have to sharpen my driver occasionally? And when
did Twenty-Mule Team Boron quit making detergent
and go into the golf business?"

"Sir, once and for all, I don't know what your fetish
is with oxen, cattle and mules, but I wish you would
leave me out of it. If it's kicks you're after, I suggest
this ceramic-headed driver."

"Ceramic, like in toilet bowls?"

"Yes sir. The manufacturer recommends that you
spray it with Lysol after each round. For a man of
your tastes, I also could recommend this state-of-
the-art, electric-powered driver made of high-tech
thermoplastic that was originally developed for the
bulletproof vest industry. It comes with a one-thou-
sand-foot retractable extension cord that stores in
the heel of the driver. For a few dollars more, it can
be converted for battery operation."

"Tell me about the irons. Are they still metal, or do
you also offer wooden irons these days?"

"They're metal, sir, but you can get them cast or
forged with a black-face, the Al Jolson model, or a
beryllium copper finish. They're all perimeter
weighted, and the lower clubs have wider flange
soles to encourage skimming."

"Skimming? I've got a banker friend serving five
years for that. And I've done all the perimeter waiting I care to do; the traffic was awful on the way over
here. Look, this is a lot more complicated than I ever
dreamed. Why don't I just buy a dozen balls and
come back some other time?"

"Fine, sir, if that's your wish. What dimple pattern do you prefer?"

"I've had it with these personal questions. I'm out of here."

"But wait a moment, sir. We haven't even discussed your putter yet."

All of this new, high-tech equipment is more than I can comprehend. But there are several things I know for sure about golf equipment:

• Whether you play ninety- or one hundred-compression balls, whether you play white, yellow, red or orange balls, they're all hard to hit under six inches of water.

• The new oversized putters are really old traditional Bullseye putters with thyroid conditions.

• The metal woods that are so chic today weren't nearly so cool when they were standard equipment at driving ranges twenty years ago.

• No matter how good the equipment is, you've still got to put the club face squarely on the ball for it to work.

• By the time a man can afford to lose a golf ball, he can't hit it that far.

AND I THOUGHT A SWING PLANE WAS AN ORGY AT 30,000 FEET

THE GOLF PRO is giving a lesson to one of his club members. "Now, first of all, just take a few swings without hitting the ball," says the pro.

"Hell, I've already mastered that shot," says the pupil. "I'm paying you to teach me how to hit it."

Okay, you want to learn to play golf. Or, if you already play, you want to learn to play better. Everybody does. To my knowledge, no one in the world is ever pleased with his golf game, or even with a single round.

If you shoot ninety-one, you spend the next three hours talking about the two three-foot putts you missed that would have put you in the eighties. And if you shoot seventy, you bore the fuzz off a peach talking about the six-foot putt you missed that would have put you in the sixties. Either way, whether you're a scruff or a scratch golfer, you're never satisfied with your score.

So how do you improve your game and get rid of that extra shot or two?

You can subscribe to golf magazines and read the tips, but that's as dangerous as reading—and heeding—your horoscope. You can always spot these guys on the golf course. They're the ones who count aloud while they're swinging.

You can rent an instructional video, but you don't find many televisions on practice tees, and every swing is beautiful in your den. Besides, I suspect Kim Basinger is the only person in the world who could make indoor golf seem like fun. I don't know how she would do it, but after watching her in the movie *9 1/2 Weeks*, I'm confident she would come up with something. My palms sweat just imagining what she could do in the front seat of a golf cart.

After that, there is only one alternative left, and this is to take a lesson from a certified, genuine, sanctioned PGA Club Professional, His Honor, Sir. He is the handsome, well-dressed, tanned person who hustles eighty-dollar golf shirts and slips off occasionally to have sex with the wife of one of the members who just teed off and won't be home for five hours.

After taking about half a million dollars' worth of lessons from at least four hundred pros (I'm not married, so I don't worry about any of them slipping off to have sex with my wife. I do live with two black Labs, but let's not get into anything like that.), I have become convinced of a conspiracy.

DOES A WILD BEAR CHIP IN THE WOODS?

Here's the deal: God picks out people and gives them Golf's Secret. These are the people who actually can shoot par or better. I'm not certain by what process God chooses these individuals.

Perhaps he does it at random. He's sitting there, dictating who will get what when they are born, and he says, "Okay, Hotchkiss gets a lot of hair, Windom gets great teeth, Matthews gets no zits when he's in high school, give Shirley Patton blue eyes and a rich daddy, and give Schwarz The Secret of Golf."

So, at any time on earth, there are maybe 10,000 people God has given The Secret of Golf.

The problem for the rest of us (I got quick hands and was born in the South) is that those who know The Secret of Golf have a pact not to tell the rest of us what it is because if everybody knew The Secret of Golf, pros who know the secret couldn't make any money giving lessons because we wouldn't need any.

So, when you take a golf lesson from a pro, consider that and the fact that nothing he says or shows you will actually work.

I will give you some examples:

• Your pro will talk a lot about the "proper swing plane." You are supposed to take the club away from the ball and bring it back in a perfect inside-out path every time you swing.

This is impossible, however, because when you take the club away from the ball, you can't see it anymore, so how are you going to bring it back on the proper swing plane when you can't see the damn thing?

• Your pro will talk about your alignment. He wants you to point your arms, hands, feet, shoulders, hips, eyes, nose, ears and pancreas in certain positions.

To do all this like he says to do it, you would need to be a contortionist, plus when you stoop over like he says to, it hurts your back and this guy is twenty-eight years old and his back hasn't started hurting yet. When your pro begins to talk about the proper alignment, take a pack of Doan's Pills out of your bag and eat four of them. They won't help your golf swing, but they will allow you to get out of the bed the next morning after our pro has made you try things with your body that are impossible after age thirty-five.

• Your pro will talk to you about weight transfer. When you take the club back, your weight should be on your right foot. As you bring the club toward the ball, you are supposed to shift your weight to your left foot. The same thing is required of you when you do the samba, the beguine and the Teaneck, New Jersey Hustle, and who does this person think you are? Fred Damn Astaire?

• Your pro will further confuse you by talking about your grip, your shoulder turn, your one-piece takeaway, your club release, the fact your head should become an immovable object and the fact your wife looks so lovely when the sun hits her hair in that special way while she's at the club pool wearing nothing but a cork and two Band-Aids.

He will use such words as "perpendicular," "horizontal" and "parallel." He will mention the rotation of the earth, gravity, the summer equinox, the equator and Norfolk, Virginia.

He will also mention that you need a complete new set of clubs and better-looking pair of golf shoes.

When your lesson is over, he will charge you forty dollars, make another couple hundred off your new clubs and shoes, and then call a friend who also knows The Secret and laugh at you for being a sucker.

So, the bad news is if you didn't come into the world with The Secret, you're not going to find it out and you'll be a hacker like the rest of us during your entire golfing life.

The only thing you can do is buy this book and read *GRIZZARD'S INSTRUCTIONS FOR GOLFERS WHO GOD LEFT OUT:*

• Keep you head down when you swing. This is made easier by pretending you are bobbing for apples. Except don't think what diseases you could get poking your nose and mouth into a bucket of water everybody else at the party has had their nose and mouth in.

• Watch the ball. Watch it go left, watch it go right, watch it go three inches, watch it land behind a tree, watch it go into the street and hit a new Saab, watch it sky, shank, dribble off the tee, hit a low-flying aircraft or your pro who is giving another sucker a lesson over at the practice range.

On second thought, don't watch the ball. Too many horrible, ungodly, unmentionable things can happen to it.

• Hold your club with a death grip. You don't want to further embarrass yourself by having the club come loose from your hands and killing a member of your foursome. Then again, if the son of a bitch wouldn't concede a two-foot putt to you on the last hole, he deserves to die.

• Swing as hard as you can. Golf is an expensive game and you want to get your money's worth.

• Swing as fast as you can. The sooner you finish, the sooner you can get to the bar in the men's grill.

• Finish high: When you go into the bar in the men's grill, drink as many drinks as you had triple bogeys. This will allow you to end your day not giving a damn how many triple bogeys you had. But don't attempt to drive home. Make the pro drive you in his new $90,000 two-seater Mercedes convertible with the power roof you helped him buy.

One other note: When all else fails, consider these inspiring words from Dan Quayle, "A wasted mind is a terrible thing to bogey."

"I just got a new set of golf clubs for my husband."
"Gee, what a great trade!"

RULES ARE BENT
TO BE BROKEN

GOLF CAN BE a humiliating, bumbling, frustrating game, especially if you have to play by the rules. And there are a million of 'em—rules covering everything from how many clubs you can carry to when you can touch your ball.

Worse than that, golfers have to call penalties on themselves. Almost every other sport has umpires and referees to be the bad guys (that's why they all wear black uniforms), but golfers are on the honor system.

Say in basketball you're under the basket and notice that the referee is screened out, so you take your elbow and bury it in the rib cage of the defender who has been frisking you all night long. The guy with the collapsed lung rolls on the floor like he's having a grand mal seizure, while you seize the moment to score an easy basket. You have broken the rules (and maybe a couple of ribs) but didn't get caught. It's a good feeling and your teammates congratulate you.

Now say you're on the golf course and hit your drive into the woods. When you finally find your ball, it's sitting down in a hole directly behind a tree with more branches than the Chase Manhattan Bank. If, however, the ball were two feet further to the right, you would have a clear shot to the green with an unobstructed swing. If the stupid groundskeeper hadn't watered the fairway last night, the ball would have rolled those two extra feet . . . after it ricocheted off the rake in the fairway bunker and scooted through the rough and into the woods.

You have obviously been victimized by cruel fate, so you seek retribution in the only way you know how—by moving your ball two feet to the right when your opponents are not looking. You hit a great second shot, make the birdie putt and go on to win the match one-up. Like the basketball player, you have broken the rules and didn't get caught. But rather than feeling good about it, you feel like a flattened skunk who's been dead on the road for four days.

So who decided to pick on golfers? The game was already difficult enough to make grown men wear skirts, so why make it harder with a bunch of nit-picking rules? I figure the wee Scotsman who first made up all those rules must have been wearing his kilt too high or his pouch too low. Or both.

Being the great humanitarian that I am, I have devised a kinder, gentler set of rules for golf. The next time you're out for a round, use these modified rules and see if you don't shave several strokes off your score and leave the course feeling much better about yourself . . . and mankind.

The Milligan Rule

Most golfers know what a "mulligan" is. That's when you hit a second shot off the first tee because your first shot went into the rose bed of the little old lady who lives across the street from the first fairway. The "milligan rule" takes that logic a step further. If you don't like your first shot on *any* tee, hit another one (that's your "milligan"). If that shot is lousy, too, hit a third shot, called a "McMilligan." If you *still* don't have a good shot, drive the cart out into the middle of the fairway about 250 yards from the tee and drop your ball there. That's called a "Grover McMilligan," named for the famous card cheat who died in a lynching accident in 1926.

Moving the Ball in the Rough

Under my modified rules of golf, you may not only move your ball in the rough, you may ignore the rough altogether and place your ball back in the fairway—ten yards closer to the hole for each form of reptilia spotted while you were over there in the weeds looking for your ball.

Sand Rule

Whose idea was it to put sand on a golf course in the first place? If I'd wanted to play in the sand, I'd have gone to the beach. When your ball goes into the sand, remove it as quickly as possible and place it on a nice flat spot on the green (no closer to the pin, however, than the length of a standard beach umbrella).

Lost Ball Rule

Let's say you hit your ball into the water and it can't be retrieved. What you do is subtract two strokes from your eventual score on that hole. You deserve it. After all, you just paid nearly three bucks for a brand-new golf ball that is now a toy for a fish.

Tree Rule

If you are aiming at a tree and hit it, you must play your ball as it lies. If, however, you are aiming down the middle of the fairway and your ball hits a tree, advance the ball fifty yards toward the green for each variety of pine tree you can name.

Two-Putt Rule

If your ball still isn't in the hole after two putts, pick it up and place it in the hole. Be careful not to touch the edge of the cup, which is a one-shot penalty. Rules are rules. If your opponent complains, pick him up and place his head in the hole.

Beer Rule

At the end of your round, count up the number of beers you drank during the round and subtract that number from your total score. If you had been sober, that's probably what you would have shot in the first place. (NOTE: Your net score must be a positive number; that is, you may not drink more beers than you had strokes during the round. Actually, you *may* drink more than that, but you can't deduct them from your score. In such cases, a bronze statue of you will be erected outside the men's grill.)

Two-Club Length Rule

Many times when a golfer hits a shot where he's not supposed to, such as under the concession stand, he is given relief and allowed to move his ball two club lengths in any direction no closer to the hole.

I think that is an excellent rule, but unfortunately

173

it has been misinterpreted for years. Under my modified rules, the two clubs in question should be your home golf club and your favorite nightspot.

My home golf course, for instance, is approximately two miles from my favorite watering hole, Harvey's Dance and Ratchet Club, where they work on your car while you drink and dance. Therefore, I can move my ball up to two miles in any direction no closer to the hole.

Snake Rule

This one deserves an extended explanation. After all, snakes rank right up there with lightning, flying in bad weather at night, dentists and revenge-minded ex-wives as the things I fear most in this life.

One day not long ago I was playing golf at the beautiful Melrose course on Daufuskie Island, South Carolina. On the par four fourteenth hole, I hooked my drive into the woods. As I drove off in my cart in search of it, my playing partner said, "Be careful. They've been seeing a lot of snakes lately."

"What kind of snakes have they been seeing?" I asked.

"Rattlesnakes, I guess," he said.

I don't know why I asked such a silly question. As far as I'm concerned a snake is a snake. I didn't pay attention enough in Boy Scouts to be able to determine when I step on a snake whether it is going to bite me, coil around me and squeeze me to death or talk about all the rats it has been eating lately.

"If they ain't got shoulders," my boyhood friend

and idol, Weyman C. Wannamaker, Jr., a great American, used to say, "I don't want to be near them."

Weyman's uncle had frightened him with stories about the dreaded "cottonmouth water rattler."

"My uncle says that's the meanest snake there is," Weyman explained. "They'll follow you home and wait for you to come out of the house the next morning."

"Do you think it's safe to go into the woods after my ball?" I asked my partner, as I reminded myself that this temporarily lost golf ball only cost $2.50.

"Just be careful around thick brush and fallen logs," he said.

I drove my cart into the woods and was about to get out when I noticed that all I could see around me was thick brush and fallen logs.

"One other thing," my partner yelled to me. "Snakes climb up trees, and sometimes they can fall off on your head."

I might have been able to deal with thick brush and the fallen logs. The part about a snake falling on my head did it, however. I declared my ball lost, took the necessary penalty, and from that point on played by the "snake rule," which clearly states, "Any player who hits a ball anywhere there might be a snake can forget about that ball and drop another in the fairway with no penalty."

I was at Melrose for four more wonderful days and, after inventing the snake rule, remained out of the woods and never saw snake one.

My partner, meanwhile, had to play golf with his wife one day.

"She went into the woods on No. 11 and saw a

snake," he explained. "Best thing that ever happened to me."

"What do you mean by that?" I asked.

"The minute she stopped running," he said, "she gave up golf . . . forever."

My modified rules of golf have proven so successful for Americans that I felt, in the spirit of international cooperation (and in exchange for a free weekend at a golf resort, which required that I write about it), I should extend my efforts to cover Mexican golf.

My research was conducted at the luxurious Club Med in Ixtapa, Mexico, where the quality of the facility is rivaled only by the dedication of the efficient, trained staff which services the 135 rooms, each with its own telephone and cable television, and the restaurant uses only the freshest ingredients, regardless of how old they are. With that out of the way, here follows *GRIZZARD'S LIBERTARIAN RULES FOR MEXICAN GOLF:*

The Burro Rule

If a burro hee-haws during your backswing, you get an automatic par on the hole as retribution for your interruption. If your ball lands on what burros occasionally leave on Mexican golf courses, get your caddy to remove the ball and wash it thoroughly, give yourself a birdie and give your caddy an extra five hundred pesos for his trouble.

The Crocodile Rule

There are lots of crocodiles on Mexican golf courses. If you hit your ball into the water, make your caddy swim out and find it. If he is eaten by a crocodile, subtract ten strokes from your score for having wasted five hundred pesos.

The Ralph Nader
Unsafe-at-any-Speed Rule

There are no brakes on Mexican golf carts. Hit two balls off the tee of any hole where you have to drive the cart down a steep embankment. If you are not maimed or killed in the cart, you may pick the best of your two tee shots.

The Night of the Iguana Rule

There are lots of iguanas—large, ugly lizards—on Mexican golf courses. If you see one, divide Roseanne Barr's weight by four and subtract the total from your score. If you don't know Roseanne Barr's weight, put three caddies and a golf cart on a scale and use that total.

177

The Tequila Rule

Take the number of tequila shots you had the night before, add the number of times you got into a fight as a result of drinking all that tequila and then go back to bed. Nobody could play golf in your condition.

The Montezuma's Revenge Rule

If you have ignored everybody's advice and drank the water in Mexico anyway, hit your ball into the woods every chance you get. You will need to.

The Pepto Bismol Rule

Better to be eaten by a crocodile in a water hazard than to be in Mexico without it.

Clifton was having a beer in the men's grill when Tony came in. "Hey, did you hear the terrible news about Newton?" asked Tony.

"No, what happened?"

"He finished his round early Saturday, went home and caught his wife in bed with another man. Shot 'em both deader than a doornail."

"Well," said Clifton, "it could have been worse."

"Worse? How?"

"If he'd come home early on Friday, he'd have shot me."

After an enjoyable eighteen holes of golf, a man stopped in a bar for a beer before heading home. There he struck up a conversation with a ravishing young beauty. They had a couple of drinks, liked each other, and soon she invited him over to her apartment. For two hours they made mad, passionate love.

On the way home, the man's conscience started bothering him something awful. He loved his wife and didn't want this unplanned indiscretion to ruin their relationship, so he decided the only thing to do was come clean.

"Honey," he said when he got home, "I have a confession to make. After I played golf today, I stopped by the bar for a beer, met a beautiful woman, went back to her apartment and made love to her for two hours. I'm sorry, it won't ever happen again, and I hope you'll forgive me."

His wife scowled at him and said, "Don't lie to me, you sorry scumbag! You played thirty-six holes, didn't you?"

POLIES, WHAMMIES, PUKIES, BONKERS & LLOYD BRIDGES

A ROTUND GOLFER was arguing for more shots when the bet was being made. "You guys have a tremendous advantage over me because I have to putt from memory."

"From memory? What are you talking about?" asked his opponent.

"It's sad but simple," he explained, patting his belly. "When I put the ball where I can see it, I can't reach it; when I put it where I can reach it, I can't see it."

I'm not certain just how many people would play golf if they couldn't gamble. You don't have to gamble when you play golf, of course, but who wants to roll in a long birdie putt and not make somebody have to pay for it?

The problem in golf gambling, however, is that most golfers are also liars, especially when it comes to their handicaps.

There are two kinds of handicap liars. One is the egomaniacal liar. When he is asked his handicap on the first tee for the purpose of arranging a fair wager, he knocks off about five strokes from his real handicap to impress his opponents.

(There is a way egomaniacal liars can actually have handicaps much lower than their actual ability. What you do is this:

Let's say you're fifteen feet away from the hole putting for par. Your partner makes his par, making your putt meaningless as far as the bet is concerned. The egomaniac announces, as his partner's putt goes in, "That makes mine good." He writes down a "4" on his scorecard and winds up shooting thirty-eight on the front having picked up for par on four holes.)

You want to avoid getting an egomaniacal liar as a partner in any form of bet. They will cost you many dollars because they cannot play to their handicap.

Often, partners are decided upon by throwing up each member of a foursome's ball. The two closest balls are one team, the two balls the furthest distance from one another are the other.

When your ball lands near a player who has an ego-reduced handicap, and you know you are going to lose money because of that fact, the smart thing to do is either refuse to play, demand another throwing up of the balls, or say, "If he's a seven, my ass is a typewriter," and perhaps get him more strokes.

DOES A WILD BEAR CHIP IN THE WOODS?

If all else fails, hit your partner over the head with your putter, rendering him unconscious and unable to play the round. And go get somebody else.

The other kind of handicap liar is the person who claims his handicap is higher than it actually is. This person is also called a sandbagger, a sandbagging SOB, a cheater, a cheating SOB, a thief, a thieving SOB, or, simply, SOB.

When asked his handicap on the first tee, he will say sixteen.

Sixteen? The sandbagging SOB shot seventy-eight on his own ball in last week's member-guest and he wants sixteen shots?

(There is a way a lying, sandbagging, etc., can actually have a handicap higher than his actual ability, too. Here's how: You are three feet from the hole, putting for par, and your partner rolls in his par putt, making your putt meaningless as far as the bet is concerned.

The LSSOB will then three-putt on purpose and write down "6" on his scorecard, when he easily could have had four. He does this four or five times a round and he's turning in eighty-eights, rather than seventy-eights, keeping his handicap inflated.)

"Why don't we just give you our wallets and you take what you want?" is what to say to somebody who shot seventy-eight on his ball in last week's member-guest, and wants sixteen shots.

You want this person for a partner, if he can get away with getting sixteen shots and can shoot a seventy-eight. If your ball doesn't land next to this player's ball on the first tee, you might say, "Look, it's Halley's Comet!" and while the other players look

183

to the sky, you move your ball next to the one belonging to the sandbagging, etc.

All that said, there is one other matter to discuss on the first tee as the bet and partners are being discussed, and that is extenuating circumstances as in, "I'm a twelve, but I hurt my back having sex with a University of Idaho cheerleader, so I need more strokes."

I've heard some incredible begging for more strokes on the first tee. I was playing with a guy who is a four handicap and he announced on the first tee, "I'm a four, but I'm playing to an eleven. My dog chewed the spikes off my shoes and I can't stay down on the ball."

What golf needs is a system where handicaps are adjusted for such circumstances. I would do so in this way:

• DEATH IN THE FAMILY: Two more strokes a side. It's hard to play golf feeling guilty because you're out on the course while everybody else is at your wife's funeral.

• INJURIES: Shots are added in relation to the creativity one shows while describing the ailment. The old "I-hurt-my-back-while-having-sex-with-a-University-of-Idaho-cheerleader trick will get you an additional shot a side if she was blonde, had big bazoogas and thought Twin Falls was the capital of her home state." "I broke my toe dancing with Juliet Prowse" will get you a couple of strokes, as will, "The little boy had gone down for the third time in icy Lake Michigan when I jumped in, swam over to him and pulled him out of the jaws of death. I've had trouble making a shoulder turn ever since."

• BUSINESS PROBLEMS: Next time you need some more strokes, try saying, "I never should have bought all that Po Folks stock."

• EQUIPMENT: An Arab terrorist stole your sand wedge. An extra shot a side. You broke your seven-iron while attempting to break into a K mart. Two more strokes on the front, one on the back.

• FOREIGN AFFAIRS: "Daniel Ortega is my brother-in-law" should get you a couple of extra shots, as will "My wife is out shopping with Imelda Marcos" or even "I've invited Manuel Noriega to be my partner in the member-guest."

• ACTS OF GOD: "We've been sleeping in the truck since the tornado hit the trailer" is a good one. So is "You should have seen what the sinkhole did to our house in Ponte Vedra."

I've mentioned the term "member-guest" often here, and when discussing various forms of sandbagging, lying and cheating, it becomes necessary to expand a bit on the aforementioned term.

Every golf club has an annual member-guest tournament. This is where you invite a friend, relative, business associate, or your proctologist to be your partner at a tournament at your club. The club charges you several thousand dollars to be in the tournament, but there are free nachos and fried frozen shrimp available after each round, and you get a photograph of you and your partner on the first tee, standing there like a couple of idiots with your drivers.

Each member-guest tournament begins with a calcutta, which works like this:

Everybody in the tournament drinks for a couple

of hours and then an auction begins. Each team in the tournament is put up for bids. All the money from the auction goes into a pot.

Let's say you've had six Scotches and you buy Stranglehammer and Forsyth for $1,200. Stranglehammer and Forsyth have the right to give you six hundred dollars for a half interest in themselves.

If Stranglehammer and Forsyth win the member-guest tournament, you and Stranglehammer and Forsyth share forty percent of the pot, which can be a substantial amount of money. Second place brings thirty percent, third brings twenty, and so on until the pot is cleaned out.

With so much money involved—plus, the member-guest winners can gloat—it becomes necessary to cheat if you want to have any chance whatsoever to win and recoup the money your ego forced you to pay for your own team, after first forcing you to drink six Scotches.

Here's how you cheat in a member-guest:

You bring in a ringer. You find somebody from Wyoming who nobody else in the club knows and you invite him to play as your guest. He carries a two handicap, but you claim he's a sixteen when you fill out your entry form for the tournament. That way, he's going to get eight shots a side (if he makes a par on any of the eight holes, it's a net birdie, if he makes a birdie, it's a net eagle, if he makes a hole-in-one on a par three where he gets a shot, you get to write down "0" on your scorecard and the two of you shoot a net forty-three and win the tournament and all the money).

Most clubs do a tacky thing known as verifying your guest's handicap. That involves your head pro calling the head pro at your guest's club and asking, "Is Marvin Stranglehammer really a sixteen?"

But if you invited somebody from Wyoming, you can say your guest is a sixteen when he's a two, because when your head pro attempts to call your guest's club in Wyoming it will be closed because the entire state is up to its armpits in snow, so you can get away with your clever ruse.

So what happens is on the first day of the tournament, your guest shoots seventy-one on his own ball and you lead the tournament by four hundred shots. When the other participants ask, "How in the hell did that Wyoming SOB shoot seventy-one on his own ball with sixteen shots?" you reply, "Hey, he just made a putt here and there and shot the best round of his life."

The next day, when he shoots sixty-nine on his own ball and you and he win the tournament by seven hundred strokes, you get your check and don't hang around for the cocktail party because nobody else in the tournament knew anybody in Wyoming with a two handicap they could bring in as a sixteen and they want to kill you and the sandbagging SOB you ran in on them.

A traditional team bet is a Nassau—a wager on the front nine holes, the back nine holes and the entire eighteen holes. This is usually a team best ball competition, with handicaps applied. In a five dollar Nassau, a team could win the front one-up, lose the back two-down and therefore lose the eighteen one-down. The net loss is five dollars.

Another typical team bet is "five and two," which means five dollars per side (team best ball with handicaps applied) and two dollars on "trash." In this bet, and sometimes in a Nassau, being two-down automatically freshes the bet, that is, starts a new bet from that point on while the old one continues.

"Trash" is an extra bet and traditionally favors low handicap golfers, but more exotic "trash" makes the game fun for everyone.

The most common trash items are *birdies, greenies* (closest to the pin on the first shot on par-three holes, but you must make at least par) and *sandies* (a natural par after being in a sand trap). Obviously low handicap golfers are going to make more birdies, be closer to the pin and make more pars from the sand than higher handicap golfers, so traditional trash items favor the low handicappers.

Less traditional items are more democratic:

SHANKY—a natural par on a hole after shanking a shot.

DIVORCEY—Your wife called you in the grill at the turn and said she was filing for divorce and she wants the house, your car, $2,000 a month in alimony and your dog. If you make par on any hole in the back nine after getting that bit of bad news, it's a piece of trash.

DO-DOEY—If there are animals around your golf course such as cows and geese, and they have, as we discussed earlier, left anything on the green and you have to putt through it and you make the putt, ring the cash register again.

BONKER or WOODY—making par after hitting a tree or limb squarely, thus producing a "bonk" sound. In Florida or other tropical areas, a *Wooshy* is the same thing with a palm tree.

DOES A WILD BEAR CHIP IN THE WOODS?

LLOYD BRIDGES—as in "Seahunt." This is where your ball skips across a body of water and you still make par.

PUKEY—You've been up drinking all night, have an early tee time and feel like pond scum. You rush into the woods to puke and return to make par.

I've seen people bet on any number of things on a golf course. While waiting to hit on a tee, I've seen folks bet on trying to chip into the trash can, or putt with their drivers trying to get a ball closest to the tee markers. And I've even seen people bet on a hole played entirely with a putter, from tee to hole.

Two guys in Atlanta (rumor has it they had enjoyed a beer or two) once made a bet on who could play a ball from the clubhouse to a neighborhood bar several miles away in the fewest strokes. The winner played out to the street corner, chipped onto a city bus, rode to the bar, chipped out of the bus and putted into the bar for a four.

189

SAVE IT FOR THE JURY

A young golf pro struggling to make it on the tour hit a shot into the deep rough. Just as he was about to chip back to the fairway, a frog hopped out of the bushes and spoke to him. "Hey, fellow," said the frog, "if you'd move your left hand back just a little, you'd be a great golfer."

The young pro looked at the frog and said, "What the hell do you know about golf? You're just a stupid frog."

"Trust me," said the frog.

With little to lose, the pro took the frog's advice and hit a great recovery shot. He put the frog in his bag and went on to play a brilliant round. Taking the frog's advice, he won that tournament and five others before the end of the year. He was the leading money winner on the PGA tour and one of the world's best golfers.

One day the frog, who had been with him the whole

time, said, "After all I've done for you, I want you to do something for me."

"What's that?" asked the golfer.

"I want you to kiss me," said the frog.

"Kiss you? I ain't kissing no slimey frog," said the golf pro. But finally he had to admit he owed the frog a great debt, and if a kiss was the payback, he couldn't refuse. So he kissed the frog flush on the lips.

To his surprise, the frog suddenly turned into a beautiful, naked fourteen-year-old girl. Lying nude on the bed, she said, "Now I want you to make love to me."

"I can't do that," said the golf pro. "You're beautiful, but you're much too young."

"After all I've done for you, you would refuse me this one request?" said the young girl.

So the golfer relented and made love to her.

"And, Your Honor, that's exactly how it happened!"

"I don't know about that new pro," said Dave. "He may be a little strange."

"Why do you think that?" asked Clyde.

"He just tried to correct my stance again."

"So?" said Clyde. "He's just trying to help your game."

"Yeah, I know," said Dave, "but I was standing at the urinal at the time."

* * *

Fred, an obstetrician, and James, a recent first-time father, had been golfing buddies for years, but James was furious about a bill he had just received from Fred.

"How can you charge $200 for use of the delivery room when you know good and well that Alice delivered the baby on the front lawn of the hospital?" James ranted.

"You're right," said Fred as he took the bill from James. He scratched out the words "Delivery Room Fee" and wrote in "Greens Fee."

WHY ARE THERE
NO REPUBLICANS
ON PUBLIC COURSES?

IN THE YEARS since I sneaked on to the Athens
Country Club course, my first taste of a private club,
I have been fortunate enough to play at many oth-
ers.

I once played at a club so exclusive you had to
have suffered your second heart attack before you
could join. The average age of the members was de-
ceased.

Of course, only a couple of clubs in the world are
as exclusive as the Augusta National Golf Club in
Augusta, Georgia, site of the Masters tournament.
Since it is truly a national club and the local membership is no more than thirty or so, and invitations
to guests are limited, members say it is sometimes
difficult for members to find a game.

There is a true story which demonstrates the point:

One beautiful fall Saturday during football season, a National member decided he would love to play golf. He called the club looking for a game, but no one had scheduled a tee time. Several phone calls later, he still couldn't find anyone to play.

Finally, he called a friend and said, "How would you like to be my guest for a round of golf today?"

"Great," said the friend.

"Excellent. I've reserved the Augusta National course for us." They were, in fact, the only golfers on the course that day. Now *that's* ex-by-God-clusive.

After years of arduous research, I have come up with a list of ways to distinguish public courses from private courses. I offer these for the personal enrichment of my readers:

• Players on private courses acknowledge good shots by saying, "Nice swing, Edward." Players on public courses say, "You lucky mutha!"

• The rough on private courses is usually cut to precisely three inches. Depending on the type of grass, that can leave very difficult shots. For example, the rough at U.S. Open courses is like Roach Motels—you check in but you don't check out. You may find similar rough on public courses, but there it is the result of a broken bush-hog rather than strategic design.

• The balls from the practice range of the private club later become pro shop inventory at the public course.

• At private courses they'll shine your street shoes

while you play. At public courses they'll steal your street shoes while you play. I know there's at least one person with taste at my club because he stole my Guccis.

• Golf carts at private clubs sound like electric fans. Carts at public courses sound like '56 Chevys with dual exhausts and glass packs.

• Finer private clubs will have a wine bar. Most public clubhouses have a wino in a corner sleeping off a drunk.

• The masseuse at private clubs will give you a rubdown. Anybody who tries that at a public course is usually light in his loafers or out on bail.

• At private courses, men restrict the days and times when women can play. At public courses, wives usually decide when husbands can play.

• Golfers at private clubs ask, "May we play through?" At public courses they hit first and ask questions later.

• At private courses, they play it as it lies. At public courses, they play it as it lays and then lie.

• Starters on private courses are usually retired executives. Starters on public courses are usually off-duty cops.

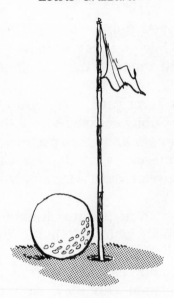

Charlie and Bruce, both low handicappers, were flying around the course and having a great round until they ran up behind two women playing together. Suddenly they had to wait before every shot.

"I think I'll walk up and ask them if we can play through," said Charlie.

"Good idea," said Bruce.

Charlie walked about fifty yards towards the women, made a quick U-turn and headed back for Bruce.

"I thought you were going to ask them if we could play through," said Bruce.

"I was," said Charlie, "but when I got close enough to see them, I realized that's my wife playing golf with my mistress."

"Are you sure? Let me go take a look," said Bruce. He walked thirty or forty yards down the fairway, did a quick about-face and came back to Charlie. "What a coincidence," he said.

HOW TO IMPROVE YOUR LIE WITHOUT GETTING CAUGHT IN ONE

CHEATING IN GOLF can range from subtle to blatant, from nominal to heinous. The universal law of relativity (discovered by either Dow Finsterwald or Albert Einstein, I forget which) dictates which it is: If *you* are doing the cheating, it usually doesn't amount to much . . . certainly not anything you'd have to worry about on Sunday morning. But if your opponent is cheating, it's likely to be a capital offense. Punishment for getting caught is being publicly humiliated in the men's grill and being forced to play with your wife in the next mixed couple tournament.

I, of course, have very little hands-on experience in this area. But in my endless quest for truth, justice and new tips for lowering my handicap, I have conducted extensive interviews with known cheaters and can now share some of their techniques with you.

(You must be over eighteen or have the consent of a parent or guardian to read beyond this point.)

Moving Violation

The most common form of cheating on the golf course is moving the ball in the rough. Even when you're playing winter rules, which allow the ball to be repositioned in the fairway, you're still not supposed to touch the ball in the rough.

But what if you're directly behind a tree, or an over-hanging limb obstructs your swing, and just a foot or so in either direction would give you relief? On a four-hundred-yard hole, what difference does twelve inches make?

There are two techniques widely used for moving the ball in the rough. One is to wait until your playing partners are a safe distance away, squat down like you're removing an unattached and non-living object from around your ball, and quickly move it the necessary foot.

The other technique is to wait until someone else actually hits their shot. At that moment, all eyes usually are on the ball. Yours, however, should be on *your* ball as you gently kick it to a better line.

Neither of these techniques works if your opponents don't trust you and therefore follow you in the woods and wait for you to hit your shot before moving on to theirs. That's usually a sign that you've gone to the well for a good line one time too often.

Should you ever get caught moving your ball in the rough, your first response should be, "My ball was sitting on a rock, and I'm not ruining a club over a five-dollar bet." If that doesn't work, try, "Hey, I thought this was a friendly game." Then act indignant and try to shift the guilt.

Finders Keepers, Losers Weepers

Another popular form of cheating is finding lost balls. Say you hit a shot into the woods. After several minutes of looking, it becomes obvious that you're probably not going to find your ball, that your opponents are probably going to win the hole by default, and that you'll probably have to get a night job to pay off the bet.

What to do? If you planned ahead, you have a replacement ball on your person and can suddenly "find" it in a place not totally cleared (nobody would believe that) but with a shot toward the fairway or green.

There are several methods for actually getting the ball on the ground. One is to have it in your pocket when you walk into the woods, pull it out, announce that you found it and simultaneously place it on the ground as you dramatically brush away surrounding debris. The only problem here is that the replacement ball may be visible between your pocket and the ground.

One way to minimize this risk is to have a hole cut

in one of your pockets (remember which one before you put your car keys or loose change in there). As you search the woods for your ball, the replacement can slip through the hole in your pocket, fall down your pants leg and roll out into a nice lie.

In cool weather, when you're probably wearing a sweater or wind breaker, another technique is to have the ball inside the sleeve on the inside of your wrist (where you take your pulse). Then you yell, "Here it is!" and as you reach down, the ball falls from your sleeve.

In all cases, be sure to pick a soft spot so the ball doesn't roll when it hits the ground.

There are also several other points to remember. For example, don't take a *new* replacement ball into the woods if you've been playing with an old one. In fact, it's best to have the same kind of ball and even better to have the same numbered ball.

Also, don't take a yellow replacement ball into the woods if you're looking for a white one. That tends to be a dead giveaway.

Finally, there's a story about this situation which brings up an interesting moral question: A golfer hit his shot into the woods, and his partner and two opponents were helping him look for it. One opponent whispers to the other, "He'll never find this one."

"How do you know that?" asks his companion.

"Because I've got it in my pocket."

About that time, their opponent yells, "Here it is!"

Do you call him a liar and explain how you know?

Didn't the same thing happen somewhere in the Old Testament? Was Adam really holding an half-eaten apple behind his back when he accused Eve?

I never knew golf was so philosophical.

Mark and Remark

Cheating on the greens requires far more finesse than cheating in the woods because everyone is there and, unless you're playing with Mr. Magoo, can watch you closer.

The easiest and most common cheat is mismarking your ball by picking it up first and then tossing down a mark. It's the golf equivalent of the game tossing to the line. With practice, you can make a dime roll eight or nine inches closer to the hole before it settles down.

Another method is using two markers. First you properly mark your ball, then two or three steps closer to the hole you casually drop another mark. When it comes your time to putt, you place your ball on the marker nearest to the hole. If you choose this method, mark with pennies; leaving dimes behind could get expensive.

And don't forget that these marking techniques can be used in reverse against your opponents. Wasn't that nice of you to mark their balls while they were making their way to the green? Isn't it funny how a putt that looks only six or seven feet long from the fairway is really fifteen feet when you get to the green?

Graffiti

On most golf courses, a white circle indicates Ground Under Repair. Any ball that lands inside can be repositioned outside the circle without penalty.

For those rare occasions when you get a bad lie or a bad line, a small can of spray paint in your pocket or in your bag can create instant Ground Under Repair and provide the necessary relief. How do you spell PAR?

Teed Off

How you ever tried hitting a driver out of the rough? Every time I've tried it, the resulting shot killed forty-seven earth worms and left a trench in the ground.

So how is it that occasionally somebody, usually my opponent, hits a driver from the rough better than he hit it off the tee? How? I'll tell you how. He teed it up. Oldest trick in the book. Some things can't be improved upon, not even by technology.

4 + 2 = 5

When I finish a round of golf, I can tell you where every shot I hit went. And most times I can tell you where every one of my opponents' shots went.

So why is it that some guys can't remember how many swings they took on one hole? You've seen them. They hack it around from tee to green, then make two passes at the cup before picking up a six-footer. I already know what they made on the hole, but just for sport I ask.

"Let's see," says Sir Isaac Newton, "I was one in the woods, two under the bush, three in the trap, four on the green and two putts for six."

"Actually you were three in the woods. That first drive you hit out of bounds carries a stroke and distance penalty."

"Penalty? It's penalty enough that I lost that ball. But I want to play by the rules, so make it an eight."

"What about the shot you banked off that passing car?"

"Oh, yeah. Nine."

"And what about that first sand shot you left in the trap?"

"Did I? Yeah, that's right. Ten."

"And you made that last six-foot putt?"

"Well, sure, you know I don't miss those."

What I do know is that the man's math is worse than Ivan Boesky's.

Was That a Forward Lateral?

When I was growing up, the Ford Motor Company used to sponsor a national Punt, Pass and Kick competition. I think some of the guys I play golf with must have been finalists in that contest.

Punting, passing and kicking all are methods of cheating as long as you do them while no one is watching. Like in extramarital sex.

Lying of Flight

When a golfer hits a shot into a water hazard, he is supposed to take a one-shot penalty and place the ball on the same line that it went into the water and no closer to the hole.

I remember something from my high school geometry class that comes into play here, something that I probably asked at the time: "How will I ever use that silly information in real life?" As divergent lines go out from a point, the distance between them increases as their length increases.

What that means is this: You hit your drive into the water on the right side of the fairway. From the tee you chose a marker, usually a tree or something in the distance, that is on the same line as your ball was. If, however, enroute to your ball you were to get your trees mixed up, you could end up placing your ball thirty yards closer to the hole. "Yeah, I had it lined up on this tree right here," you say to your skeptical opponents.

Another favorite trick of mine is to line up my ball on a bird. Nine times out of ten they'll fly away before I get there, and I have to remember where they were.

The Checkered Flag

Finally, one of the keys to successful cheating is choosing a fast golf cart. Get the picture: Your foursome is on the tee when you hit a drive near a hazard. Someone asks, "Is it in the creek?"

What you think but don't dare say is, "Not if I get there first."

You and your partner jump into your cart while your opponents clamber into theirs. If you get to the ball well ahead of them, the odds that your ball is *not* in the creek increase dramatically.

I have found that a small tip, usually two to three dollars, to the cartmaster before teeing off is a good investment. It's amazing how often my opponents get carts that barely make it around the course, while mine run like they were built by Maserati.

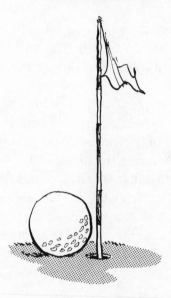

Fred had tried to be particularly careful about his language as he played golf with his preacher. But on the twelfth hole, when he twice failed to hit out of a sand trap, he lost his resolve and let fly with a string of expletives.

The preacher felt obliged to respond. "I have observed," said he in a calm voice, "that the best golfers do not use foul language."

"I guess not. What the hell do they have to cuss about?"

I'M NOT SAYING THEY WERE SLOW, BUT WINTER IN CHICAGO WAS QUICKER

SLOW PLAY IS the bane of good golfers. After following a particularly slow elderly gentleman for seven holes without being invited to play through, a younger man yelled, "Could you speed it up just a little bit?"

The old man yelled back, "I'll have you to know that I was playing this game before you were born."

"That's fine and good," said the younger golfer, "but I'd be obliged if you'd try to finish it before I die."

In certain parts of the world, most notably Scotland, an average round of golf takes only about three hours. Scottish golfers tend to play quickly because they're generally good and because they're trying to finish before the next squall comes ashore.

The average round in America takes approximately four and one-half hours, unless, of course, you're playing a resort course, in which case the average time is about six agonizing hours.

I used to think that slow play could be attributed directly to televised golf. Joe Bologna, a twenty-six handicapper, sits at home and watches the pros play on television. They discuss the shots with their caddies, take a couple of practice swings, and hit the shots. Then when they get to the green, they study their putts from all sides, step up, and knock it close if not in.

Joe watches this and figures, "Hey, if that's the way the pros do it and shoot even par, I'll do the same and shave some shots off my score." So the next time he plays, Joe discusses his shot with his partner, takes a couple of practice swings, and hits the shot . . . about twenty yards to the right.

He gets in the cart, drives twenty yards, changes clubs, discusses the shot with his partner, and hits it again . . . this time about thirty-five yards to the left.

Five shots later, following more discussion than an international summit, Joe reaches the green. He's got a forty-foot, uphill putt; odds are he'll win the lottery before he makes this putt. But, just as he saw on television, he studies the putt from all sides, sets up, and hits it halfway to the hole. Now he again studies the putt from every angle, sets up, and knocks it fifteen feet past the cup. Finally Joe scrapes it in the hole for a natural eleven. Have you ever noticed how slow play becomes the week after the Masters has been on television?

In recent years, however, I have decided that televised golf is only part of the slow play problem. The rest, I conclude, can be attributed to (1) nouveau riche foreigners, (2) company tournaments, (3) Canadian and Yankee tourists and (4) women.

I took a couple of weeks off not long ago and went to one of my favorite Southern golf resorts, the Hyatt Grand Cypress in Orlando.

There are forty-five holes at Grand Cypress, eighteen of which make up one of my favorite Southern golf courses, The New Course.

The New Course is named that because its designer, Jack Nicklaus, tried to make it look and play like The Old Course in St. Andrews, Scotland. I have played The Old Course in St. Andrews, and The New Course at Grand Cypress could be its cousin. First cousin.

There are the dreaded pot bunkers just like St. Andrews, and a burn, which is Scottish for creek, runs throughout the course and eats golf balls.

As much as I enjoy Grand Cypress and The New Course, I encountered four of the five main reasons for slow play. Here's a hint: My round was not televised. If it had been, Jerry Lewis would have been there raising money for some charity. We're talking telethon. Marathon. Homicide. Suicide.

Obstacle No. 1 was the recently wealthy foreigners. Grand Cypress charges about a hundred big ones for a round of golf. This, of course, is nothing for people who pay the equivalent of the GNP of a Third World country just to play back home.

So they descend on such resorts as Grand

Cypress, buy out the pro shop and play from dawn to dusk. That's how long it takes them to complete eighteen holes.

A guy who worked at another Orlando golf course told me that four foreign guys who showed up to play had leased a local television station's helicopter; it hovered over them for eighteen holes, videotaping every shot, as seen from three hundred feet above.

I got behind a Japanese foursome at The New Course. Not only did they take five-and-a-half hours to play, but when I suggested they speed things up a bit, they handed me a camera and asked me to take their picture. Then they took one of me and told me if ever I were in Tokyo to give them a call and they would arrange a game for me, provided I could qualify for a substantial loan at the Bank of Tokyo.

Obstacle No. 2 was a company tournament. Many companies hold their annual conventions at Southern golf resorts in the winter, not to mention their annual company golf tournaments.

Here's how it works: The company president gets up at the Registration and Welcome cocktail party and says, "Tomorrow is our annual company golf tournament, and we'd like a good turnout.

"It doesn't matter if you don't play golf. We're just out for a good time, so come on along and join us. There will be lots of beer on the course."

Six zillion furniture salesmen hit the course the next day, and your tee time is always just after the last foursome in the tournament goes off.

Prepare for another six-hour round. One of the few things that moves slower than a company golf tournament is winter in Chicago. On my second day at

DOES A WILD BEAR CHIP IN THE WOODS?

The New Course, I played behind the National Association of Tank Truck Owners.

There was a twosome playing out of one bag. There was a guy who whiffed it three times on one tee and then threw the ball fifty yards down the fairway. There he whiffed it three more times, and I cursed the sun.

When I arrived at the seventeenth tee, there were two foursomes waiting to hit. So everybody started spraying everybody else with beer.

As I stood over a putt at the seventeenth three days later, one of the guys in the foursome that was departing asked me, "Hey buddy, whar's eighteen?"

"In Palatka," I answered. I missed my putt.

Obstacle No. 3 was the dreaded Canadian or Yankee tourist, down from Cleveland or Detroit or some god-awful place in New Jersey or Toronto. You can recognize them by the way they dress for the golf course. Look for white legs with no hair on them. Look for tennis shorts and black stretch socks pulled up as close to their armpits as they can get them. Look for silly hats.

I saw a Yankee tourist playing golf in a pair of tennis shorts, black socks and a long-sleeve shirt. He was the best dresser in his foursome.

The fifteenth hole at The New Course is a par five, eight hundred yards long. There is water on the hole, not to mention a pot bunker every six yards and then a bunker down by the green that is large enough to film a scene from *Lawrence of Arabia.* I am convinced Jack Nicklaus's wife was having PMS cramps when he designed the fifteenth at The New Course.

So my foursome, all Southerners, had been behind these four Yankee honkers all afternoon. Cross-town traffic in Manhattan moves faster than they played, for God's sake.

When we arrived at the fifteenth, they hadn't teed off yet. "Y'all haven't teed off yet?" I asked.

"It's the foursome ahead of us," said one of the honkers, who was wearing a silly hat. I looked at his bag and there was a tag from some course in New Jersey.

"Do you mean," I said, "the foursome that is walking off the fifteenth green three miles ahead of you?"

"They're slow," he said. "Very slow." (Yankee golfers are bad to repeat themselves.)

They finally teed off. One topped it fifty yards and didn't make the ladies' tee. We thought of explaining the Ft. Worth Rule to him, but then we thought better of it. It would only slow things down more.

The next guy hit it in the water on the right. The next went into a pot bunker, and the fourth hit his in the monkey grass which guards the left side of the fairway.

We timed it. Twenty-eight minutes after the Yankees teed off, they were out of range so we could hit our drives.

A guy in my foursome who lives in Orlando said, "If the SOBs didn't come down here and spend all that money, there'd be a bounty on 'em."

A lot of Southern golf resorts have alligators. Alligators do not know how much money Yankee tourists spend. So there is some hope.

Obstacle No. 4 was women. I once wrote in a column that women should have their own golf courses so they wouldn't slow down male players. Lady golfers at my home course burned a sand wedge in front of my locker, and my secretary, the lovely and talented Miss Wanda Fribish, who is also an officer in the 303rd Bombadier Wing of the National Organization for Livid Women, said, "Die, scumbag!" as she threw her daggerlike letter opener at me.

Luckily, I was able to dodge her missile. It stuck in the photograph of the October playmate that hangs on my wall.

Perhaps I should attempt to clear up my stand on women on the golf course:

First, there are many, many women who can beat me playing golf. I am to golf what Moammar Khadafy is to world peace. Who I'm talking about are the female versions of me, the lady hackers. They are the ones who slow down play, and here is why:

When the male high-handicapper reaches a score of double-bogey or triple-bogey and he still doesn't have the ball in the hole, he avoids further embarrassment by moving on to the next hole so as not to slow down golfers behind him. Not so with many women high-handicappers. They are resolved to get the ball into the hole regardless of how many strokes it takes.

I was playing behind a woman at Grand Cypress. After she took two hours to complete the first six holes, I counted her strokes on the seventh.

She made a twenty-six. It was a par three.

Men and women could get along on the same golf course if women simply would PUT THE DANG BALL IN THEIR POCKETS AND MOVE ON AFTER THEIR SCORE REACHES DOUBLE DIGITS.

This will never happen, of course, which is why women should have their own golf courses so they can hack the ball around as long as their hearts de-

213

sire. Women have their own restrooms and bridge clubs, don't they? So what's wrong with their own golf courses?

As far as Ms. October is concerned, she was hit by the letter opener in such a location that she certainly won't be playing golf anytime soon.

There is this place in south Florida—I can't tell you the name of it or exactly where it is—where they have solved the problem of women on the golf course. The reason I'm not going to put a name or location on it is because some feminist might read this and decide to file suit, and I might never be invited back as a guest.

At this golf club, women are not only forbidden from the course, they aren't even allowed on the grounds except once a year. For the annual Christmas party.

Your wife drives you to the club. She lets you off at the front gate. Phone calls from women are even discouraged.

"And you can play gin rummy naked," a member explained to me. I'm not certain I'd want to play gin rummy naked, but I saw the member's point.

There aren't any women within miles of the club, so you're safe to belch or curse or make funny noises with your armpit, or, if you so desire, to play gin rummy naked.

"When will men ever grow up and get over such as this?" flared-nostril women readers are asking.

Most of us never will because of the Treehouse Syndrome. When men are boys, they build treehouses, or other assorted edifices, in order to have a secret place to go with their friends where there aren't any girls to tell them how stupid they are, or how they should move the orange crate over near the cardboard box that serves as a table in order to give the room more symmetry.

We need this getaway all our lives in order to gather our wits and share the goodness that is brotherhood.

And to play gin rummy naked if we want to.

Men have given up so much of what was once their exclusive space as it is. And some of it we needed to share. Like boardrooms and mastheads and offices on the top floor.

But at this club at least, men have drawn the line at golf.

"What I like most about this club," said a friend who was also a guest, "is there aren't any ladies' tees. You can hit from all the way up front and not feel like a wimp."

Indeed.

My own baptism in the necessity of picking up came when, after nearly a decade away from the game, I launched my comeback at Myrtle Beach, South Carolina. A companion and I paid a week's salary for green fees, rental clubs, electric cart and a half-dozen golf balls. (I could have sworn they were white when I quit playing.)

On the first tee my playing partner and I made the obligatory small wager and then proceeded to tee off. Unfortunately, my first drive sliced into the back-yard of somebody's condominium where a Tupperware party was in progress. I got a free container suitable for serving congealed salads and a free drop off the coffee table.

My second shot, a three wood, caught a tree limb and bounced back toward the Tupperware party, coming to rest on a plate of cheese and crackers the ladies were munching with their white wine. This time I bought six cups and a casserole container to pay for the damages and pitched back into the fairway. I took a twelve on the first hole. My companion went one-up with an eleven. We agreed to pick up before we reached double digits again.

We both went into the water on the second hole— the water in a swimming pool located behind somebody else's condominium where a woman sat reading a copy of *Cosmopolitan.* My companion removed his tennis shorts and waded into the pool to retrieve our errant shots. The woman went inside and fetched her husband, a very large man who threatened to call the authorities if we weren't off his property within thirty seconds.

In our haste to leave, we drove the cart over one of the pool chairs, which wouldn't have been all that bad had it not been the one the woman was sitting in at the time. Luckily, the poor woman was unhurt, but her *Cosmo* got caught under one of the cart wheels, and we scattered a series on unsightly liver spots for several hundred yards. I finally shot a sixty-six on the front nine. My companion had a sixty-two and took me for a dollar.

Undaunted, we drove to the strip on Myrtle Beach and got in a quick eighteen holes at Jungle Jim's Carpet Golf, where they don't care if you take off your shirt just as long as you don't steal the scoring pencils.

Relieved to get away from the pressure of the regular links, I got my dollar back on the last hole by sinking a long putt that rolled into the monkey's mouth, out through his tail, then under the giraffe's legs before dropping squarely into the cup. It must have been finishing on that high note that brought me back to the game for good. Or bad. Or whatever.

NO MATTER WHAT YOU CALL IT, IT STILL GOES SIDEWAYS

THERE ARE CERTAIN words in every environment that are inappropriate. For example, you probably shouldn't talk about your favorite *Kool-Aid* flavor at a convention of Jim Jones followers. At a brith milah ceremony, you shouldn't brag about the new *carving set* you bought your wife. You never mention the words *no-hitter* when a baseball pitcher is actually throwing one, and you most certainly never say the S-word to a golfer.

The S-word is the most dreaded of all golf diseases because there is no known cure, short of a frontal lobotomy, which tends to have an adverse effect on other parts of the golf game. Like remembering how to get to the course. Or what to do when you get there.

219

The S-word is like a cancer that grows slowly in the golfer's brain. Even on days when you feel great and are playing well, it lurks in the recesses of your mind, just waiting for the chance to strike. To spread. To drive you looney.

The word itself is so intimidating that golfers have created many euphemisms for it:

— Chinese hook
— lateral
— three o'clock
— snap fade
— power push
— "thang"

Although many teaching professionals claim to be able to cure the S-word, those afflicted with the disease say it ain't so. Not even the CDC has been able to wipe out this scourge of golf.

The only thing we all know for sure is that the shot is created by hitting the ball with the hosel of the club. This can be done by leaving the club face open or by closing it. One way or the other, the ball makes contact with the hosel instead of the club face.

There are stories of pros being driven from the tour by the S-word. My club pro told me about a man who came to him in tears because of the S-word. A good friend of mine, Boom-Boom Boyd, who played on his college golf team and has actually won a legitimate golf tournament in his career, contracted the disease a couple of years ago and has been struggling since.

When I told him I was writing a chapter for this book on the S-word, he offered a personal testimony about what it's like to suffer this fate. His hope is that by sharing his experience, others may be spared the same humiliation . . . or at least give him more shots next time they're making a bet:

"The S-word is a life-altering disease. In one quick flash of flexible steel, your entire personality and outlook on existence is changed for all eternity.

"You are embarrassed; you are emasculated; you are stripped naked of all self-worth. You lose control of your private bodily functions, sometimes on the very spot. It is the sensation of being struck with a cold bolt of lightning. It sends a flash of nausea through your entire body, churning your bowels.

"You immediately look for a place to hide, but it is hopeless. To relieve the pain and embarrassment, your soul seeks to leave your body. You see Jesus in reverse.

"You are panicked. You consider surgery. A sex change operation is not ruled out.

"My experience leads me to conclude that the S-word is not a physical disease but rather a spiritual sickness. Somewhat akin to demonic possession. Could I have committed some travesty in an earlier life that would warrant this type of punishment?

"The S-word is contagious, so your golfing comrades avoid you. You go to your club. The parking lot is filled with automobiles, but no one is inside. You are reminded of the closing scene from the movie *On the Beach.* You search the premises for your friends, and, alas, find them huddled and trembling in the far corner of the locker room hiding in a darkened shower stall.

"Life seems hopeless. But it goes on.

"There are more remedies for the S-word than there are cures for the common cold, and all are equally ineffective. Yet in desperation you try them all. Eventually you seek professional assistance. Your local teaching pro promises to cure you. In fifty-five years of golf, he says, he has never S-worded a golf ball. The fundamentals of the golf swing were instilled in him at a very early age by his father, who was also a professional.

"After two hours on the practice tee, you have given him the disease.

"Word of your trouble is spreading. It has reached a friend who is a touring professional. He calls to offer help. On a break from the tour, he meets you on the practice tee one Sunday afternoon. He watches you S-word practice balls for the better part of an hour without comment. Then he asks if you might be able to teach him the shot to be used as a psychological weapon in Australian match play.

"You are awakened at night by a dreamy remedy. Could this be a heavenly vision? You slip silently from your bed in hopes that you do not awaken your wife, who is sleeping in a deep state of exhaustion brought on as a result of having to carry the entire financial burden of providing for the family during your illness.

"You put on your golf shoes in the darkness and stuff whiffle balls into your bathrobe pockets. You take your wedge outside and experiment with the newfound solution. In the headlights of your automobile, on your small front lawn, it works! You rush inside and euphorically call your pro from his sleep to analyze the experience.

"His conclusion: 'If the whiffle balls are going

straight, then you need to start playing the sons of bitches.'

"I remain bowed but not broken. Like so many others, I must survive until a cure is discovered."

Don't it just break your heart? A man stricken in his prime. But fate is a cruel mistress.

This same poor soul was part of our group which went to Scotland to play golf for two weeks. Before our first round, my friend went to the men's locker room to relieve himself. Suddenly we heard a blood-curdling scream and rushed in to find him standing there paralyzed. On the front of every urinal, dyed into the porcelain like fine Wedgewood china, was the name of the manufacturer—Armitage Shanks.

The justice of the peace in a small town was about to tee off with two other friends one day when the club pro volunteered to join them. It seemed like the perfect opportunity for a free lesson. But instead of being helpful, the pro was openly critical of the JP's game. At every bumbled shot, the pro made a joke about the justice.

But the criticism didn't even stop at the end of the round. The pro continued to embarrass the JP in the clubhouse among his friends. Finally the pro got up to leave and said, "Judge, let's do it again sometime. If you can't find anybody else to make it a foursome, I'll be glad to play with you again."

The justice of the peace said, "How about next Saturday? I don't think any of my friends can join us, so why don't you invite your parents, and after our round I could marry them."

An Italian, a Frenchman and a Scotsman were playing golf on a links course when they spotted a stunning mermaid on the shore. They all dropped their clubs and ran down for a closer look.

The mermaid was incredibly beautiful and voluptuous. The Italian, burning with desire, asked the mermaid, "Have you ever been fondled?"

"No, I haven't," whispered the mermaid. So the Italian walked over and hugged and fondled her warmly. The mermaid said, "Hmmmm, that's nice."

The Frenchman, not to be outdone, said, "Have you ever been kissed?"

"No, I haven't," answered the mermaid. So the Frenchman went over and kissed her long and slow. "Hmmmm," sighed the mermaid, "that's nice."

Finally the Scotsman asked her, "Have you ever been screwed?"

"No, I haven't," said the mermaid.

"Well, you have now," said the Scotsman, " 'cause the tide's out!"

THE FIRTHS,
FOURTHS AND FIFTHS,
OF FOREIGN GOLF

I HAVE PLAYED tennis in three foreign countries.
Except for an occasional sign in a strange tongue,
usually forbidding spitting or playing without a
shirt, the experiences were identical. I don't remember one overhead from another, because the tennis
court, by design, is the same in Europe as it is America.

I also have played golf in three foreign countries—
four, if you count Hawaii. Each experience was
unique, each course different, each round memora-
ble. The only thing that was the same in each instance was the caliber of my game, which is beside
the point.

That's one of the glories of golf. Every course you
play—whether domestic or foreign, public or private,

long or short, mountain or beach—is a new and wonderful experience. Even bad courses usually have a couple of great holes on them.

In addition to the courses being different throughout the world, the nuances surrounding the game also are different. Nowhere are they more distinct than in Scotland, the birthplace of golf and the site of my ancestral home—Glen Close.

Twice I have been to Scotland with a group of golfers to play the most historic courses in the world. Each time I came back a bloody pulp but never more in love with the game.

It's amazing to me that any American golfer has ever won the British Open, because the courses and the elements are so unlike ours that it's almost a different game.

Maybe that's what my caddy meant one trying day when I said, "I want you to know this is not the game I usually play." He answered, "I should hope not, sir. But tell me, what game do you usually play?"

The links courses of Ireland and Scotland are topographical wonders. Situated next to bays (sometimes called firths, a Scottish word for "large water hazard") or directly next to the ocean, they are always wind-blown. And rain-blown.

You've heard the old joke: If you don't like the weather, just hang around a few minutes and it'll change. That joke must have originated near a links course.

One day at Lahinch in Ireland, we teed off in beautiful Irish weather (that means cloudly, fifty degrees, and winds gusting up to thirty miles an hour).

Before we finished nine holes, the wind was at gale

force and rain was blowing horizontally. My caddy, a nine-year-old boy, could no longer move forward into the wind, so I had to abandon him and carry my clubs the rest of the way. I hope the nice lad was found.

I had my doubts about him before we even started. The first tip that the youngster might have trouble was the fact that he was barely taller than my bag. I complained to the caddymaster about having a nine-year-old boy as a caddy.

"Better to have them very young, sir," said the caddymaster. "The lad probably can't count past ten."

By the time I finally left him on the course, he looked and walked like Walter Brennan. Bad golf will age a man—or boy—quickly.

I finished the round, of course. That's part of the thrill of Irish and Scottish golf. No matter what the elements, you persevere. One of our group, leaning into the wind at a forty-five degree angle, yelled, "Next time there's a hurricane warning off the Georgia coast, why don't we call down and get tee times for the group?"

Another member of our group had washed a pair of pants in the hotel the night before. He apparently had not rinsed them very well, however, because as the rain soaked through his pants, they began sudsing. Every time the man took a step, suds bubbled out of his shoes. And from between his legs. It looked like he had taken an Oxydol enema.

The wind blew so hard that you couldn't spot a ball on the green without its blowing. If you were downwind, you didn't even have to hit the putt; you just spotted it and let it go. If you were upwind, you had to make an indentation in the green and place the ball in it, and then you had to take a full shoulder turn to drive the putt into the wind.

At the Old Course at St. Andrews, Scotland, the wind was gusting to fifty miles per hour. My caddy said, "Aye, sir, you should be here when the wind really gets up." Moments later, as he handed me a club for a shot into the teeth of the wind, he said, "Best to keep it low, sir." Oh, really?

Beautiful and intimidating land formations are created by these elements. No bulldozer has ever set tread here. Huge mounds rise up in the middle of fairways, and cliffs are formed by the pounding of the sea. Pot bunkers—deep, hellish depressions all over the courses—were created by sheep seeking shelter from the wind and rain. Three hundred years ago, that's all this land was good for—grazing sheep. And then some sadistic soul designed a golf course on it. They left the natural bunkers and, not content with mere punishment, even added sand in the bottom of some of them.

There's a joke about one of the bunkers at Muirfield in Scotland which tells the story:

One day a priest playing the fabled course found himself with an impossible lie in one of the deep fairway bunkers. His ball was buried in sand and the wall of the bunker was four feet high.

The priest looked at his ball, turned his face toward Heaven and said, "God, help me." Then he looked back at the ball, the part of it that was showing, turned again to Heaven and said, "And, God, don't send Jesus. This is no shot for a boy!"

Amen.

* * *

Unlike in America, most of these wonderful courses are open to the public. Nonetheless, I recommend that you travel with a golfing group if possible because a lot of things can go wrong between Ireland and Scotland, as you'll soon read.

Since portions of these trips are not perfectly clear in my memory (must have been something in the water . . . or over the ice), I have asked my friend and erstwhile correspondent, Mikey "The Mouse" Steed, playing out of the Social Circle Sewing Center in Ft. Deposit, Alabama, to offer advice to any aspiring masochist who wants to play golf in Ireland and Scotland. You're up, Mike.

"When contemplating such a trip, you can make no more important decision than who is going. Choose wisely those companions you enjoy, because ten days at close quarters will test friendships.

Our group was led (astray, most often) by Lewis McDonald Grizzard, "a legend under the kilt," as he told us frequently. The group consisted of redneck raconteurs, good old boys and middle-aged professionals (Muppies). You know the type—they hang around bars, playing gin and telling lies.

The coveted invitations were extended to almost anyone who could gather enough money to put up a deposit and produce a handicap of fifteen or below, which is required for play on many Scottish courses.

Seeking a name that blended the character of the group with the homeland of golf (where everything is either "Royal" or "McSomething"), we named our event "The McNeck Invitational." The runner-up name was "Floggers of the Firth of Feces." Rejection

232

of that name was the final display of good taste exhibited by the travelers.

Arrangements

There are many good tour operators who specialize in golf packages that are nearly idiot proof. We tested this claim and found it to be true. They book the flights, the hotels, transfers, and, most importantly, the tee times.

Both times we were graced by the world's best bus driver, Scotsman Tommy Hanlon, who told some of the best and raunchiest jokes we ever heard. Usually by the third telling of a joke, we caught enough of his Scottish brogue to understand it. He also taught us local swearing and got us to the course on time.

It was Tommy who, when questioned about the existence of the Loch Ness monster, said, "Of course I believe in her. I divorced her only six months ago."

Women

Your trip likely will be celibate unless you bring your own. There just aren't that many women around the golf courses in Scotland and Ireland . . . and those who are there are difficult to distinguish from the ubiquitous sheep.

Without mentioning any names, one member of our group was always attempting to befriend attractive desk clerks and waitresses. Lewis's first move was to ask a comely lassie her name. She might reply, "My name is Abigail." From there the exchange was predictable.

"Ah, Abigail, what a lovely name. Are you married?"

"Yes."

"And are you happily married?"

The man was persistent if not successful. After awhile, I devised a plan to help keep this dog under the porch. I learned that nearly half of the Irish people speak Gaelic and virtually all understand it. I learned a Gaelic phrase from my Irish caddy at Ballybunion which goes, "Pog ma thoin." It means, "Kiss my ass."

I taught the phrase to Lewis, but rather than encourage him to use offensive language, I told him it meant, "You're very lovely." It was worth the price of the trip to hear the exchange with the waitress that evening.

"What's your name, Darling?"

"Colleen."

"Ah, Colleen, pog ma thoin," he said passionately.

Equipment

You are advised to eschew the "big hog" golf bags so often strapped on the back of American golf carts, because there's a great likelihood that bag will be strapped to your back in Scotland. While most courses have caddies, they look at you like you have a pox if you ask them to haul one of those "tour" bags.

A lightweight bag is essential, but that doesn't necessarily mean small. It should be large enough to hold your dirty underwear for the trip home.

Take two pairs of comfortable golf shoes, for you will be walking. No carts. You can wear the second pair while the first one dries out. And take a good rain suit. It's the outfit you'll be wearing in most of your photographs.

You'll be surprised how few balls you will need—a sleeve per round is usually adequate. The caddies rarely lose one, and there is very little water on the courses. Of course, the price you pay for the caddies' skill is often verbal abuse. Allow me two examples.

As we were tromping the heather looking for an errant shot one day, someone asked, "What kind of ball is it?"

The caddy answered quickly, "A brand-new one— never been properly hit!"

Another time a caddy pointed out a ball in the rough which he claimed was mine. "That can't be my ball," I said. "It looks far too old."

"But, sir," said the caddy, "it's been a long, long time since we started."

More about caddies later.

Clothing

You'll need a variety of clothing, from short sleeve golf shirts and sweater vests to turtleneck and warm sweaters. Remember that you'll be wallowing in the mother lode of woolen sweaters and will probably want to bring some home.

For ectomorphic golfers, silk long underwear provides warmth and comfort as well as a few winks in the locker room.

Food

It's hearty, good, stick-to-the-ribs fare. They have lots of cows in Ireland and sheep in Scotland, as well as fresh fish in both places, so all three make excellent choices.

Be sure you know what you're doing before you order the Scottish staple haggis. It was cooked in a sheep's stomach. And if you think you know everything that can be done to a pig to make it edible at breakfast, you'll learn a lot in Scotland.

The presentation of food is done with great élan in hotel restaurants. Usually, you are served by a team. The food is unveiled ceremoniously, and your expressions of delight are well received.

One member of our group had the best response of the trip when he was served chocolate mousse for dessert. It was grandly placed before him, three thick lines of dark brown chocolate mousse squeezed from a pastry bag onto a large, pristine white plate.

He looked at the waiter and said, "My compliments to the dog."

Spirits

The drinking kind, not the haunting kind. You have arrived in the motherland. Don't order a "Scotch" in Scotland, because it's all "Scotch" to them. They just call it whiskey.

You will recognize certain blends from the shelves in the U.S., but there is a plethora of single-malt whiskeys from little known regional distilleries throughout Scotland. Each is distinctive and worthy of debate among Scotch lovers in choosing *the* very best.

There are more brands to choose from than the A&P has cereal selections. I recommend taking home some of the obscure brands for gifts. Your friends will like it just because they can't get it at home; so what if it really tastes like creosote?

There also are wonderful regional beers, each with its own character and body. In gluttonous quantities, each can change your character and lead to out-of-body experiences.

International Relations

There can be no friendlier, sweeter people on this earth than the Scots and Irish. You should be loathe to insult them. Read *The Ugly American* before you go, and don't invite Lewis Grizzard. Even friendly, sweet people have their limits, and we tested them trying to fly from Ireland to Scotland.

It was chaotic at the Shannon, Ireland, airport. We had played eighteen holes at Ballybunion and were hustling to make a flight to Edinburgh, Scotland, with a change of planes in Dublin. Murphy's law took over, and six of us were somehow dropped from the computer for the last leg of the flight.

By the time the problem was discovered in the Dublin airport, the flight was sold out except for two seats. Four of us would have to stay behind and find alternate transportation.

In the meantime, Lewis had made a startling discovery of his own—that the plane for the last leg of the flight was a commuter with propellors and an overhead wing. For a man who hates to fly in the best of circumstances, this was too much. He began preparing himself for the coming ordeal by taking on supplemental fuel. I think it was double screwdrivers. By the time the plane was ready for boarding, he was charming enough to be considered "tanked."

With reality staring him in his glazed eyes as he walked across the tarmac toward the waiting plane, Lewis made a quick decision to drive to Scotland (across the Irish Sea, we presume). He jumped into a fuel truck belonging to the Irish airline, Aer Lingus (which I think is Gaelic for "Fly My Tongue"), and started the truck's engine.

Forty-seven ramp attendants and two security guards with their hands on their weapons appeared from out of nowhere and convinced Lewis to get out of the truck. He was again aimed at the airplane, but before boarding, he decided to kick the tires to see if they were worthy. He reserved his verdict for a nun he encountered on the plane—"Pray for us, Sister," he said, " 'cause this damn thing is going to crash!"

Meanwhile, back in the terminal where four of us waited for a plan to get to Scotland, Aer Lingus officials tried to placate us by saying there might be one additional seat to open up on the plane. Security personnel were about to remove one unruly passenger. We begged and pleaded with them not to remove that passenger—it could only be one person—that to do so might imperil the country. Lewis stayed on the plane.

The four stragglers, including your correspondent, were flown to London and then driven to a waiting train destined for Edinburgh. Overnight. Full of unwashed travelers from the Middle East and poor German students. With no stops for food, water, or beverage.

We arrived in Edinburgh, battered and bruised, just in time to catch a taxi to nearby Muirfield for our 10:30 A.M. tee time. Not even Jack Nicklaus misses a tee time at Muirfield.

Unfortunately, Aer Lingus had not, as they had promised, put our clubs and bags on the plane to Edinburgh. The result was that we had to tackle the legendary course with borrowed clubs and shoes.

As our weary group sat trying to piece together the proper ensemble, one member said, "I saw a man who had no shoes and I wept, until I saw a man who had no clubs."

Caddies

Don't tee off without them. For one thing, the courses are not marked like the ones you're used to.

There are no cart paths to guide you and, by definition, links courses are very natural and have many blind shots. The only disadvantage to a caddy is that they usually won't carry a cooler of iced-down beer like a cart will.

My advice is to listen to what the caddies tell you. They know the courses, and after a few holes they know you and your game. Nonetheless, I did manage to fool one for several holes at Gleneagles.

There is a pecking order of sorts when caddies choose the bags they want to carry; that order is based on seniority. I'm sure they look at the men to spot good tippers, the equipment to spot good golfers, and so forth.

This was my first encounter with a Scottish course. Combine that with jet lag, and I was as nervous as a man wearing trifocals at a strip joint. I hooked my first tee shot into a fairway bunker, got out OK and salvaged bogey. The next two holes produced solid double bogeys. My drive on the fourth tee again went off the fairway. As we walked toward the ball, my caddy, who had been extremely quiet, suddenly said with great scorn, "Normally when a man carries a *one* iron, he can play."

Caddies for afternoon rounds can be scarce, so it's best to book them for the entire day. Even that has its pitfalls, however. At St. Andrews we played The New Course at 8 A.M. and were scheduled to tee off on The Old Course at 3 P.M. Our caddies used the three hours between rounds to drink their profits in the local tavern. By the time we got on The Old Course, they were loop legged.

When I occasionally hit a good shot and held the pose at the top of my swing, my caddy would scream, "ICHIBAN! ICHIBAN!" Seems that he had been caddying for too many of the Japanese golfers who flock to St. Andrews with cameras in hand.

We picked up a lot of local color from these wonderful, surly ambassadors of mirth and golf history. Just their phrases alone are worth the price of admission:

• "Sir, hit it on a line directly between the paps in the distance." Say what? When he told me that "paps" means breasts, the terrain in the background became unmistakable.

• "Take it on a line just a wee bit right of the Scotsman lying on his back." This was a reference to a tall silo in the distance.

But they also can be demanding and critical:

• "Damn you, sir. I said *drrraw* it, not *hoook* it!"

• After I hit a particularly bad shot, my caddy turned to me and said, "And you call yourself a golfer."

• Another member of our group, trying to make conversation, said to his caddy, "I'll bet you caddy for some pretty bad golfers." The caddy replied, "Aye, laddie, I'm caddying for one now."

• Lewis's caddy at Nairn said to him, "You have a great short game, sir. Too bad it's off the tee." At the end of that round, Lewis tried to retaliate by saying, "You must be the worst caddy in the world." To which the caddy responded, "That, sir, would be too great a coincidence."

• Finally, after another string of bad holes, I tried to make light of the situation with my caddy. "You know," I said, "golf is a funny game." With an absolutely straight face, he said, "It's not supposed to be, sir."

A golfing trip to Scotland and Ireland is a dream you can live. There is nothing quite like it for those who love the game and its history. The charm of the Olde Sod may be oft imitated but never duplicated. And if anyone tells you otherwise, just tell 'em, "Pog ma thoin!"

In Mexico, plush golf resorts have been built along the coasts. These are virtual leisure compounds, where the beautiful people eat, drink, swim, tan and play games. Just outside these compounds, however, is a very poor country with a low standard of living. People work hard for little money. The American dollar is strong, and everything is relatively cheap.

Several of us once spent four days playing courses around Ixtapa, Mexico. The green fee, for a plush facility, was about four dollars, and a cart for eighteen holes was less than that.

As we prepared to tee off the first day, a Mexican man in his late forties offered to serve as our forecaddy. Even though we had electric carts and didn't need a regular caddy, it was helpful to have someone along who knew the course and could help us find stray shots.

At the end of the round, Lupe had done an excellent job, so we each gave him ten dollars. His eyes bulged, and he asked excitedly if we were playing again the next day.

For four straight days, Lupe met us on the first tee

and served as forecaddy, and each day we paid him ten dollars apiece. We knew that was a good deal of money to him, but we didn't fully realize how much.

I suppose we should have been tipped off when, on the third day, Lupe's wife met us at the turn with sandwiches she had prepared.

At the end of our round on the fourth day, Lupe again asked about the next day. When we told him we were leaving, that our vacation was over, he cried. The man wept because we were leaving. No, actually he wept because our American dollars were leaving.

The courses I played in Hawaii were mostly around mountains and volcanos. Of course, every one of them was plush, but that's no big deal in a land so fertile that tropical fruit trees grow out of what appears to be solid rock.

Many of the courses were on cliffs overlooking the ocean. And the wind blew steadily. And it was not a good idea to wear baggy shirts that could fill up with wind and become balloon-like. With you inside them.

Basically, there are two things that describe golf in Hawaii—long waits and pineapples.

I was looking forward to playing golf in Bermuda. I had seen photographs of the beautiful courses carved out of that tiny island. Pink sand. Clear blue water. It was like playing on a postcard.

I had arranged an invitation to play at the prestigious Mid-Ocean Club, one of the island's few private courses. Ve-dy British, photographs of scowling old men on the wall. Before I left the states, I had purchased a new pair of golfing shorts and a new shirt for the occasion.

Shorts are popular in Bermuda, especially Bermuda shorts. Makes sense, doesn't it? Men actually wear them to the office with knee socks, shirt, tie and coat. I couldn't help thinking of Little Lord Fauntleroy.

Anyway, I catch a taxi from my hotel to the golf course and am greeted there by a man who appears to be doorman.

"May I help you, sir?" he asks in a clipped British accent with his nose in the air.

"Yes, my good man," I counter. "I'm here to play golf."

"Not in those shorts, you're not," he says.

"What's wrong with these pants?" I ask, wondering who died and made this fellow king for the day.

"They're too short, sir. All you Americans think you can come over here and dress any way you like. Well, not on this course. This club has strict standards, sir, and your pants are definitely too short."

I argued for a good while longer, just out of principle. But when they started to call the U.S. Embassy, I figured maybe my pants were a little too short.

Not coincidentally, I was able to buy a pair that were the proper length—approximately one and a half inches longer than mine—in the pro shop. For a king's ransom.

If that scam were tried in the U.S., Ralph Nader would be on them like hair on a leg.

My round was most enjoyable, except for one embarrassing episode. I was still feeling a bit harassed when we teed off, and even when we reached the first green I was still thinking of ways to maim that uppity doorman.

Suddenly I was struck by the beauty of the green. The grass was so perfect, firm yet soft like carpet, with just a hint of blue in its deep green color.

"This green is beautiful," I said to my host. "Is it bent grass?"

He looked at me without a smile and said, "No, Bermuda."

MORE STORIES ABOUT THOSE CATTY CADDIES

NEAR THE END of a particularly trying round of golf, during which the golfer had hit numerous fat shots, he said in frustration to his caddy, "I'd move heaven and earth to break a hundred on this course."

"Try heaven," said the caddy. "You've already moved most of the earth."

Standing on the tee of a relatively long par three, the confident golfer said to his caddy, "Looks like a four-wood and a putt to me." The caddy handed him the four-wood, which he topped about fifteen yards off the front of the tee. Immediately the caddy handed him his putter and said, "And now for one hell of a putt."

* * *

The golfer sliced his drive deep into the gorse, and the diligent caddy followed him in. After several minutes, they found the ball under a thick branch.

"Do you know what kind of shot I'll need here?" asked the golfer.

"Yes, sir," answered the caddy. And he pulled a hip flask from his back pocket.

"Caddy, why do you keep looking at your watch?" asked the curious golfer.

"It's not a watch, sir. It's a compass."

For most of the round the golfer had argued with his caddy about club selection, but the caddy always prevailed. Finally on the seventeenth hole, a 185-yard par three into the wind, the caddy handed the golfer a four-wood and the golfer balked.

"I think it's a three-iron," said the golfer.

"No, sir, it's a four-wood," said the caddy.

"Nope, it's definitely the three-iron."

So the golfer set up, took the three-iron back slowly, and struck the ball perfectly. It tore through the wind, hit softly on the front of the green, and rolled up two feet short of the pin.

"See," said the caddy. "I told you it wasn't enough club."

The golfer tried three straight times to hit the ball over the inlet of water between him and the green, but each time the ball splashed into the drink. In utter frustration, the golfer said, "Caddy, take my clubs on in. I'm going to jump in the water and drown myself."

"I doubt that, sir. You couldn't keep your head down long enough to drown."

The man came in from a long afternoon of golf. His wife met him at the door with a kiss. A few minutes later their son came in looking tired and weary.

"Where's he been?" asked the father.

"He's been caddying for you all afternoon," said his wife.

"No wonder that kid looked so familiar."

YOU PROBABLY DON'T
REMEMBER ME, BUT . . .

A COUPLE OF years ago, I was invited to play in that elegant golf tournament known simply as The Crosby. It is whatever happened to the Bing Crosby tournament in California that drew the stars and the game's top players for so many years.

The late crooner had indicated that if there came a time that less than fifty percent of the proceeds of his tournament were going to charity, it should be halted, moved or somehow altered to return to its roots as an event held primarily to help the less fortunate.

The demands for a large purse for the pros finally did deplete the charitable funds, and Crosby's widow, Kathryn, packed the whole thing up and moved it to Burmuda Run Country Club in Winston-

Salem, North Carolina. The tournament raises approximately one million dollars for charity each year.

It was an incredible experience. For four days I played between the ropes, just like the stars of the PGA.

The Saturday crowd was estimated at over twenty thousand. I, an eleven-handicapper who shouldn't be that low, hit a screaming three-iron twelve feet from the pin on the watery seventeenth hole in front of five thousand people.

When I arrived at the green to applause just like at the Masters, I did my best Jack Nicklaus smile and waved.

I missed the putt, but I made par and it was bigger than the time in high school when I hit the pop fly that rolled into the weeds by the concession stand, and before the ball was found, I was around the bases for the winning run.

I also topped a few off the tee, left one in the trap on eighteen, and lost my players badge and was nearly thrown off the course by a security guard, who said with a sneer, "You don't look like no golfer." But I didn't hurt anybody.

I also got to meet a lot of famous people. Bob Hope was there. I shook his hand. I met Dale Robertson (who played in *The Tales of Wells Fargo*), McClean Stevenson, Claude Akins, Efrem Zimbalist, Jr., football's Dick (Night Train) Lane and Jim McMahon, the goofy quarterback.

I also played a round with Jim Palmer as my partner. Jim Palmer is the former pitcher for the Baltimore Orioles who now shows up on billboards wearing nothing but his Jockey underwear.

Women love Jim Palmer.

"You're absolutely gorgeous," one woman said to him at the sixth hole.

"Jim Palmer!" exclaimed another at the tenth. "I didn't recognize you with your clothes on."

It went on like that all day and I, quite frankly, got a little tired of it. It was difficult to putt with a large group of women offering up various mating calls.

Finally, however, one woman did say to me, "Lewis, what kind of underwear do you have on?"

"Not any," I replied, leaving her eating the dust of my golf cart.

Another time I played in singer Larry Gatlin's tournament, which benefits the Muscular Dystrophy Association. In my group was a monstrous professional football player named Glen Titsensor. He was a Dallas Cowboy at the time.

On one hole Titsensor swung a four-iron so hard that the head of the club came off the shaft and traveled farther from the tee than my ball had.

"I used to hit the ball like that before my operation," I said to Mr. Cowboy.

"What did you have?" he replied. "A muscle-ectomy?"

I didn't laugh because I didn't think it was that funny. But one more smart aleck remark from this palooka, I thought to myself, and I'm not going to send him a Christmas card next year.

But that's not the point of this story. The point is that on the sixth hole we were off the edge of the fairway, searching for a men's room, when someone yelled, "Snake!"

As I have explained earlier, I am afraid of snakes. Make that terrified. Even more afraid than I am of obnoxious Dallas Cowboys. I don't even look at pictures of snakes in magazines.

Mr. Cowboy, of course, was not at all afraid of the snake. He picked it up by the tail and said, "It's just a little garter snake."

I disagreed with his identification. It looked a lot like the dreaded copper-headed water rattler to me. They all do.

Mr. Cowboy just laughed, put the snake down on the ground, and jiggled his size-sixteen tennis shoe at it. The snake tried several times to bite the shoe. Mr. Cowboy laughed. I didn't need the men's room anymore. The snake slithered off into the bushes.

A couple of minutes later, when order was restored, I dubbed my shot off into the bushes where the snake had gone. I left it there for the weeds and the ages.

One fact of life I know for sure: Never give a snake that has just been embarrassed by a Dallas Cowboy the chance to get even on somebody with a physique that strongly resembles a four-iron.

Probably the highlight of my pro-am career came before the 1987 Heritage Classic at the Harbour Town Golf Links at Hilton Head, South Carolina.

The week before, Australian golfing great Greg Norman had lost the Masters golf tournament in overtime when Larry Mize chipped in from the next county. Before he could even recover, Norman suffered another traumatic experience at the Heritage— he drew me as one of his partners in the pro-am.

I figured that after losing the Masters, Norman would be justifiably quiet and maybe even pout a little. But not so. He signed about three thousand autographs and posed for at least that many pictures during our round.

As I watched him smile his way through all that, I thought of a young sportswriter who had tried to interview baseball's Darryl Strawberry of the Mets during spring training. The kid had asked Strawberry a simple question.

"Out of my face" is how Strawberry had answered him.

Norman had a bad round in the pro-am; he shot five over par.

I lost control of my game and birdied the fifth hole. On No. 6, I chipped in from off the green for another birdie.

"I've seen that shot before," said Norman, referring to Mize's winning chip against him in Augusta. "And it was going the same speed," he added, referring to the fact that both Mize's shot and my shot would still be rolling had they not gone into the hole.

I've played golf with a number of golf's best, as a matter of fact. Want a list? Okay.

• TOM WATSON: Nice person. Told me I wasn't turning my hips.

• PAUL AZINGER: Hates sportswriters. I didn't mention I used to be one.

• ANDY BEAN: Could have been a linebacker.

• HALE IRWIN: At the Federal Express Pro-Am in Memphis. It was 200 degrees. He didn't sweat.

• CHI CHI RODRIGUEZ: I told a joke to the gallery. They laughed. He said, "I'm the comedian here."

• KEITH CLEARWATER: My girlfriend wanted to marry him.

• GEORGE ARCHER: At the Doral Pro-Am. Never spoke.

• ARNOLD PALMER: Yes, I played eighteen holes with Arnold Palmer at Bay Hill in Orlando. Arnold Palmer praised my good shots, didn't say anything about my bad ones, made an eagle on Bay Hill's par-five sixteenth and got just as excited as he did when he was winning everything in sight. I made a three on a hole he made four on and we were playing from the same tees. Arnold Palmer has a dog named "Riley," hit a 270-yard three-wood, his secretary brought him a portable phone on the course so he could return his calls, and he's in his sixties and looks about forty-five.

I have eaten dinner with two presidents, sang on stage with Larry Gatlin, shook hands with Bob Hope, been to New York City several times and Paris once, kissed the best-looking cheerleader in the history of the Atlanta Falcons square in the mouth and have played golf with Arnold Palmer. My life is complete.

GATEWOOD DOOPER
AT THE MASTERS

AS ONE WHO earned his rent money on the working side of the press for a number of years, I had the opportunity to cover a lot of professional golf tournaments.

I was in Augusta when Roberto DeVecenzio signed an erroneous score card. I was there years later when an aging Jack Nicklaus roared one more time. I was at the U.S. Open when Fuzzy Zeller almost pulled it off; that's what America needed, I wrote—a U.S. Open champion named Fuzzy.

Each of the tournaments I covered was different, each with its own brand of excitement and pageantry. But two things were always the same, no matter where you were. One, the sandwiches always tasted like they had been made the day before, because they had. And two, the post-round interviews always sounded the same.

You may have seen one or two of these interviews if you watch a lot of ESPN. After a good round, a golfer is invited into the press area and asked to go over his round, shot by shot.

Once at a U.S. Open I listened as Ben Crenshaw went over his round, which had momentarily tied him for the lead. In the middle of his summary, he said, "On eleven, I hit a four-wood to the corner, had about 175 yards to the green, and hit an eight-iron to about twelve feet. Then I missed the . . ."

"Whoa, just a minute!" I said, surprising even myself. "You hit an eight-iron how far?" I mean, he's a little fellow.

"About 175 yards," said Crenshaw matter-of-factly. Seeing the bewilderment on my face, he added, "It was downhill."

Downhill, molehill. I don't think I could hit an eight-iron 175 yards with Hurricane Hugo behind me.

But most of the guys on the PGA tour are so good, and so strong, that listening to them recount their rounds has as much meaning to me as listening to someone explain mathematical equations.

I have this recurring fantasy about listening to a different kind of golfer go over his round at the Masters. I know what Nicklaus did. He hit a drive down the middle four thousand yards, hit a wedge to the stick and tapped it in with his middle finger. And on sixteen, he walked across the water to the green after holing his tee shot. That's everyday stuff.

I want them to bring in Gatewood Dooper from the Clubfoot Links in Oshkosh, who got into the tournament by some strange quirk of Masters eligibility fate and then played like a goat with muscular dystrophy.

Let me hear *him* go over his round with the world's press assembled. Here is Gatewood Dooper describing his 107, the worst round in Masters history:

"On the very first tee, I wet my pants. That's a two-stroke penalty and very embarrassing. I was hitting three on my opening drive. It landed in a trap. I wound up with a nine. My wife went back to the car.

"On No. 2, I went into the trap again. The one behind No. 3 green. I managed to save double bogey. My sponsor made an obscene gesture and went looking for my wife.

"On three, four and five, I had bogeys. My caddy agreed to stay for one more hole. I triple-bogeyed No. 6 and he went back to my car, too. To slice my tires.

"At seven, I hit a spectator. I had to. He came at me with a rock.

"I made the turn at seventeen-over. Before I teed off on ten, the tournament committee asked me to withdraw, my wife came back to the course and asked me for a divorce, and my sponsor stripped his company's name off my bag and hat.

"I fell into the lake on No. 12. One of the marshals pushed me. My drive went into the crowd lining the fairway at thirteen. I had to take another penalty. They hid my ball.

"No. 14 and No. 15 were both disasters. At sixteen, they threw beer at me. At seventeen, I twisted my ankle. My playing partner tripped me. At eighteen, they sang "Turkey in the Straw" while I tried to hit out of the rough.

"After I finally putted out, they put my card in the

paper shredder and I had to hightail it to the locker room. The tournament committee had ordered sniper fire from the roof of Ike and Mamie's cottage."

Tough luck, Gatewood, but hang in there. There's more of us who understand your round than understand a 175-yard eight-iron.

DOES A WILD BEAR CHIP IN THE WOODS?

A Tale of Two Lifestyles

Here is a twist on an oft-told story. I'm sure we've all been here at one time or another.

All his life, the dignified State Supreme Court Justice from South Carolina had dreamed of playing a round of golf at that Southern holy of golf holies, the Augusta National. But he had never met a member or been able to wrangle an invitation from someone who did. While passing through Augusta one day, he couldn't resist the urge to at least drive by and gaze at the course—or actually at the stately gates which lead to it.

Though he knew better, the primal pull led him to drive up to the gatekeeper. As the frowning man approached, the Judge rolled down his window and said, "I am Judge Poteet from Charleston, and I'm in town on business. Would it be possible for me to just drive down Magnolia Lane once?"

261

"Sorry," replied the eloquent guardian.

As he was turning around to leave, another car was turning in to the driveway. Losing all sixty-three years of dignity, he rolled down his window and stuck his head out as a signal for the driver to stop. He began talking fast.

"Are you a member of this marvelous club?" he prayed aloud.

"Of course," came the unamused reply.

Pressing forward, he continued, "Sir, I am Judge Poteet of Charleston, South Carolina, and I have been a lifelong devotee of golf. Although I have attended the Masters golf tournament for the last thirty-seven years, I have never had the privilege of playing this course. My life will not be complete until I've struck a golf ball inside these walls. Is there any way, sir, that you could help me?"

"Let's get out of the driveway," the member answered, and he gestured for the highly excited judge to follow him in.

He couldn't believe it. He was actually driving his car down the historic, picturesque, magnolia-shrouded lane leading toward the most beautiful and restricted golf club in the world. Could this be happening?

When they got to the parking lot, he jumped out of his car and rushed over to the member.

"I appreciate your taking a moment to consider my request, sir. I know this is completely out of order, but I would consider the opportunity to play here the crowning achievement of my life—and a great personal favor."

The member gave the judge a long look, shut his car door and asked, "Handicap?"

"Eleven, sir, though during my younger years I was a scratch golfer."

"Education?"

262

"Duke, undergrad, Harvard Law School—magna cum laude."

"Athletics?"

"Duke golf team. Was medalist on the '58 ACC champion team that beat Palmer's Wake Forest team in a play-off. Also lettered in all four sports in high school."

"Military?"

"Army intelligence, Korea. Purple heart and Bronze Star."

"Community involvement?"

"State coordinator for American Heart Association, '72 through '79. Chamber of Commerce, Lions' Club, church deacon."

"Club membership?"

"Charleston Country Club, Melrose, Pinehurst."

The member pondered briefly, then nodded to the young man from the club who had walked out to see if his assistance was needed, and said, "Let him hit a bucket of balls."

DIVORCE: AN AMERICAN GOLF TRAGEDY

THE MOST DIFFICULT tickets to obtain in all of sport are those which allow the holder to walk upon the hallowed grounds of Augusta National Golf Club during the annual Masters Tournament.

There are no sales to the general public. Those who have tickets either inherited them or got on the list for the privilege of buying them years ago.

What follows is a warning to those men . . . and maybe a demonic tip for their women.

Jack, an acquaintance, first began buying tickets twenty-three years ago.

"They were just fifteen dollars back then," he said, "but they went up to seventy."

Jack used to go to the tournament each year with three friends, Bill, Gene and Sid.

"We would leave home at six in the morning," he recalled. "There was a little beer store on the way. We'd wait at the door with the pulpwood workers until the guy came to open up. We had some great times and saw some great golf. But then my wife got to be a big problem for me and my Masters tickets."

"I heard that," I said.

"She just hated for me to have a good time," Jack went on. "She didn't like me going to the Masters or playing golf or fishing or running with my buddies. I was on a leash. I was a salesman and my territory was the Southeast. On Friday afternoons on my way home, I enjoyed stopping by the Elks Club and having a few beers with my buddies."

"And your wife didn't like that?"

"Of course not. She'd start yelling at me the minute I got home: 'Jack, you stopped by the Elks Club, didn't you? How many beers did you have?'

"I always said two. I usually had twenty-seven. She'd say, 'Why do you always say two?' and I'd say, 'What difference does it make what I tell you? You don't believe anything I say anyway.' One day she got so mad at me she went to my closet and took out all my clothes, and then she got my golf clubs and went out on the deck and covered them with charcoal lighter and set them on fire."

"But what about the Masters tickets, Jack?"

"Several years ago," he continued, "they cut my allotment down. I used to get four but they cut me to two. Well, that ended our group going to the tournament, and by this time my wife had gotten herself a job at the courthouse, and she started thinking she was pretty high and mighty and she wanted to be seen in all the right places. So she began going to the

Masters with me just to be seen, but she never wanted to stay over an hour.

"One thing led to another and we finally got a divorce. I was so sick and tired of everything I wanted it to be over as fast as possible.

"So when the lawyers came to me, I told them my wife could have everything, the house included. I signed the papers without really looking at them. And do you know what she had put in those papers?"

"Don't tell me."

"Yep. She had them put in that she got my two Masters tickets. And she doesn't even like golf. She did it out of spite."

"That's one of the saddest stories I've ever heard," I said. "To have once had Masters tickets and then to have lost them to an ex-wife. Have you ever tried to get them back from her?"

"I'm afraid to," said Jack. "A woman who'll take your Masters tickets would kill you if she got half the chance."

I heard that, too.

President Dwight D. Eisenhower was an avid golfer with a good sense of humor, and one of his favorite golf jokes was told by Tennessee Ernie Ford, also a golf fan. Anytime the two were together, Eisenhower urged Ford to tell this joke:

One spring day the Lord and Moses were sitting in Heaven looking down at the Earth when their eyes fell upon the beautiful Augusta National Golf Course. There was no one on the course, and the two had the same idea at the same time: "It's so beautiful, why don't we drop down and just play the back nine."

When they came to the sixteenth hole, the picturesque par three over water, the Lord said, "I think I'm going to hit a seven-iron."

Moses thought for a moment and then said, "I'm not sure that's enough. I think you should hit a six-iron."

"No," said the Lord, "I'm going to hit the seven. That's what Arnold Palmer hits, so that's what I'm going to hit."

So the Lord hit the seven-iron, but it came up about six yards short and landed in the water. Without a word, Moses parted the water, walked out and retrieved the Lord's ball.

"Maybe now you'll hit the six-iron," said Moses.

"No," answered the Lord, "I'm going to hit the seven-iron again. If Palmer can do it, so can I."

"Well," said Moses, "if you hit it in the water again, I'm not going after it this time."

Sure enough, the Lord hit a seven-iron again, and again it

fell short into the water. The Lord lay his club down and walked across the water to fetch his ball.

Just at that time, another foursome came up from behind them. One of the men spotted the Lord walking on the water and said to Moses, "Who does that guy think he is, Jesus Christ?"

"He *is* Jesus Christ. He thinks he's Arnold Palmer!" said Moses.

The great Sam Snead, known in some circles for his biting sarcasm as much as for his golf, was conducting a clinic at a chic club. A woman raised her hand and asked, "Mr. Snead, how do you make a three-iron back up?"

Snead thought for a moment and then asked, "M'am, how far do you hit a three-iron?"

"About 150 yards," answered the woman.

"Then why in the hell would you want to back it up?" said Snead.

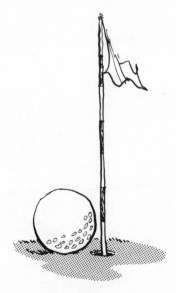

269

After being away from home for three months trying to make it on the European tour, the golf pro was finally back in bed with his wife, hoping to make up for lost time. Later in the evening when they were asleep, there was a loud knock at the door, and they both sat up straight.

"My god, that must be your husband!" exclaimed the golf pro.

"No, it can't be," said his wife. "He's in Europe playing golf."

Bob stood over his tee shot on the eighteenth hole for what seemed like forever. He'd waggle, look down, look up, waggle, look down, look up, but would never start his backswing. Finally David, his playing partner, asked, "Why on earth are you taking so long on this shot?"

"My wife is up there watching me from the clubhouse, and I want to make this shot a good one," said Bob.

"Good Lord," said David, "you ain't got a chance of hitting her from here."

QUAYLE IS BEING
KICKED IN THE PUTT

AS SOON AS George Bush nominated Dan Quayle to be his running mate, the young senator started taking a licking from the press. Even after two years as vice president of the United States, he is better known as a joke writer than a politician.

I have, until now, tried to be supportive of Vice President Quayle, because he reminds me of an old hound dog of mine who used to chase cars. (He finally caught one.) But a recent revelation about the vice president has undermined my confidence in him.

An article in *Sports Illustrated* cited Quayle's fondness for golf. He has, in fact, been referred to as "Florida's third senator," because of all the time he

271

spends in that golfing paradise. But that's not the big deal.

The article also quoted Randy Reifers, who was a golfing teammate of Quayle's at DePauw University. When asked to describe Vice President Quayle's game, Reifers, who lives in Dublin, Ohio, said: "Quayle still can't beat me. He never could putt."

As everyone who plays golf knows, putting—the actual stroking of the ball into the hole—is where the head gets involved in the game more than at any other time.

Putting is a touch. Putting is confidence. Putting is a test of the nerves.

The pro players know the axiom "Drive for show, putt for dough." Everybody on the pro tour is a marvelous golfer. But those who win tournaments and the big bucks are the ones who can sink a four-foot, downhill birdie putt on national television with a couple hundred big ones on the line.

My point is simply this: Putting is not only a true test of one's nerves; it's also a true test of one's character.

People who can't putt are lily-livered chokers who eventually commit suicide or go insane and take up bowling.

I know this to be true, because I, as much as I hate to admit it, am a terrible putter.

I can make a putt for double-bogey occasionally because there is very little pressure involved in it. But give me a short putt for par or birdie and . . . I perspire heavily. My mouth becomes exceedingly dry. I begin to breathe laboriously. My pupils dilate. My hands shake.

And I miss the blankety-blank putt.

DOES A WILD BEAR CHIP IN THE WOODS?

Another couple of bad putting years and I'll have to decide whether or not it's worth going on living if I have to become a bowler.

My question here is, Are we safe with a man who can't putt only a heartbeat away from the Presidency?

Doesn't this revelation prove that Vice President Quayle, like myself, can't take the heat? Can't make the big one when he has to?

I realize many Americans feel the press has been very harsh on Quayle, but I cannot stand idly by and not make the American public aware of this flaw in the vice president.

When I think of a national leader, I think of someone who never leaves a putt short, who firms a ball into the hole with a smooth, steady stroke despite any pressure.

I say Ben Crenshaw for vice president in '92!

A man called the pro shop to get a tee time for the afternoon.

"I'm sorry, sir," said the pro, "but we're all filled up."

"Wait a minute," countered the man. "If Dan Quayle called and said he wanted a tee time this afternoon, could you get him on?"

"Well, of course we could, sir."

"Well, fine. I happen to know that the Vice President is out of the country today, so I'll take his tee time."

Two guys from New Jersey are playing golf together, both using Titleist DT2 balls. On a long par four, they both hit great drives right down the middle. When they get to the balls, however, one of them has a very bad lie while the other is sitting up perfectly.

"I'm sure this is my ball," says Vinnie, standing over the good lie.

"No, you're wrong," says Harvey. "That's definitely my ball."

The two argue about whose ball is which for ten minutes. Finally they decide to go get the pro and let him settle the argument.

When the pro returns, he says, "Well, guys, I think I can settle this for you pretty quick. Who's playing the yellow ball?"

"If I died, would you remarry?" asked the wife.
"Probably so," answered the husband.

"And would your new wife take my place as your golfing partner?" she asked, a bit hurt.

"Probably so," answered the husband.

"And would you give her my new golf clubs?" she asked indignantly.

"Of course not," said the husband. "She's left-handed."

KISS MY ACE, IT REALLY WENT IN

ON A GLORIOUS November day in 1989, I made a hole-in-one on the St. Simons, Georgia, Island Club course.

Honest, I did. This isn't one of those make-believe things I sometimes write. I mean that I hit a golf ball on a par three and it went into the hole for a "1."

Do you know the thrill of writing a "1" on a golf scorecard next to your name?

I've had my thrills in sports before. Playing for dear old Newnan High back in '63, I hit a jump shot at the buzzer to defeat the top-seeded team in the region tournament. That got my name and picture in the paper. (I wanted a kiss from a certain red-headed cheerleader, but she remarked how she detested kissing anyone covered in sweat.)

277

I also pitched a no-hitter in Pony League, finished second in a tennis tournament, hit a hard-way six on a crap table in Vegas, made back-to-back net eagles playing with Greg Norman in a pro-am golf tournament in Hilton Head, and once had dinner with the girl who used to say, "Take it off. Take it *all* off," in the old shaving-cream commercials.

(I realize having dinner with a girl who made a shaving-cream commercial has nothing to do with sports, but she made the commercial with Joe Namath, so there.)

But none of that compares with my hole-in-one.

Get the picture:

I'm on the par three, twelfth hole at the lovely Island Club in coastal Georgia. I admit No. 12 isn't that long a hole, but I didn't design the course, so it's not my fault.

The hole is 128 yards over a small pond.

It was Saturday morning, November 4. I was playing in a threesome, comprised of myself, Tim Jarvis and Mike Matthews, two players of lesser talent with whom I often hang out.

It was a lovely morning, having warmed to the low seventies as I approached the tee. I was wearing an orange golf shirt, a pair of Duckhead khaki slacks and my black and white golf shoes, the ones my dogs have not chewed up yet.

I was first on the tee.

"What are you going to hit?" asked Matthews.

"None of your business," I said. We were playing for a lot of money.

OK, so we weren't playing for a lot of money, but you never tell your opponent what club you are hitting.

"Tell us," said Jarvis, "or we'll tell everybody how you move the ball in the rough when nobody is looking."

"Nine-iron," I said.

The green sloped to the right. I said to myself, "Keep the ball to the left of the hole."

(Actually, I said, "Please, God, let me get this thing over the water.")

I hit a high, arching shot. The ball cut through the still morning air, a white missile against the azure sky. (That's the way Dan Jenkins or Herbert Warren Wind would have described it.)

The ball hit eight feet left of the pin. It hopped once. It hopped again. It was rolling directly toward the hole.

An eternity passed.

It has a chance to go in, I thought. But that's not going to happen, of course, because I'm terribly unlucky and I've done some lousy things in my life and I don't deserve for it to go into the hole.

It went into the hole.

A "1."

It was a joyous moment when my first hole-in-one fell snugly into the hole. But the best moment came at the next tee, the par-four thirteenth.

For any non-golfers, the person with the lowest score on the previous hole gets to hit first on the next hole. I strode to the tee with my driver, teed up my ball and then said to my opponents, "I think I'm up, but did anybody have a zero?"

Jarvis and Matthews were good friends, and I shall miss them.

Wayne, who was seventy-two years old, still loved to play golf, but his eyesight had become so poor that he couldn't follow the flight of his ball anymore. He was about to give up the game when the club pro suggested a solution. "Why don't you take old Harvey with you when you play?"

"Harvey? He's eighty years old and can't even play," said Wayne.

"Yeah, but his eyesight is perfect, and he could watch your ball for you."

Wayne decided to give it a try. At least it was better than giving up the game he so loved. The next day Wayne and Harvey stood on the first tee. Wayne smacked his drive squarely. He turned to Harvey and said, "Did you see it?"

"Yep," said Harvey, "sure did."

"So where is it?" asked Wayne.

"I forget," said Harvey.

* * *

"Kathy, if you don't stop nagging me," said the golfer to his wife, "you'll drive me out of my mind."

"That wouldn't be a drive. It would be more like a gimme putt."

THE MEN'S GRILL:
THE FINAL FRONTIER

AS YOU MAY have noticed while reading through this book, golf is full of rituals—getting up the bet, talking in clichés, razing the guy who's playing poorly. But no ritual is as sacred as that of the Nineteenth Hole.

This is when, at the end of a round, the participants adjourn to the men's grill to enjoy a cold drink, to settle the bet, and to replay the highlights and lowlights of the just completed round.

In a men's grill, a man can be himself. He is surrounded only by his own kind, by golfers and gin players and drinkers, and a strong camaraderie develops over time.

Recently, however, at one of the clubs where I belong, this sanctuary was challenged. Female mem-

283

bers of the opposite sex petitioned the club's membership in an attempt to be admitted to the men's grill.

An emergency meeting of the men's grill gang was called to address this crisis. Due to the seriousness of the issue, I feel it is my duty to release the confidential transcript of that meeting so that other men's grills, should they be confronted by the same challenge, may be better suited to deal with it. (Didn't Daniel Ellsberg go to jail for something like this?)

"This meeting of the Potookie Golf and Country Club's Men's Grill and Grab-ass Association will now come to order . . . or close to it," announced Shorty Milsaps, president of the group.

The boys gunned down the last swallows of their beers and gave Shorty their attention.

"Men," Shorty began, "as most of you know, a bunch of pinheaded women's libbers have petitioned the membership of this fine club to be admitted to the men's grill. They want to sit down here amongst us and ruin our good times. And it's my job to level with you and tell you that they got a chance to win this one."

"Are you serious, Shorty?" asked Cooter Carnes.

"As serious as your mother-in-law's drawers," replied Shorty.

There was much murmuring and cursing, and finally Gilbert Harskins said, "We got to fight this, men. This is the last place we got. You can't get away from women at work no more. They are on television giving the news. They are even driving buses and attending the Rotary Club. I wouldn't be surprised to see one playin' outfield for the Pirates before it's over."

"Hell," said Marvin Coddlemeyer, "if we get women in here, we going to have to change a lot of things."

"Like what?" asked Gilbert Harskins.

"Well, for one thing, we won't be able to spit on the floor or have the weekly belchin' contest. Women don't go in for spittin' on the floor or belchin'. We'll also have to quit telling nasty jokes, and Leon Caldwell won't be able to do that funny thing where he paints eyes on his belly and uses his navel for a mouth and pantomimes, 'She Was Just a Stableman's Daughter, But All the Horsemen Knew Her.' "

"That'd be a shame," said Cooter Carnes.

"I'll tell you what else," said Marvin Coddlemeyer. "Women will want to have congealed salad and celery sticks in here 'stead of Vienna sausages and beef jerky. And I guarantee you it won't be a month before they'll be sittin' around here drinkin' white wine and talkin' about their hair stylists."

"Marvin's right," said Cooter Carnes. "A man's just got to have a place he can go now and then and just be himself and say what he wants to and scratch where it itches. Dammit, Leon, quit spittin' on my shoes."

Curtis Knowles hadn't said a word during the entire discussion. Curtis had been married four times—once to a lady lawyer—and was held as an expert on females.

"Boys," he said, "if a woman can sit here with us and listen to all the bull and put up with chewin', spittin', belchin', cussin', and Leon Caldwell's navel, I say she's what I've been lookin' for all my life and hadn't been able to find. A woman who would put up with a man just bein' himself."

A hush fell over the crowd.

"I move we put an ad in the paper," said Cooter Carnes. "I'd like to meet a woman like that myself."

DOES A WILD BEAR CHIP IN THE WOODS?

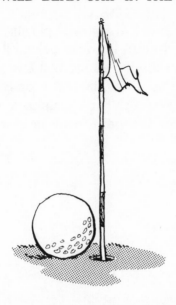

"Why don't you play golf with Dick anymore?" the inquiring wife asked her husband. "You two used to have a regular game."

"Well," said the husband, "would you play golf with a man who talks during your backswing, moves his ball around in the rough, forgets to take penalty shots, and never pays his bets when he loses?"

"Certainly not," said the wife.

"Well, Dick won't either."

George and his wife were playing a round of golf together when he sliced a drive behind a barn adjacent to the course. When they found his ball, his wife noticed that doors on both ends of the barn were open and suggested that George try to play through the opening. He took a mighty swing and hit the ball squarely. Unfortunately, it hit the frame of the door squarely and ricocheted backwards, striking his wife right between the eyes and killing her instantly.

About a year later George was playing the same hole with a friend and sliced his drive behind the barn again. When he started to pick up the ball and take a penalty shot, the friend said, "Hey, the doors on both ends of the barn are open. Why don't you just play through there?"

"Oh, no," said George. "Last time I tried that I made triple bogey."

WHEN DID YOU
GET THAT HITCH
IN YOUR SWING?

THIS IS A chapter about all the other things about golf I couldn't figure out where to put into another chapter.

Like gamesmanship. Gamesmanship is a way to cheat in golf without breaking any of golf's 417,000 rules. It's a mental thing, a way to get inside your opponent's head and remember that ninety percent of golf is half mental, which Old Tom Morris said one day after a round at Old Prestwick in Scotland as he was sipping some Very Old Scotch in a country where everything is old.

There are many ways to play mind games in golf.

There's the old 'When did you get that hitch in your swing?' ruse. Your opponent is two-over after fourteen holes. He nails one down the middle on fif-

289

teen. You say, "Great drive, Earl, but when did you get that hitch in your swing?"

Earl's mind says to Earl, "Hitch. What hitch? I don't have a hitch. But if I don't have a hitch, why did he mention it? Could it be the old 'When did you get that hitch in your swing?' ruse? It could be. But maybe it isn't. Maybe I do have a hitch in my swing. When did I get it? Sitting on a dirty commode stool in a truck stop?"

The very next time Earl swings he will have his mind on the hitch thing, and he'll hit the ball sideways. Your mind says to you, "You devil, you."

Then there's the old, "Didn't I see your wife in Goalby's the other night?" trick. Goalby's is a pickup bar and your opponent's wife has never been there, but the seed has been planted. Your opponent will forget all about his golf game after that and concern himself with finding either a good lawyer or a large gun.

If your opponent hits his ball into the deep rough, golf etiquette requires that you help look for the lost ball; however, it doesn't require you to look all that hard.

Nonetheless, great skill is required to act earnest and concerned on the outside while howling on the inside. The proper dialogue is, "I just don't understand; it wasn't hit *that* bad"; or, "I'm sure it's around here somewhere"; or, "Maybe a squirrel ate it."

Gamesmanship sometimes takes on the appearance of courtesy. Dangerous animals live on some golf courses. You can use this fact to your advantage, as well. Say your opponent has you down three-and-none and is already talking about how much fun he'll have driving your car. Suddenly he duck hooks one deep into the woods.

If he doesn't find it, he must go back and retee the ball and you will win the hole. It becomes necessary, then, to insure that he doesn't find his original shot.

You might say, "Be careful in there, Grover. The pro said he saw a snake as big as his arm in there last week." This will do two things. It will cut down on how deeply Grover goes into the woods to look for his ball, and if he does find it and can hit it, the notion a snake as big as the pro's arm is somewhere around him will ensure a quick swing and perhaps he won't be able to get the ball back to the fairway.

There are other animals that live in the woods on golf courses besides snakes. You can say to your opponent, "Herb Gaines said he saw a wild pig in there last week."

Or, "Phil Daniels was in these very same woods Sunday and a big black dog walked up to him and bit him. He'll be taking rabies shots for a month."

Or, "Did you hear the gorilla got loose from the circus last week?" or, "Watch out for wooleyboogers in there."

Your opponent will ask, "What's a wooleybooger?"

You answer, "I don't know, but they say the sons of bitches have three eyes and carry machetes."

You devil, you.

Then there's what's down in the lagoon on coastal golf courses.

Alligators:

• "I think you stopped just short of the hazard, Al, but be careful because there's a lot of alligators in this lagoon."

291

• "Walter Sommers hit his ball in the same place you did, over near the lagoon, and just as he was about to hit it, an alligator the size of a Greyhound bus swam up on the bank. Walter never heard it. I'd have gone to his funeral today if I hadn't already scheduled this game. They never did find his other leg, by the way."

• "I think your shot stayed up. It's just on the edge of the lagoon. Did you know alligators can run sixty miles an hour?"

I was in a foursome at Melrose once, and my partner went over the green on the par five third hole. His ball stopped just short of the lagoon. He had a shot, but his ball had landed three feet from an alligator lying on the bank getting a bit of sun.

My partner said, "There's an alligator near my ball. I'm going to drop in over there."

One of our opponents said, "It will cost you a shot. You're in the hazard."

Not allowing an opponent an alligator drop is very mean-spirited. What my partner did was declare himself in his pocket and left the ball next to the alligator. Several days later, he went over to our opponent's house and set fire to his car.

Here are some other things you can casually remark to an opponent to ensure his mind will turn to mush:

• "If you took a little bigger swing, you really could get out there on your drive."

• "I called the office at the turn. The market's down thirty points."

- "Have you had your house checked for radon yet?"
- "You really do keep your left arm straight, don't you?"
- "There's an out of bounds on the left. Don't hit it over there."
- "You mean I'm past you? I just hit a three-wood."
- "Did you hear that Alice Farnsworthy has herpes? You used to date her, didn't you?"

And, in conclusion, the following:

- The hardest course I've ever played. Bay Hill, Orlando, from the tips, 7,100 yards, with Arnold Palmer. Into the wind. I was so nervous my caddy's hands were shaking. I shot the national deficit.
- The best recent innovation in golf: Carts with two container holders on each side. There's a place for your can AND your cup of ice. Before, you either had to put your can or your cup of ice on the floorboard of the cart and it would spill all over your new Foot-joys three seconds later.
- My favorite golf clichés: "Hit it, Alice" or, "Does your husband play golf, too?" on a putt left short. And, "Good roll," which everybody says when you miss a putt.
- The most certain thing in golf: "Good rolls" never go in.
- A good true golf story: I was at the Masters the year Nicklaus won his last one. I was sitting on sixteen, behind three guys from New York or Ohio or New Jersey. All I know is that they talked funny, and when Nicklaus's tee shot on the par three almost

293

went in, stopping eight inches short of the flag, one of them said, "Never up, never in, Jack," and his fellow honkers laughed mightily.

Later, I went to get a beer. I noticed the four guys on the other side of the concession hut. One of them looked at the posted menu and said, "A Masters' sandwich, huh? That really sounds tip-top, guys."

Then he asked the young girl behind the counter, "What's in a Masters' sandwich?"

She answered with a very Southern, "Thar's ham, turkey, roast beef, cheese and ma-naise."

"Super. We'll have four Masters' sandwiches."

To which the girl replied, "We ain't got no more."

• My favorite golf balls: Slazengers. I like the package they come in.

• My favorite kind of golf shirts: Slazengers.

• Why I mentioned those two things: Maybe Slazenger will send me some free golf balls and shirts.

• A Ben Hogan story: Hogan was sitting in a locker room before a round, looking at golf balls with a magnifying glass.

Somebody asked him what he was doing.

"I'm throwing out the balls that have excess paint in the dimples," he answered.

• Most gentlemanly pro I ever played with: Dow Finsterwald. He also used only twenty-eight putts in the round.

• Best golf cartoon: Two guys are on a green. In the background is a large city. A nuclear bomb has sent a mushroom cloud rising above it. Says one guy to the other, "Go ahead and putt out. It'll be another four seconds before the shock wave hits."

• An absolute must read if you like golf: Besides

this book, of course, don't miss *Dr. Golf,* by William Price Fox.

• Why restrooms on golf courses wouldn't be necessary except that women play occasionally: A man, when given a choice, will always take a leak outside rather than inside.

• What not to do when it begins to lightning on a golf course: Hold up a one-iron and say, "Even God can't hit this!" God is tired of hearing that story.

• One of the few things I would enjoy more than shooting a par round: Being naked with Kim Basinger in a sand trap at Pine Valley.

• Best recent golf rumor that probably isn't true: Nicklaus has trouble managing his money.

• Best tort and retort I've heard: "If I had your swing and my brain, I'd be on the tour."

"Yeah, and if I had your swing and you had a feather up your butt, we'd both be tickled."

• If there was one more Masters story to be written, who I'd like to see write it: Dan Jenkins or Furman Bisher.

• Somebody once asked me if I were really a redneck and what I replied: "Yes, but that's a four-iron in the gun rack of my truck."

• Something I've never understood: What's a "trace," and why does that word show up in names of new golf courses with a lot of expensive home sites?

• What American golf courses need: Names for each hole like they have in Scotland.

At Ansley Golf Club in Atlanta, an attractive nine-hole course that is a mean test of urban golf, I actually have named each hole. Here are the names and why:

No. 1: State Farm. That's because if you slice the ball off the first tee, it winds up on Montgomery Ferry Drive, and as soon as your insurance agent gets off the golf course, he'll have a message to call the irate owner of the new Saab that you hit.

No. 2: AIDS. Clear Creek runs across No. 2. Clear Creek isn't clear clean, however. The city found a bunch of used syringes in Clear Creek and put up a sign on it at Ansley that declares it a health hazard.

No. 3: Wino. To get to the par three third hole, you have to drive by a railroad underpass where a lot of winos sleep.

No. 4: Seaboard Coast Line. There are railroad tracks on the right of No. 4, and once I hit a shot that hit a passing freight train and it bounced off a Fruit Growers' Express car and onto the green and landed four feet from the pin where I made birdie.

No. 5: The Road Hole. You tee off about an 8-iron from Interstate 85.

No. 6: Greg Norman. If you hit the ball to the right side of the fairway, it can hit the cart path and roll all the way to the hole, four hundred yards away.

No. 7: Dammit All to Hell. What everybody says when they try to carry the lake in front of the green and don't make it.

No. 8: Halter Top. For the woman who lives in the house behind the green.

No. 9: The Pool Hole. They had to put up a big screen on the left side of the hole, a par three, because people were all the time hooking their shots into the pool. One day somebody in the men's grill asked, "Any good looking women out by the pool?"

An older gentleman replied, "I haven't looked today, but there haven't been any in seventy-six years."

• My last words: No, I can't get you two tickets for the Masters.

Golf Lingo

A glossary of golfing terms:

Addressing the ball—Be sure to use zip codes for prompt delivery. Or, "Hello, I'm Lewis, and I'll be your driver."

Caddy—A person paid to lose balls for others and find them for himself.

Chili-dip—A shot that goes half as far as you intended it to go, or a party dip that goes half as far as you intended it to go.

Divot—A flying carpet.

Drive—An afternoon spin, usually to the left or right, through a scenic, heavily wooded area.

Flag—A rallying point where players meet every twenty minutes or so to exchange alibis.

Fore!—The golf equivalent of an air-raid siren. When

299

you hear it, fall flat with your face down and cover the back of your neck with your hands.

Gimmee—An uneasy agreement between players who can't putt.

Green—An area covered by a special grass that prevents balls from traveling in a straight line.

Handicap—A device for collective bargaining.

Improving your lie—Your wife didn't believe the first one, so you embellish it and try again.

Missing the cut—After being caught in the act of cheating, you outran the guy chasing you with a knife.

Par—Mathematical perfection, usually attained with a soft pencil and a softer conscience.

Put a good move on the ball—"What's your sign?" or, "Haven't we met somewhere before?" Also swinging properly.

Score—A fable in eighteen chapters.

Mixed scramble—A kinky breakfast.

Tee time—The last moment when golfers are seen laughing and joking.

Shot-gun start—A lot like a shot-gun wedding: you do it out of sequence and stroke it before you're ready.

Golf Clichés

What they really mean:

"Get it close."—Don't even think about making that putt.

"Good roll."—You didn't, and I'm delighted.

"Hold your head up."—If that sucker doesn't stop slicing soon, it'll land in Bulgaria.

"That'll play."—It ain't in the rough.

"Hit it, Alice."—Sexist remark for, "You left the putt short."

"Does your husband play golf?"—Same as above.

"All I had to do was hit it."—You left the putt an inch short, square in the hole. Your partner gives you half of the peace sign.

"Never up, never in."—Short again. Also the motto of the National Society of Impotence.

"Giraffe's ass shot."—High and stinky.

"That one leaked on you."—More like gushed.

"I'll take it if you want to hit another."—Stop your bitching. That's the best shot you've hit in a month.

"That dog'll hunt."—A keeper.

"Ain't no pictures on the scorecard."—It doesn't matter that it ricocheted off a rake before it bounced in the hole.

"Anything that travels that far ought to have a stewardess on board."—Compliment for a long drive.

"That one air-mailed me."—A drive that flies past an earlier one.

"Air-mailed to the wrong address."—An errant long drive, usually followed by snickering.

"That one took a victory lap."—A putt that circled the hole before falling in.

"How did it stay out?"—I know I missed the hole, but why didn't the wind blow it in?

"That's a teen-age putt."—It exploded in your hands.

"There's an Oral Roberts ball."—Shot hit off the heel of the club.

"You're playing Catholic golf—cross over here, cross over there."—Comment after a player chips back and forth over the green several times.

"That's a Baptist ball."—One that disappears under the water.

"That's a Methodist shot."—One that skips over it.

"You're playing Army golf—left, right, left, right."—Hitting it all over the golf course.

"Got enough club?"—Question asked of man urinating in the woods.

"Damn, this water is cold."—Spoken by man urinating into stream from the bank.

"Deep, too."—Spoken by man beside him who doesn't want to be outdone.

SOUTHERN
BY THE GRACE
OF GOD

Edited by Gerrie Ferris

BORN RIGHT

ALL OF US native Southerners knew it was coming. And now, it is here. The Sunday paper carried a large article about Northern migration to the capital city of the South.

In the metro Atlanta area, the article said, native Georgians still have the edge, but it's not an overpowering one and the margin is dwindling. Said the article, "The migration patterns that brought Northeasterners to Atlanta's elite northern suburbs also sent people from other regions to spots around the metro area. These settling patterns . . . have brought a new sense of place to dozens of Atlanta neighborhoods, influencing everything from local politics to the inventory at the corner grocery store."

The article also quoted a Yankee population expert, William Frey of the University of Michigan, as saying, "The nice Southern flavor of Atlanta may be diluted a bit with all the Northerners moving in."

The nice Southern flavor of Atlanta may be diluted a bit. . . .

I certainly understand why somebody from the land of freeze and squeeze would want to seek asylum here. A friend, also a native Southerner, who shares my fear about losing our Southern flavor, put it this way: "Nobody is going into an Atlanta bar tonight celebrating because they've just been transferred to New Jersey."

So what should I expect as my beloved Southland becomes more populated with migrating honkers? (Honker: Northerner with a grating accent who always talks at the top of his or her voice.) Will Southerners start dropping the last part of everybody's first name like the honkers do? Will I forever be Lew? Will Mary become Mare? Will Nancy become Nance? Will Bubba become Bub?

Will the automobile horn drown out the lilt of "Georgia on My Mind?" Will they dig a tunnel through Stone Mountain so native New Yorkers can remember the dark, choking atmosphere of the Lincoln and the Holland Tunnels? Will Harold's barbecue, 45 years in the business, lose its clientele to delicatessens where you have to scream at the top of your voice to get somebody to take your order for pastrami on pumpernickel?

Will the downtown Atlanta statue of the Phoenix, symbolic of the city's rising from the ashes, be replaced by a statue of Sherman holding a can of lighter fluid? Will grits become extinct? Will corn bread give way to the bagel? Will everybody, including native Southerners, start calling Atlanta's pro football team the "Fall-cuns" like Yankee sportscasters, instead of the way it's supposed to be pronounced, "Fowl-cuns?"

Will "freeway" replace "expressway"? Will "soda" or "pop" replace "Co-coler?" Will Southern men start wearing black socks and sandals with Bermuda shorts? Will "Y'all come back" become "Git outta here?"

I was having lunch at an Atlanta golf club recently. A man sitting at another table heard me speaking and asked, "Where are you all from?" He was mocking me. He was mocking my Southern accent. He was sitting in Atlanta, Georgia, making fun of the way I speak.

He was from Toledo. He had been transferred to Atlanta. If I hadn't have been 46 years old, skinny, and a basic coward with a bad heart, I'd have punched him. I did, however, give him a severe verbal dressing down.

I was in my doctor's office in Atlanta. One of the women who works there, a transplanted Northerner, asked how I pronounced the world "siren." I said I pronounced it "sireen." I was half kidding, but that is the way I heard the word pronounced when I was a child.

The woman laughed and said, "You Southerners really crack me up. You have a language all your own."

Yeah, we do. If you don't like it, go back home and stick your head in a snow bank. We really don't care how you said it or how you did it back in Buffalo.

I read a piece on the op-ed page of the *Constitution* written by somebody who in the jargon of my past "ain't from around here." He wrote white Southerners are always looking back and that we should look forward. He said that about me. He was reacting to a bumper sticker that shows the old Confederate soldier saying, "FERGIT HELL!"

I don't go around sulking about the fact that the South lost the Civil War. But I am aware that once upon a long time ago, a group of Americans saw fit to rebel against what they thought was an overbearing federal government. There is no record anywhere that indicates anybody in my family living in 1861 owned slaves. As a matter of fact, I come from a long line of sharecroppers, horse thieves, and used car dealers. But a few of them fought anyway—not to keep their slaves, because they didn't have any. I guess they simply thought it was the right thing to do at the time.

Whatever their reasons, there was a citizenry that once saw fit to fight and die and I come from all that, and I look at those people as brave and gallant, and a frightful force until their hearts and their lands were burnt away.

I will never turn my back on that heritage. I am proud to be a Southerner. If I've said it once, I've said it a thousand times: I'm an American by birth, but I'm Southern by the grace of God.

PUT SOME SOUTH
IN YO' MOUTH

Look Away, Look Away,
and Watch What You Say

AS SOON AS Bill Clinton was elected president,
along with his running mate Al Gore, I knew "y'all"
would be thrust upon the public like white on grits.

Clinton, of course, is from Arkansas and Gore is
from Tennessee. I don't count either man as having
all the characteristics of a true Southerner, since
both passed up their state universities for George-
town and the Ivy League.

But both obviously understand "y'all" and use it
often. "Y'all" is, to be sure, a Southern thing that
most people living outside the South don't understand.

I have long been involved in y'allism. I find it a

charming word that is pure Southern, but because it is so often misunderstood, I thought it would be wise to discuss "y'all" at some length.

The biggest mistake people from outside the South make in the y'all area is they don't think we say "y'all" at all. They think we say "you all."

A Southerner visiting the North surely will be mocked the first time he or she opens his or her mouth and out comes a Southern accent.

Northerners will giggle and ask, "So where are you all from?" I answer by saying, "I all is from Atlanta."

For some unknown reason, Northerners think Southerners use "you all" in the singular sense. How many movies have I seen where a Northerner is trying to do a Southern accent, failing miserably, saying you all, while addressing one other person?

Southerners rarely use "you all" in any situation but they never, never, ever, ever, use it when addressing just one person. If you were in my home and I offered you a cup of coffee I would say, "Would you like a cup of coffee?" If you and your brother-in-law and your cousin were in my home, then I'd say, "Would y'all like a cup of coffee?"

"Y'all" is, of course, a contraction of "you all," and most Southerners use it in all verbal situations involving more than one other person.

And another thing: Northerners also tend to think Southerners say the following when bidding a farewell to a visitor: "You all come back now, you heah?" Maybe the Clampetts said that, but very few real Southerners do.

We might say, "Y'all come back to see us when you can," or, "If y'all can't come, call."

But this "you heah" business is the concoction of some Yankee scriptwriter trying to be cute.

I rarely get into a punching mode, but I was in New York doing a tape version of a book I had written and the producer had hired an actor to speak some of the lines.

"Can you do a Southern accent?" I asked the actor.

"Would you all like to hear me?" he answered.

"I've already heard enough," I said. Then I turned to the producer and said, "This man isn't going to be on my book tape because I will not have the Yankee version of Southern accent in or on anything that bears my name."

The actor became enraged and said he could, too, do a Southern accent, and I replied, "If you can do a Southern accent, pigs can fly."

We got into each other's face, but before we came to blows, the producer fired the man and ordered him out of the studio and the script was altered so I would be the only one speaking on the tape.

I take the Southern accent and the preservation of its purity quite seriously. And if any of y'all don't like it, just keep it to yourself, you heah?

Lewis Grizzard

Crossing the Mason-Diction Line

It was the 1991 Poulan Weedeater Independence Bowl between the Universities of Georgia and Arkansas, the Dawgs and the Hawgs respectively.

One would think television people wouldn't have a problem repeating the above paragraph correctly, but that hasn't been the case, and so once again I must assume my role as Slim Pickens, Professor of Speaking Correctly.

Let us begin with Poulan. A local announcer pronounced it POH-land, as in the Eastern European country. (Not as in the recession-ridden United States.) It's POO-lahn, I think. What the announcer should have done anyway is not try to say Poulan at all, but simply call it the Weedeater Bowl.

I like a football game named after such an aggressive piece of equipment as the weedeater. A coach could say, "Boys, they're grass and we're a bunch of souped-up Weedeaters."

Coaches say things like that, as well as things like, "Remember, boys, they put their pants on one leg at a time, just like we do."

Whenever a coach said something like that to me, I always thought, "Well, I guess so. Who the hell could jump into a pair of pants two legs at a time?" I'm certain it's POO-lahn, and if it's not, it should be. The professor has the last word.

Now, to Dawgs and Hawgs.

A dawg is a Southern man's best friend, as in, "That dawg'll hunt."

A hawg is Southern for, "You can lead a hawg to water, but all he'll try to do is waller in it."

But I was watching a network telecast of the Atlanta-New Orleans NFL playoff game recently and one of the announcers was hyping the telecast of the Independence Bowl. It came out: "It's the Dugs and the Hugs in the Independence Bowl."

It was quite obvious the announcer wasn't, as they used to say back home, "from 'round heah," which basically meant he was a Northerner.

Read my lips: "Dawwwwwgs." Put your tongue to the roof of your mouth. Then bring it down forcibly and spit out "Dawwwwwgs" by forming the mouth into a circle. If it comes out a little nasal, more the better.

For "Hawwwwwgs," it comes from deep in the throat as in "Haw!" Pretend you're spitting out a bad oyster.

Some announcers also say the Atlanta "FALL-cuns." It's "FOWL-cans." And they say "aw-BURN" when they should pronounce it "AW-bun."

Television, I believe, is responsible for the slow disappearance of all sorts of accents in this country. I'm afraid one day everybody will sound alike, and that would be a shame.

Professor Grizzard would be out of work, and who would care about an athletic event between the Dugs and the Hugs? Sounds more like an encounter group than a bunch of fired-up weedeaters trying to take each other's heads off, which builds character both on and off the field.

The Dawgs and the Hawgs. It's a Southern thing. The rest of y'all just wouldn't understand.

I Wish I Was . . .
Politically Correct in Dixie

I certainly agree with all those who have protested the playing of "Dixie" at Southern football games.

Although slavery isn't mentioned in the song, it still makes people think of the Old South, where every white person owned African-American slaves.

"Dixie" is definitely a politically incorrect piece of music. Even the word is offensive to some, and I apologize to those who are offended by my use of it.

But I'm proud to say my alma mater, the University of Georgia, years ago rid itself of any connection with the song or the word you-know-what (see, I didn't use the word that time, as I despise offending people).

The Georgia band used to play the song at football games. But not anymore. The only place they still play the song is at the University of Mississippi. They also wave Confederate flags and they allow prayer before a football game.

I'm not certain how long it will be before members of the Speech Police move in and shut down such reprehensible behavior, but it could be any day now.

Georgia not only stopped playing the song, it even changed the name of the band, formerly known as the Dixie Redcoat Band. It became simply the Redcoat Band.

That prompted my stepbrother, Ludlow Porch, the famous radio talk show personality, to fire off a letter to the editor suggesting the following: "I applaud the dropping of "Dixie" from the name of the University of Georgia band, but let us not stop there.

"How can we allow the word 'red,' which stands for communism? And the word 'redcoat' itself is an affront to the memory of all those Americans who fought against the redcoats of England in the Revolutionary War.

"And 'band.' Poncho Villa had a 'band' of desperadoes and we had to send brave young soldiers into Mexico after him. So 'band' should go, too, and that just leaves 'The,' which is a dumb name for a large number of musicians, so I guess they're just out of a name altogether."

I believe if we really try we can wipe away all symbols of the Old South forever. There's a company in Savannah that makes Dixie Crystal Sugar. Sorry, it's just Crystal Sugar from now on, and don't give me any grief about it.

And there's even a Dixie Highway in the South. It should be referred to from now on only as Highway. As in, "Well, you take Highway, then go down three blocks and. . . ." There are even some people named Dixie, believe it or not. They will have to get new first names, or go by their middle names. And if anybody named Dixie lives on Dixie Highway, the Speech Police will likely demand they be shot.

And if the song and word "Dixie" are symbolic of the Old South, I guess we ought to stop using "Old South" as well. Instead of saying "Old South" perhaps we can refer to it as "Back Then," and we can roll our eyes when we use it so everybody will know we aren't talking about when dinosaurs roamed the Earth, but when slaveholders used to go around singing songs like "Dixie" and "Eating Goober Peas."

315

But wait. "Eating Goober Peas" is a song from Back Then, too, so don't anybody dare play that at a football game.

Rap songs about killing innocent people, incidentally, are just fine.

No Offense, but
I Am Taking Offense

I'm offended.

I never thought I would say that because I'm an easy-going type of guy who figures it's a lot less stressful not to let anybody get to me.

But these are the '90s, and getting offended is "in," like drinking bottled water, refusing to eat red meat, and cursing smokers.

Hardly a day passes that somebody doesn't make the news by getting offended.

Sister Souljah, the rap person, rapped about killing white people, and then she became offended because Bill Clinton said she was a racist for doing such a thing.

Jesse Jackson, who was born offended, also got offended by Mr. Clinton's remarks, so it was a 2-on-1 fastbreak, two offendees on one offender. Hardly sounds fair, but that's baseball these days.

And that brings up Native Americans becoming offended by Atlanta Braves fans' tomahawk chop and criminals becoming offended by the name Texas Rangers, since Texas Rangers are law enforcement people who nab a lot of criminals and send them to jail.

So why should I be left off the bandwagon of offendees? It's a free country, isn't it? Here's why I'm offended.

There was an article on the front page of the Atlanta newspaper the other day concerning suburban Clayton County promoting itself as a nice place to live in order to persuade more Atlanta area people to move there.

The second paragraph began: "Feeling that the county has been treated for years as metro Atlanta's redneck stepchild. . . ."

That offended me.

In the first place, I know the origin of the term "redneck," and several members of my family fell into that category.

"Redneck" got its start when ruralites came to town on Saturdays to buy feed, seed and maybe a new pair of brogans.

These people made their living working in the fields under the hot sun growing food, a very worthwhile endeavor, and their necks often became sunburned.

Townfolk, who tend to be snooty, thought these people ignorant, uncouth and undesirable because they tended to drive pickup trucks, to listen to the Grand Ol' Opry on the radio on Friday nights, and to be humble.

They were easy to pick on, in other words. My grandfather was one of those people. He made his living from behind a mule, and his neck got red. He also liked Ernest Tubb, and I never heard him make a loud, bodacious statement of any kind.

He also was the most gentle, caring person I've ever known, and I'm glad he didn't live long enough to see the term applied to him become such a derisive label.

In the second place let us discuss the term "stepchild."

In the context it was used—redneck stepchild—it

seemed to indicate someone of that description was a most undesirable individual.

I spring from those who worked the soil and became red of neck, and I had a stepfather, so I was a stepchild, and that makes me twice offended.

Now, if you'll excuse me, I'm going to ride around in my red Blazer—a sort of pickup truck—and pout.

Lewis Grizzard

"Bubba Bashers" Use Stereotype That Doesn't Fit

For years, I have attempted to enlighten those individuals who hold biased and ill-based opinions about the name "Bubba."

Most think men named Bubba are nothing more than ignorant swine who wear caps with the names of heavy equipment dealers on the front, shoot anything that moves, listen to music about doing bodily harm to hippies and put beer on their grits.

There may be Bubbas who fit the above description, but there are plenty who don't.

I once wrote of a man college-educated, with no tobacco juice stains on his teeth, whose family had always referred to him as Bubba.

"I got that name," he explained, "because my baby sister couldn't say brother. She called me Bubba."

The man's problem was that he had taken a job with some sort of high-tech corporation, and his boss insisted he drop the name "Bubba" because he thought clients wouldn't respect a man with such a name. Our Bubba refused to use any other name, however, and became quite successful with his new company and wound up with his former boss's job. The former boss now refers to his old employee as "Mr. Bubba."

Anyway, I happened to pick up a back issue of *Southern* magazine recently, and on the very front cover were the following words: "Bubba! You don't have to be dumb, mean, fat, slow, white or male to be one!"

I turned to page 37 and began to read: "Of all the Southern stereotypes," the story began, "the one that answers to 'Bubba' is probably the least flattering."

The article went on to do portraits of eight Bubbas. Do any of the following fit the typical "Bubba stereotype?"

Keith "Bubba" Taniguche: lawyer, Austin, Texas. Full-blooded Japanese. Into Zen.

John "Bubba" Trotman: state director of the U.S. Agriculture Department's Agricultural Stabilization and Conservation Service, Montgomery, Alabama. On people moving into Alabama: "At first, they say, 'Alabama, that's Tobacco Road.' Then you can't blow them out of Alabama with a cannon."

Efula "Bubba" Johnson: narcotics officer, Savannah, Georgia. Johnson is a large man, and he carries a large gun.

Walter "Bubba" Smith: minister, Ashdown, Arkansas. Claims no relation to Bubba Smith of football and beer commercial fame.

James "Bubba" Armstrong: surgeon, Montgomery, Alabama. Careful poking fun at anybody who knows his way around a scalpel.

Paula "Bubba" Meiner: owns a barbecue joint in Winter Park, Florida. Nice lady.

Bernard "Bubba" Meng: state administrator for U.S. Senator Ernest Hollings, Columbia, South Carolina, He's "Little Bubba." Dad was "Big, etc."

Kyle "Bubba" Patrick: elementary school student, Auburntown, Tennessee. He wants to be a basketball player when he grows up.

One more thing: The University of Georgia veteri-

nary school produced the state's first test-tube calf,
a Holstein bull, weighing 100 pounds.
    They named him Bubba. What else?

U.S. of the South Still a Good Idea?

An Atlanta *Journal-Constitution* survey has uncovered the rather astounding fact that one in five lifelong Southerners still thinks the South should be its own nation.

This is even more astounding: The poll also indicated 27 percent of black Southerners "lean toward Southern independence."

That's a lot of people. That's a lot more "Fergit, hell!" bumper stickers than I would have thought.

"You would think the idea would have died by now but it hasn't," the papers quoted Emory Thomas, a Civil War historian at the University of Georgia.

I'll say. It's been 130 years since the Civil War. It's been 60 years since *Gone With the Wind* debuted in Atlanta.

What could all this mean? As far as the 27 percent of black Southerners who favor independence, the Rev. Joseph Lowery of the Southern Christian Leadership Conference said he didn't think blacks understood the question.

"I can't see anybody seeing an advantage to the United States of the Confederacy," he went on.

But maybe they can.

I don't think you would find many white Southerners and certainly no black Southerners who would want to return to a slave state, but perhaps this has to do with something else.

Many of us Southerners might think we could simply do a lot better on our own if we didn't have Washington and New York and that Eastern corridor of arrogance and eggheadedness with which to deal.

323

The rest of the North I don't really worry about. We probably even would let Minnesota into the new confederacy if it weren't so cold.

But what has Washington ever done for us in the South besides take our money, close our military bases, use us for a dump and foul up our schools? If we were the United States of the South, we wouldn't have to deal with Bill and Hillary anymore, either, and I still don't consider them Southern even if they are from Arkansas.

They both went to Yale and couldn't identify a razorback hog if it walked into the White House.

And New York? Why do we need to be in the same country with New York?

They think we're still one big pellagra belt and we're not even sure New York could still qualify as an American city. Try to find a cabdriver who speaks English or a dope dealer who can tell you the name of one co-signer of the Declaration of Independence in New York. The more I think of this concept, the more I like it.

There would be immediate problems, of course. What to do about South Florida would be one. It's about as Southern as wearing black socks with Bermuda shorts and sandals. And could the Yankees already living there pass citizenship tests? Would they stop wearing black socks with Bermuda shorts and sandals? But at least we could tighten the immigration laws and keep a lot more out. Yankees aren't bad people, but you have to spend a lot of time dressing them correctly and explaining we never use "you all" in the singular.

This has some exciting possibilities, like putting the new capitol in Little Rock just for spite.

Chicago-Like Weather Chills Urge to Gloat

Wait a minute. If I had wanted to continue to live like Nanook of the North, I'd never have packed my sled and moved back South from Chicago years ago.

I spent three winters in Gulag Chicago. One year, Lake Michigan froze solid. Another year, it snowed in May. The third year, the heat went off, and my apartment froze. My entire apartment. My clothes froze. My furniture froze. I froze.

I had to move downstairs with my landlord. His heat went off, too, but he had a wood-burning stove. We huddled around the stove for a week.

Finally, he said, "This is ridiculous. I'm moving to Orlando."

"You're right," I said. "I'm moving back to Atlanta."

So I did. Back to the sunny South. One of the best parts about getting out of Chicago was I knew I would never have to wear a pair of galoshes again.

You have to wear galoshes over your regular shoes during Chicago winters. If you don't, your shoes will fill up with snow and your toes will freeze and fall off.

Just fall right off. Imagine life without toes. There would be precious little left to wiggle.

The problem with galoshes is they look dumb. Seriously dumb.

The only Southerners who wear galoshes are nerds whose mothers came from up North somewhere.

These mothers give their children names such as

325

Manny, and Vito, and Melvin and say, "Melvin, don't forget to wear your galoshes," when their children leave for school.

It doesn't matter if the sun is shining and it's 70° outside, a nerd whose mother is from up North and still hasn't got over it will insist he wear his galoshes, and the other students will throw rocks at him and hoot him off the playground.

Another great part about moving back South is, although we do have a winter, it doesn't last nearly as long and isn't nearly as severe as in Chicago.

I've played tennis outdoors while wearing shorts on Christmas Day in Atlanta.

Atlanta usually has an ice storm or two in January, but by the middle of February you often can go outside and catch a few rays.

But what's with this year? I looked in the paper the other day, and it was just as cold in Atlanta as it was in Chicago. That just isn't right.

I also noticed it was snowing in Florida. That just isn't right, either. It's not supposed to snow in Florida. Isn't that in the Bible someplace? I don't know what meteorological aberration has caused the South to have to suffer through these Chicago-like temperatures lately, but I would just as soon it stop.

For one thing, I'm missing my annual gloating period. During winter, I look at a color weather map in the newspaper. I notice it's white in Chicago, which means your toes could fall off if you don't wear galoshes. Then, I notice the South is a pleasant warm orange. I still have friends in Chicago. I call them and gloat.

"So," I usually begin, "got enough whale blubber in to last the winter?" That, or, "Getting out of the igloo much?" I usually close by saying, "Hey, it's been real, but I'm late for my neighbor's pool party."

But how can I gloat when I think I saw a penguin waddling down Peachtree Street the other day? Not only am I missing my gloating period, but I'm also afraid if it doesn't warm up soon, I may have to search through the bowels of my closet to see if I still have my galoshes, a fate worse than death. I honestly never thought I'd have to wear a pair of galoshes again. But I also never thought the normally mild early winter of the South would be gone with the arctic wind.

Lewis Grizzard

Y'all, Let's Teach Yankees a Lesson

Southern readers recently have flooded me with copies of articles written in Northern newspapers concerning Atlanta and the Olympics, the Braves in the World Series, the tomahawk chop and the fact that Ted Turner and wife, Jane Fonda, dozed off during one of the Braves' playoff games against the Pirates.

Much of it is the same old tripe, with the worn references to Bubba, the Southern accent, General Sherman and Petticoat Junction.

There even was a reference to me, saying I was a cross between Buck Owens and David Letterman. It could have been worse. They could have called me a cross between Boxcar Willie and Pat Sajak.

I continue to protest such stereotypical references to the land I love, and it's interesting that a Northern transplant to the South, in a letter to the editor, compared me to David Duke as a spreader of geographical hatred.

So what does that make Twin Cities columnist Nick Coleman, who wrote, "Somebody has made off with these people's [Atlantans'] brains?" Sadly, the Chicago *Tribune's* Mike Royko fell victim to all this, as well.

The reason I use the word "sadly" is because Mike Royko is my idol.

I consider him to be the best newspaper columnist in America.

I've never met Mike Royko, but I did have the pleasure of reading him the three years I lived in Chicago, and I still search for his syndicated column when I travel.

Royko is hilarious. He is inventive. He can take out your appendix with a broken Budweiser bottle.

He took offense to the instance of Ted and Jane going to sleep in Ted's private box at Atlanta–Fulton County Stadium.

"True baseball fans stay awake, even the drunks," he wrote. "So these two snoozers don't deserve a world champion team."

He wasn't through.

"Nor do the fans in Atlanta with their Indian tomahawk chop and the terrible noise they make, like a giant herd of pregnant moo-cows."

I could have lived with most of that, especially the part about Ted and Jane going to sleep during a playoff game. What I have against Ted Turner is he married Hanoi Jane, and what I have against her isn't going to get in this column.

But then Royko takes off on the Southern accent with a trite explanation of how we say "snowin" instead of "snoring" and "mowf" instead of "mouth."

He also makes fun of the way the Puerto Ricans pronounce "Blue Jay" and one wonders where all the politically correct editors in Chicago have gone.

Mike Royko is better than all that. He must have tarried too long at Billy Goat's Tavern.

I also received a clip from USA Today. Somebody named Taylor Buckley was perplexed about golf being considered for the 1996 Atlanta Summer Olympics as a "signature" event.

Writes he, "Why not 'signature' in these games with a genuine Bubba sport? Like a monster-truck tug of war, complete with Confederate flags, gun racks and trucks named 'Dixie Dawg Kicker' and

329

'Roadkill Rebel?' " These readers who took offense to all this asked me to write a rebuttal.

I've got a better idea: Let's win the World Series again, put on a marvelous 1996 Summer Olympics and if you're traveling through the North and see a state flag, turn it upside down.

Call Me Violent? I'll Buy a Knife!

Here at the Southern Anti-Defamation League, we have received yet another example of what I believe to be a continuing, unwarranted attack upon Southerners and their lifestyles from other parts of the country.

An alert reader sent along an article out of *Psychology Today* concerning a study by a University of Michigan researcher who has concluded Southerners are more violent than Northerners.

Richard E. Nisbett, Ph.D., says Southerners are more likely than Northerners to resort to violence when insulted. He says that makes the South "a hotbed of homicide."

And why are we so touchy? "All the violence stems not from some intrapsychic source, but a cultural code of honor borne of a pig-herding past," concludes Mr. PhDuckBrain. He continues, "It's the legacy of Scotch-Irish settlers who brought with them the tough defensive stance herders the world over assume to protect their livelihood from rustlers."

Well, I guess so. Somebody steals your pig, what are you supposed to do? Look him up and ask him to dance? And if indeed Southerners are a little quick-tempered about an insult, it's because we've been insulted by the rest of the country long enough.

I'm tired of being referred to as a "bubba," a "redneck" and worse.

Damn straight. Some Northern greaseball (if you can call me a redneck, I can call you a greaseball) gets on my case, then, in the immortal words of my boyhood friend and idol, Weyman C. Wannamaker, he'll have to settle the matter with "me and King Hardware."

King Hardware was the concern back home where one might purchase a knife.

You want to talk about Michigan, home of Mr. PhDonkey. OK. I recently received another letter from William L. Nix, an attorney in West Point, Georgia. He told of a trip he and his wife and two sons took to the Upper Peninsula of Michigan. The family stopped for dinner at a Red Lobster at Jackson, Michigan.

The waitress asked the two boys if they would like to see a children's menu. Both boys answered, "Yes, ma'am."

"Like all self-respecting Southerners," wrote attorney Nix, "we have taught our children to say 'please,' 'thank you,' 'yes, ma'am' and 'no, ma'am.' After our meal, our waitress said, 'You folks are from the South, aren't you?' I proudly replied that we were and inquired if it was our accents that she noticed.

"She said, 'No, it's just that your kids have manners. The kids up here are brats.'" William Nix ended with, "I relate this story not because my kids have exemplary manners. They don't. But it points out the fundamental difference between our way of life and theirs. Gentility and common courtesy still mean something to us. Let's hope it remains that way."

The reader who sent in the *Psychology Today* article asked me, "Are you going to take this lying down?" Getting out of my usually genteel mode, for a moment, I must say, not a chance. And I hope to kiss a pig if I ever do.

SOUTHERN BY THE GRACE OF GOD

I'm disgusted at Southern smearing. I think Mr.
PhDumb's research is a farce and as Weyman also
used to say, "As long as King Hardware stays open, I
ain't budging an inch."

Lewis Grizzard

Frankly, My Dear, I Don't Understand

Let me see if I have all this straight: Three metro Atlanta counties—Clayton, Douglas and Henry—are all bidding for a $30 million *Gone With the Wind* theme park.

At the same time, an Atlanta foundation is conducting a fund-raising campaign to restore a building where Margaret Mitchell, who wrote *GWTW*, once lived.

Margaret Mitchell House Inc. needs $1 million to $3 million to restore what Ms. Mitchell called "The Dump" on Crescent Avenue and Peachtree Street.

Supporters of the renovation are even planning to try to raise money in Japan. "They adore *GWTW* in Japan," said a spokesperson for the Margaret Mitchell House.

OK. All that's fine. Nobody's complaining. *Gone With the Wind* is important to Atlanta's heritage and Margaret Mitchell is our most beloved literary figure.

Gone With the Wind, of course, is about plantation life in the Old South.

There were all those magnificent balls. And the happy slaves were singing in the cotton fields.

Then the Yankees came, burning and plundering. Miss Scarlet even had to shoot one of them and a way of life was gone forever. But certainly not its memory. *Gone With the Wind* has assured that, and we never want to forget.

Thus the efforts for the theme park and Margaret Mitchell's former place of residence.

334

But what's this? The Georgia state flag reminds us of the Old South, too. It is modeled after the old Confederate battle banner.

But the flag, it seems, is politically incorrect. How some lash out against it. Said a recent letter to the editor: "How can anyone honor a flag, conceived in such hatred, or respect a banner designed to symbolize segregation? Where is the sensitivity toward the feelings for Georgians of African descent?"

So how do Georgians of African descent feel about a theme park that would remind them of a time when their forebears were enslaved? How many African-American families would visit such a place? How many African Americans will be willing to donate a few bucks to make certain Margaret Mitchell's residence is spared? Symbols of the past.

How can we rage against one and not include the others? Isn't the Cyclorama in Grant Park a symbol, too? What about the carving of Robert E. Lee and other Confederate generals on the side of Stone Mountain? Shouldn't we raze the Cyclorama and remove the Stone Mountain carving or at least cover it until the Olympics are over? There is so much concern the Olympics are going to come to Altanta in 1996 and there will still be references to our rebel days and ways.

There's Tara Boulevard named for the plantation in *Gone With the Wind,* for God's sake. Change that to Malcolm X Boulevard, if we want to name a thoroughfare for him as has been suggested.

There are a lot of Confederate dead buried in Atlanta cemeteries. What do we do about them? Dig them up and move them to the Okeefenokee swamp? Just think what might happen in a *GWTW* theme

335

park. Somebody might try to play Dixie. Somebody might suggest park personnel wear Confederate gray. Could you pay for your admission in Confederate money? Certainly African Americans would be hired to work in a theme park. How would they feel surrounded by vestiges of the Old South?

Somebody set me right here. How can there be so much objection to the state flag and not one fiddle-dee-dee about a $30 million theme park or a restored home — both of which would assure old times are not forgotten? I'm not condoning and I'm not condemning. I've simply got an inquiring mind that wants to know.

HONKERS, SANDALS WITH SOCKS, AND OTHER ABNORMALITIES

Delta's Ready When You Are

LITHUANIA HAS VOTED for independence from the Soviet Union. Other Soviet provinces want the same thing. The sweet wind of freedom is blowing.

OK, then. What about the South seceding again? I realize it didn't work the first time we tried it, but the North wouldn't fight fairly. As it is told, that great Georgian and Confederate, Robert Toombs, was trying to recruit men to fight for the South at the outbreak of the Civil War.

"Why, we can beat the Yankees with cornstalks," he told an audience. After the war, Toombs was running for governor. During a campaign speech a voice cried out from the audience, "We listened to you when you said we could beat the Yankees with cornstalks. That was a lie, so why should we believe you now?"

Toombs replied, "We could have beaten the Yankees with cornstalks, but the SOBs wouldn't fight that way."

I don't think there would be any hostilities if the South should decide to secede again.

If we did it in the winter, how could anybody who lives where it's always blue on the weather map blame us? And any of the millions of Northerners who had the good sense to move South before the secession could gain their citizenship in the All-New-and-Improved South quite easily.

All they would have to do is agree to go to speech school and learn how to lose their Northern accents.

Think of what it would be like if the South broke away from the Union again.

No more heavy taxes to bail out decaying Northern cities. No more stupid federal regulators.

There would be a few things we'd have to agree to do in the spirit of becoming good neighbors with the North.

We would agree to be equal partners in the Persian Gulf—which is more than can be said about any other ally.

We would also agree to come to the North's rescue in case it needed help for something like moving Philadelphia to somewhere in southern Illinois to make room for a parking lot when all the parking spaces in New York were taken.

I'd make Atlanta the capital of the South this time. Richmond's too close to Washington.

I would want minorities to have a chance in all leadership roles.

The Atlanta Braves and Falcons wouldn't have to play the New York Mets or Giants anymore. The Falcons could play Tampa Bay every week and actually have a chance for a break-even season.

A man can dream, can't he?

Lewis Grizzard

Kooks of the Klan
Fascinate Yankees

Big-Time media seems obsessed by the Ku Klux
Klan. Give them anything that has a sheet or a
pointed hat involved in it, and it's time to pull out all
the stops.

David Duke wasn't about to be elected in Louisiana, but he was a former Klansman, so he wound up
on front pages across the country.

And David Duke was a Southerner, as well. A
white Southern male with a Ku Klux Klan background can get more press than Mario Cuomo flip-
ping a coin to see if he's going to run for president
and then putting off the decision again to go for two
out of three.

The Northern media are especially fond of the Klan
as the basis for a news story. It's their geographical
ignorance showing. What many Northerners know of
the South they learned watching *The Beverly Hillbil-
lies* or *Mississippi Burning.*

I was on the phone with a New Yorker, and he
asked me, "What time is it in Atlanta?"

"What time is it in New York?" I asked him back.

"4:30," he said.

"You're not going to believe this," I said, "but Atlanta is in the same time zone as New York. It's 4:30
here, too."

Where did he think Georgia was? Next to Texas?
One of those talk-show hostesses came to Atlanta.
Apparently she couldn't find any Southern left-
handed lesbian cross-dressers who were being de-

340

nied their right to marry goats, so she rounded up a few Klansmen, or people who said they were in the Klan in order to get on television.

Several years ago, Larry King came to Atlanta to do his show and I was asked to appear on the second half. The first half, Larry King interviewed some kook from the Klan.

"How can you do this to me, Larry?" I joked with him. "Everybody watching this show sees me following a nut in a robe and a pointed hat and they figure my outfit's in the cleaners or something."

The Klan hasn't had any influence in the South in decades. What few members remain are too stupid, for one thing. What wears robes and pointed hats and has three teeth? Fifty-eight members of the KKK—which is about how many you could turn up given a year, a gasoline credit card and a road map of the South.

During the horror of Atlanta's murdered and missing children experience in the early 1980s, the rest of the world wanted the Klan involved. A Northern reporter walked in my office one day and asked if I knew how to get in touch with Atlanta's grand wizard. "I'm certain the Klan is involved in this," he said.

"Call 1-800-GET-REAL," I told him.

But what a story it would have made had the Klan been involved. The Ku Klux Klan killing black children in Atlanta, which is in Georgia, which is in the South. Think of the books. Think of the movie starring Northern actors and actresses trying to fake Southern accents.

Forget the Klan. Want something to worry about? OK, how about black men murdering other black men day after day? Getting laid off from your job? The Soviet nuclear arsenal winding up in the wrong hands? Or, the fact that the booger you wound up with under the sheets last night has AIDS.

Even Klansmen probably have enough sense to use Kondoms.

New York, New Yuck for This Southerner

In a recent column I wrote that I had refused an invitation to spend a weekend in New York with friends. I didn't go. I explained I wasn't afraid of the terrorists. I just didn't want to be around that many New Yorkers for that long.

In case you didn't know, if I get around a lot of New Yorkers I suffer from a number of reactions.

First, my ears hurt because New Yorkers are loud. They grow up having to scream in order to be heard over other New Yorkers.

This all stems from the fact New Yorkers are the most opinionated people on earth and can never learn to listen.

Secondly, I become extremely nervous and frustrated around New Yorkers. That is because they all talk so loudly and they all talk at once with New York accents, so I can't make out anything they are saying.

Let's say I'm in New York riding the subway. I'm always afraid New Yorkers around me are saying something important like, "I think the train is on fire," and I can't understand them.

Also, under certain circumstances, I become embarrassed around New Yorkers because of what they are wearing.

I was at a golf resort in Tampa recently. All over the course were guys wearing long black socks with their golfing shorts. They had to be New Yorkers. Only New Yorkers would wear long black socks with a pair of golfing shorts. People from other parts of the country, especially the South, know you never wear black socks with any kind of shorts.

I tried to tell a New Yorker that once, but he couldn't hear me because he was screaming his opinion on various Third World issues at the time.

The column elicited some reaction. A perfect example came from an Atlanta woman who said she grew up on Long Island.

"Probably," she began, "you're afraid of New Yorkers because they have a breadth of knowledge that you obviously can't touch. I'm sorry you are so afraid of us."

The lady was correct concerning the fact I am afraid of New Yorkers. But it is not because of their breadth of knowledge.

I'm afraid I'll go deaf if I spend too much time around New Yorkers. I'm afraid I'll start screaming my opinion. I'm afraid I'll show up at the golf course wearing black socks with my golfing shorts and my friends will point at me and laugh at me and ask, "Where's your sandals?" That's something else New Yorkers do. When they are wearing shorts and black socks somewhere besides the golf course, like at the beach, they wear sandals, another fashion miscue.

To New Yorkers who will be further offended by this column, I have just one thing to say: So sue me.

Let's Run These Ideas Up the State's Flag Pole

I've been trying to figure out a compromise on the controversy regarding Georgia's state flag.

The controversy is that one side says that because the flag features part of the old Confederate flag, it symbolizes racial oppression and hatred and it will be an embarrassment to the state and the city if it isn't changed before the 1996 Olympic Games in Atlanta.

The other side says all the Confederate flag is doing on the state flag is offering a symbol of the state's heritage. I can understand that. My great-great-grandfather, General Beauregard Grizzard, was in charge of keeping the Yankees out of Miami Beach during the Civil War.

And the two sides continue to go round and round. Somebody thought maybe the governor could figure this out.

But when asked his thoughts, Governor Zell Miller said he had a lot of other things more important than the state flag to handle.

I've used that sidestep myself when one of my ex-wives asked me where I'd been until 3:30 the previous morning. I said, "Don't bother me with little stuff like that. I'm trying to figure out who to pull for in the Iran-Iraq war."

But I've always been big on compromise. If I can't scream louder or argue the other side down, and if hitting them over the head with a baseball bat is out of the question because they're bigger than me, I go for compromise every time.

345

So let's see what we've got here: We've got a state flag that is causing divisiveness. What do we do? The most logical thing to me would be simply not to have a state flag. What does a state need a flag for? If Georgia ever decided to invade South Carolina and try to get Hilton Head back from all the Yankees who have moved there, we might need a state flag under which to march.

But I think it's too late to save Hilton Head. I was there recently and ordered grits for my breakfast. The waitress said, "Where do you think you are buddy, down South? With eggs you get potatoes."

But why else would we need a state flag? To fly atop the Capitol building? What they ought to put up there is a lighted sign after the Legislature goes home saying, "It's OK to come out now, they're gone."

The state flag flies over the governor's mansion, too. Is that really necessary? Why couldn't we get a flag with Governor Miller's smiling face and put it up there? No. Then Atlanta mayor Bill Campbell would want a flag with his picture on it flying over City Hall and imagine how much something that big would cost city taxpayers.

OK. So we keep a state flag, but how do we design it to keep everybody happy? How about a flag with a big peach on it? We're the Peach State, aren't we? How about a flag with Herschel Walker's picture on it? Heisman Herschel helped win a national football championship for the University of Georgia. And personally, I'm a lot more proud of that than the fact the South lost the war and its objective, making Northern men dress better when they visit our beaches. (No long black socks with sandals, you guys.)

The *Wall Street Journal* once praised local barbecue in an article leading up to the Democratic National Convention in 1988. A flag with a giant hog on it maybe? But not everybody likes barbecue. Some people in the state don't even eat meat at all. And they would be screaming for a flag with an asparagus spear or a broccoli stalk, and I'd throw up every time I saw it.

A flag to suit everybody. I'm still thinking.

I've got it. If it's a given we really need a state flag, then in order to please everybody we should fly a flag with all sorts of colors on it.

One that is red and yellow, black and white, and green for the vegetarians.

You look up at the state flag and figure out for yourself what you want it to symbolize. People in Atlanta once saw the image of Christ on a billboard advertising spaghetti.

And if the ghost of great-great-granddaddy Beauregard comes back to me and wants to know what happened to the Georgia flag, I'll just say, "Don't look at me. You're the one who lost Miami Beach to the Yankees."

Are Clinton, Gore
Really Southerners?

It has long been my conclusion that if you happen to be a Straight Southern White Male (SSWM), as I happen to be, you're in a mess in the politically correct '90s.

Most of us are automatically branded as racist, sexist, anti-gay, and it is often said we drink beer and listen to Willie Nelson albums instead of sipping expensive wines while listening to a recording of Mozart's Opus No. 28 in G-flat out, Asia Minor. None of that is necessarily so, except for the part about the beer and our Willie Nelson albums.

Willie singing the phone book would, in fact, be a symphony, and most wines are overpriced and overrated, and who among us would remember to bring a corkscrew to a stock car race? But look at this, will you: The two highest ranking men in our government are Straight (I assume) Southern White Males. Pass the butter beans.

Two good ol' boys (a term Northerners, especially women with hyphenated last names who hate college football and pickup trucks, came up with) occupying the White House.

Jimmy Carter of Georgia lived in the White House for four years, but he picked Fritz Mondale from Minnesota as his running mate and nobody named Fritz ever once said, "I heard 'dat"—this is what we beer-swillers and politically incorrecters say instead of "I, indeed, concur."

But then I began to ask myself, do Bill Clinton and Al Gore really fit the SSWM mold?

I wrote in an earlier column how I once saw Al Gore cooking barbecue in Memphis. But how many of us SSWM's have a wife named Tipper? We marry women named Bonnie Lou, Ann Sue, Doris and Joe Betty Mavis.

Bill Clinton's wife is named Hillary. Hillary? Once Prince Charles gets rid of Princess Di, he'll probably marry somebody named Hillary.

And both these guys went to Ivy League schools. Most little boys who grow up in Arkansas, as did Bill Clinton, want to go to the University of Arkansas, wear a silly hat and scream "Pig Soooooooie!" when the Razorbacks score a touchdown.

Al Gore didn't go to the University of Tennessee, either, where the mascot is a blue tic hound named Smokey and the band never stops playing "Rocky Top" from the opening kickoff to the final whistle.

What they do at Yale, where Bill Clinton went to school, is sing, "Boola, Boola," which is translated loosely into Southern as, "How 'bout them Dawgs!"

Does either one of these guys own a pickup truck and have a dog named Tater or Rattler or Biscuit Eater that crawls under the truck in order to sleep in the shade and emerges with oil on its back? Does either one of these guys know all the words to even one country music song?

Can they use their mouths to blow gnats off their face, or do they try to swat them away with their hands? Would either ask Congress to pass legislation outlawing instant grits?

Do they say "wrestling" or "rasslin"? Did they have a problem pronouncing "Shiite" during the Gulf

War? Do Hillary and Tipper still fry chicken, or serve it baked under some awful sauce? Do they still cook at all? Before I make up my mind whether Bill Clinton and Al Gore are true SSWMs, I want answers to these questions.

SOUTHERN LIVING

Watching the World from
My Front Porch

I'VE BEEN DOING a lot of sitting on my front porch lately. I do this late in the evenings after the intense summer heat has subsided.

I supposed there are two primary reasons. One is, television just gets more rotten by the day. I've got 50 channels but I still have trouble finding anything worth watching. I'm even tired of the Spice Channel. The plots simply never change.

I also come from a long line of front-porch sitters, and before air-conditioning and television, that's the way a lot of people used to spend their evenings.

I did that with my own family when I was growing

up. My grandfather and I used to count cars and listen for trains.

I've been sitting on my front porch with my dog Catfish, the black Lab. I count BMWs. He growls when Volvos come by.

I live on a nice street and I have a nice front porch. I have a swing and two rocking chairs. I sit in one of the rocking chairs.

The swing is a little hard on what is left of my rear. Where do men's butts go when they get older?

One thing I have noticed is there are a lot of other people, at least in my neighborhood, who aren't sitting inside watching television in the evenings, either. They aren't sitting on their porches, however. They are out engaging in some sort of exercise.

There aren't just joggers anymore. In fact, there seems to be fewer joggers everyday.

(I was sitting in my doctor's office a few weeks ago when a nurse looked in and said to him, "CNN is on the phone. They want to know your advice on running in the Peachtree Road Race in this hot weather. My doctor looked up and said, "Don't." A man had a heart attack and died in that race.) A lot of bicycle riders come by my house while Catfish and I are on the porch. They wear helmets and tight pants and race past in large packs. The other evening, maybe 15 came by in a blur. Three minutes later a lone cyclist raced past. He appeared to be attempting to catch up with the others.

"He reminds me of horses I tend to bet on," I said to Catfish.

I get a lot of people out walking their dogs. A man comes by walking a dog that looks like a rat. He sort of looks like a rat, too. They say people often begin resembling their pets after a time.

Catfish and I have been together for over a decade, but my ears seem to be the same length as always.

I get roller skaters. They tend to be younger than the other exercisers. A roller skater came by my house recently, going down hill at what must have been 35 miles an hour. If he had fallen, they would have had to scrape him up.

There's another group that comes by my house that is exercising in a manner to which I am not familiar. They aren't jogging, but they aren't simply strolling, either. They are walking very fast and slinging their arms back and forth.

"That's power walking," somebody told me. "It's not as hard on your knees as jogging."

It looks like prissing to me, but I'm nearly 50 and don't own a Nordic Trac.

It once was the custom to speak pleasantly to anybody who happened to come past while one was sitting on one's porch. I wondered how that would play in a large American city in the '90s.

So one night whenever the joggers, power walkers or dog walkers would come by (the roller skaters and cyclists were going too fast,) I would call out, "Good evening."

Amazing. To a person, each called back, "Good evening."

I must have said "Good Evening" twenty times, and not once did anybody ignore my attempt to be pleasant.

That made me feel awfully good. Made me feel good about myself, my neighbors and my region.

We may even take up front porch sitting full time,

me and ol' Catfish. He said he thought the power walkers looked like they were prissing, too, by the way.

We don't look alike, but I guess we're starting to think alike as we enter our rocking chair years.

As 50 Looms, There Are Still a Few Surprises

Once you begin staring at the half-century mark as I am, you figure it rather unlikely there are any completely new experiences left.

I'd already been to Paris and the Texas State Fair, and I played golf with Arnold Palmer once.

But.

Her mother and I have been keeping company, and when it was Daddy Day at her pre-school, Jordan picked me to go with her.

Jordan is 3 and she has blonde hair and she wore a pretty white dress and had a yellow ribbon in her hair.

We had a difficult time finding her school. Every time I would turn, following her mother's directions, Jordan would scream, "No, no, you are going the wrong way!" Here I was, a grown man trying to locate a school in rush hour traffic with what turned out to be a terrible set of directions and a 3-year-old screaming, "You're going the wrong way!" Women.

We found the school, however, and there I stood with 15 other pre-schoolers and their daddies.

The first thing we did is paint with a golf ball. I know it doesn't sound possible, but it is. What you do is take a golf ball, dip it into some green paint and then dip it into some blue paint.

Then you put the golf ball on a piece of paper in a box. You put a lid on the box, and then you shake the box and make the ball roll around inside it.

The result is a piece of paper with a lot of green and blue lines and splotches on it.

I gave Jordan the Grizzard Golf Ball Blot Test. "What does this look like to you?" I asked her, holding the piece of paper in front of her.

She pondered for a moment and then said, "Catfish."

Catfish is my dog, the black Lab. Jordan likes to pull his tail. He likes to hide from Jordan.

Actually, the green and blue lines and splotches didn't look like Catfish at all. They looked like the *USA Today* weather map gone berserk. Or like a blue-and-green Edsel. What do I know about golfball painting?

After that, we went to the music room. The daddies had to sit down on a rug with their children.

Each child was given a felt outline of a different farm animal. When that animal was called by the music teacher, the child with that animal went to a board and stuck his or her animal on it, and then we all made the sound that particular animal makes.

It had been a long time since I sat on a rug and did animal sounds. I oinked like a pig, barked like a dog, baaa-ed like a lamb, whinnied like a horse, meowed like a kitten and mooed when Jordan went to the board with her cow.

I was a little disappointed they didn't have a donkey, because I do a dynamite donkey. A college roommate of mine, George Cobb, who was in West Virginia the last time I heard of him, taught me.

You whistle through your front two teeth and then go "Ha wwnk!" Well, it was fun in college when you'd had a few beers.

I made a note to teach Jordan how to do a donkey in case they get one at her school.

The last thing that happened was the children

sang a song, and when they got to, "I love you," they were supposed to point to their daddies.

Jordan pointed to me.

It was, in fact, a completely new experience, and it was also the first time, I was thinking, a female had ever asked me out.

As the daddies were leaving, all the children gave their hug. Jordan put her arms around me, and I think she really enjoyed having me there.

I may have missed something in my first 45 years. I really may have missed something.

Lewis Grizzard

Springtime, Flowers Seem to Grow on You

Why is it the older you get the more you begin to notice things you really never paid much attention to before? Simple things. Quiet things. Natural things.

It's been that way for me, for instance, with flowers. When I was growing up in Moreland, my Aunt Jessie's yard was the flower capital of the county. People drove from as far away as Grantville, Corinth, and Smith City to gaze at the color show Aunt Jessie's yard put on each spring.

I never paid much attention to her flowers, myself. The only time I ever thought about them was when Aunt Jessie would berate me for tromping through her flowers in search of the baseball I just hit from my yard to hers.

"Get out of those flowers, young man!" she must have screamed at me a million times. I never understood her concern. There I was practicing to grow up to be Gil Hodges, and how could I continue without my baseball?

Now flowers slay me. The azaleas will be blooming in Atlanta soon. So will the dogwoods. Their beauty decorates the city in pinks and whites and takes an ol' flower stomper's breath.

This week there have been days that were certainly whispers of spring. It was warm and still and it chased away the dreariness of winter. I spent one afternoon on the golf course. On one hole, the sprinkler system was wetting the grounds around it. I smelled a smell I hadn't thought of in years. The smell of water upon dry soil.

I can't describe that smell in words, but I remembered it from when the rain used to hit the dusty dirt road in front of my grandmother's house. Also, I remembered it from when I would be in my grandfather's fields, following him as he followed his plow and his mule, and it would "come up a cloud," as the old folks used to say, and the rain pelted down upon the freshly plowed earth and produced that smell again.

I looked up at an absolutely clear, blue sky this week. Its brilliance was remarkable. Up there somewhere was a hole in the ozone layer, but I couldn't see it. All I saw was a blue so clear and so bright it was like looking into eternity.

It's also difficult to describe the feeling of warmth. It's a secure feeling, somehow. I just sort of stood out there on the golf course and wallowed in it.

When chill turns to warm, it may be whoever created all this reminding us an end does finally come to winters of discontent. This is my forty-fifth spring. But it was only the last several years that I began to take a few moments to relish them.

I vividly remember that first time I really noticed and appreciated the coming of spring. I was on a golf course then, too. Augusta National. I had just turned 30. I was covering the Masters golf tournament for the Chicago *Sun Times*.

I was standing on number 16 on an April Sunday that was spectacular. It was warm and cloudless. There was the green of the turf, the blue of the sky, the pink of the azaleas. I would be catching a flight in a few hours, back to Chicago. I'd called the office earlier. They said it was snowing.

I stood out there and soaked it all in for the first time. It did something to my soul. It also did something to my future. I vowed at that moment I'd never miss another Georgia spring.

Twenty-two days later I was back at home in Atlanta with a job as a typer of words upon blank sheets of paper.

Fifteen years later I am still taking the time to smell and feel the glory of springtime. Getting older does have its benefits.

Sorry about the flowers I stomped, Aunt Jessie. I never learned to hit a curve ball anyway.

Alcohol, Tobacco and Firearms

Just about the time we finally are convincing the rest of the nation that we don't do things like eat mud in the South and that we have paved roads and indoor toilet facilities, the following had to hit the news: According to newspaper reports, Georgia Department of Revenue officials say the consumption of untaxed whiskey in the state is on the rise. "Untaxed whiskey" is an Atlanta way of saying moonshine, or white lightning.

Here the state of Georgia is going to be the host of the 1996 Olympics and the Department of Revenue tells us, not to mention the rest of the nation, Pappy's back at the still cooking up a new batch of corn liquor. The department came out with its statement after a 77-year-old Morgan County man was arrested for bootlegging Mason jars filled with moonshine.

The reason given for the increasing taste for moonshine was the rise in prices of legal liquor. And what are the chances you could get your hands on a Mason jar filled with enough kick to send you to the cemetery? "Bootleggers," Georgia's chief revenue officer was quoted as saying, "are starting to pay more attention to the quality of their product. They're a lot smarter than they used to be. They don't want to kill off their customers."

One wonders if the airlines and the tobacco industry could learn from that. I come from rural Georgia and I partook of a Mason jar one night. We were all about 15. We held the jar against a light and noticed

361

a lot of unidentifiable things floating around inside the 'shine.

"Probably just a few sticks and bugs," said my boyhood friend and idol, Weyman C. Wannamaker Jr., a great American, who proceeded to purify the liquid by straining it through his T-shirt. I was terribly ill the next morning. My mouth felt like the entire Chinese army had bivouacked in it the night before. My head felt like it had gotten into a disagreement with Mike Tyson's fists.

I never drank any more moonshine after that, and Weyman didn't either. "Dang stuff ate right through my favorite T-shirt," he said.

So we're headed back to Thunder Road, huh? Recall Robert Mitchum outrunning the revenuers in that '50s black and white classic? It wasn't that far from the truth. A Georgia mountain man once entered a stock car race at the old Lakewood Raceway in Atlanta when stock car racing was still on red dirt.

Revenuers appeared on the scene after receiving a tip his car was a tanker and loaded with white lightning. The mountain man won the race, but he never stopped to get his trophy or cash. He crossed the finish line and just kept going and escaped from the tax boys again.

But as interesting as all that is, the idea of moonshining making a comeback in Georgia is unsettling to me. We've come a long way to prove we no longer live on Tobacco Road, or God's Little Acre.

So, as much as it goes against my raisings, I'm pulling for the revenuers this time. The Falcons are enough of an embarrassment to Atlanta and the state. We didn't need this, too.

See This Badge? Watch Your Step in My Fife-dom

I recently purchased a parcel of land with a house on it on the banks of Lake Oconee in Georgia. A beautiful new golf course called Great Waters is almost at my door.

There is serenity here. I often need it. I'm only an hour and a half from Atlanta, but it's a completely different world.

I haven't heard a single siren so far, and I can watch the sun rise over the lake in the morning. There's a constant breeze off the water, and my dog Catfish, the black Lab, spends more time in the lake than out of it when we are here.

It's all got to do with getting older, I suppose, when it's lake breezes and sunrises that make me the happiest instead of being out there running where the neon can blind a man and do terrible things to his priorities.

All this to give you a sense of the place where something very extraordinary has happened to me.

This is one of those type things one never tells without first saying, "You aren't going to believe this, but. . . ." OK. You're not going to believe this, but the sheriff of Putnam County had me over to his office the other day and swore me in as a deputy. He gave me a badge. It has my name on it.

The reaction I have gotten when I mention I'm now a law officer person comes in the form of two questions: First people have asked, "Do what?" After that, they follow up with the same second question.

"Did they give you a bullet?" It's the Barney Fife thing. Sheriff Andy Taylor of Mayberry would never allow his deputy, Barney, to have more than one bullet, and he made him carry it in his shirt pocket.

So these individuals think they are very witty and clever when they make the references to Barney.

No, I wasn't given a bullet. I wasn't given a gun, either. I didn't want a gun. Guns frighten me. And recall that Andy Taylor didn't have a gun either. Yet he was able to maintain order in Mayberry quite well. And also recall in *Walking Tall* that Sheriff Buford Pusser cleaned up his town with a big stick, not a gun.

After the sheriff gave me my badge, I asked him where I should keep it.

"Attach it inside your wallet," he said. I did. And I've been practicing opening my wallet and flashing my badge, as in "I'm the heat, ma'am, all I want are the facts."

Joe Friday. Lewis Thursday.

I am, of course, certain the Putnam sheriff made me a deputy just for laughs, and that my position is an honorary one. But I'm proud of it, anyway. I feel like I'm a part of this area now, not just some city slicker who needs to get away from the madding crowd on occasion.

But I'm also aware of this: My position might be an honorary one, but I've still got the badge, and if you're passing through Putnam County, be careful you don't let me see you speeding, making illegal turns, or failing to slow for a yield sign.

Motorists who do such a thing and get away with it might think they can get away with other violations as well. You've got to stop small crimes before they become large ones.

Jaywalk today and commit a 117 (running naked through town) tomorrow.

You've got to nip it in the bud. Nip it, nip it, nip it.

Roots and Berries

The way I figure it, you spend the first half of your life attempting to get away from your roots and the second half trying to get back to them.

My roots are deeply bedded in the Georgia soil. My grandfather had 12 acres of the stuff, and from it he grew countless tables full of fresh vegetables.

Perhaps what made them even better was the fact he did most of his growing from behind a mule. Tractor vegetables are OK, but mule vegetables have a more honest and genuine flavor, I think.

I was drafted at an early age to help in the activity of growing. My grandfather even allowed me to hold the plow occasionally as the mule trudged down the row.

Many times, the mule took control of me and began veering off course and ignoring my pleas of "gee" (go right) and "haw" (go left). But my grandfather was always right there to bring the mule to order.

But I did other things, such as gathering plowed-up potatoes, hoeing weeds and pulling corn.

To be honest, it didn't take long to realize agriculture wasn't in my future. It was hot, dirty, tiring work. I envisioned myself in an air-conditioned office rather than as a toiler in the fields.

So when the opportunity arose, I split. And it had been 30 years—the reign of Johnny Carson—since I had involved myself in any sort of activity that dirtied my hands.

But then, I began to notice those smells again, the smell of rain, the smell of rain upon dusty earth, even the smell of freshly plowed ground. Most of

366

these scents came back on golf courses, oddly enough.

They began to haunt me. I even began picking up handfuls of southern soil, just to smell it and feel its wondrous texture again.

There was something missing in my life.

Get a grip.

Here's what I decided to do: Plant a garden.

Long removed from the furrowed fields of my youth, I decided to see if I could grow anything.

I had some help. Tom broke up a small plot in my urban backyard. Dedra and Jordan helped with the planting. I dug the holes with my hands and Jordan, who is nearly 4, dropped in the speckled-heart butter beans.

Tom had brought me some gloves. I refused to wear them.

"Real gardeners don't wear gloves," I said to him.

So the three of us set out butter beans, tomatoes, squash, okra, peppers, cucumbers, and watermelon, and Tom took pictures so I would have proof.

I also worked barefoot and got my feet, between my toes, and my hands marvelously dirty.

That was a week ago. I've watered and fertilized and things do seem to be growing. Even the butter beans Jordan and I planted are meekly sprouting.

So if I can keep the bugs and the birds away, I might soon be able to sit down to a plate of food I actually grew myself. Imagine that.

The headline should read: Grizzard returns to the soil; garden said mild success.

I may even expand next year and plant the entire backyard.

Anybody know where there's a good mule for sale?

GREENS, GRITS, GRAVY AND OTHER GOOD EATIN'

Kiss My Grits

AS ONE OF the nation's leading experts on grits (my mother served them every morning for breakfast), all I can do is try to light the way for those still blinded by prejudice and fear.

Grits won't bite you. Grits taste good and they're good for you.

Just sit back and relax and put yourself in my hands and let's go.

GRIZZARD'S GUIDE TO A SOUTHERN DELICACY
FOR FOLKS FROM NEW JERSEY
AND PLACES LIKE THAT

☞ *The origin of grits:* Cherokee Indians, native to the Southern region of the United States, first discovered grits trees growing wild during the 13th century. Chief Big Bear's squaw, Jemima Big Bear, is said to have been out of oatmeal one day, so she gathered the tiny grits growing from the grits trees and cooked them in water for Chief Big Bear.

After eating the grits, Chief Big Bear ordered his squaw, Jemima, burned at the stake.

Later, however, Southern planter Jim Dandy found grits taste a lot better if you put salt and pepper and butter on them. Grits really took off in the South after that. Today, grits orchards may be seen from the Carolinas to Florida and west to Louisiana.

At some orchards, tourists may "pick their own grits." If you decide to give it a try, make certain each grit you pick is ripe and firm. Raw grits tend to stick to the roof of your mouth and have been known to choke even large goats.

☞ *How grits got their name:* From the Cherokee word, *grayette,* which means "corn pebbles." The Cherokees thought grits were tiny versions of corn. They even tried to make bread from grits, which brought about another big run on squaw-burning.

☞ *What does the word "hominy" mean?* It is Southern for "blended voices," as in, "That quartet sure makes nice hominy, don't it?"

☞ *How do we prepare grits?* First, go out to your grits trees and pick a peck of grits. Wash, then allow to soak in warm buttermilk for an hour. Add two tablespoons of Jack Daniel's (Black Label) Tennessee sippin' whiskey and one cup branch water. Stir, bake at 450° for approximately one hour. Cover with sawmill gravy, add butter, then salt and pepper to taste. Cheese (Kraft American) optional.

Must be served hot. Cold grits tend to get gummy.

You wouldn't serve cold, gummy grits to Communist sympathizers from New York.

☛ *What are some other uses for grits?* Patching blowouts. Snake bites. Bathroom caulking. In some parts of the South it is even believed grits will grow hair. This is doubtful.

Grits do make a delightful party punch, however. Just add more Jack Daniel's.

☛ *How can I order my grits tree?* By sending $38.95 for each tree desired to "Grits-a-Grow-Grow," in care of Grizzard Enterprises. Add $15 if you want to take advantage of our special offer for our handy "Grit-Picker," which will save time and wear and tear on your hands when you go out to gather grits off your new grits tree.

☛ *What else may I order from "Grits-a-Grow-Grow"?* A special brochure outlining how you can purchase valuable vacation property at our new Alligator Point resort in Florida and about six zillion copies of Amy Carter's Washington Coloring Book. Order now while they last.

Lewis Grizzard

Verily, Putteth Not Sugar into Ye Corn Bread

I can pride myself on two recent, major accomplishments. Both have to do with my fondness for down-home Southern cooking. I favor down-home Southern cooking because I am from a down-home Southern home. That, and it tastes good.

I want my chicken fried, gravy on my steak, and I want my green beans cooked and my tomatoes served raw. Too many fancy restaurants serve their green beans raw and then they cook their tomatoes—and give you some sort of hard, dark bread with it. This is an unholy aberration I cannot abide.

I find some of the best down-home Southern cooking at the Luckie Street Grill in Atlanta, which features fried chicken, country-fried steak, meatloaf and, on Fridays, beef tips on rice and home-cooked vegetables—and uncooked tomatoes, of course. Imagine my shock, however, when I went to order my vegetables one day and the list on the menu included "Northern beans."

"There must be some mistake," I said to my favorite waitress, Jo.

"This says 'Northern beans.' How can you list Northern beans in a down-home Southern cooking place?"

"What do you call them?" asked Jo.

"White soup beans, of course," I answered.

My mother used to cook white soup beans for me. It's a little-known fact, but when Jesus fed the

372

masses he served white soup beans with the fish and bread. "Northern" beans aren't mentioned anywhere in the Bible.

Jo said, "I'll see what I can do."

I come in a week later and it says "White soup beans" on the Luckie Street menu. Praise Him.

That was accomplishment No. 1.

Where else I often eat is at the Ansley Golf Club in Atlanta, which has good chili.

Chili is down-home as long as you don't put mushrooms in it. They serve corn bread with the down-home chili at Ansley. The problem is, the corn bread is sweet. Corn bread is not supposed to be sweet. That's in the Bible, too. The book of Martha White, 7:11.

If you want something sweet, order the pound cake. Anybody who puts sugar in the corn bread is a heathen who doesn't love the Lord, not to mention Southeastern Conference football.

Anyway, in late December I went to Ansley and ordered the chili.

"You ought to try the corn bread," said the waiter. "The chef got tired of you complaining, so he quit putting sugar in it."

I tasted the corn bread. No sugar. I called out the chef.

"Verily," I said unto him, "it's about time you stopped making a sacrilege out of corn bread."

Accomplishment No. 2.

I feel so good about my two feats, I've got two new targets for next year.

I'm going to see if I can convince fast food places to start cutting up their own french fries instead of using frozen ones, and I'm going to see if I can help white bread make a comeback in this country.

Do not underestimate me. I'm on a mission from God.

Sweet Memories, Right Off the Vine

Thanks to the generosity of a couple of friends, I scored some home-grown (vine ripe, if you please) tomatoes the other day with a street value of at least seven or eight bucks.

You can get these tomatoes only in the summertime, and if you have no garden of your own, you must have a tomato connection. The rest of the year, one must be content with those tasteless pretenders somebody grows in a hothouse somewhere. They lack the juice and the flavor of the summertime home-growns to which, I freely admit, I've become addicted.

I grew up eating home-grown tomatoes from the family garden. It was only after I became an urban creature living far from the tilled soil that I realized what a blessing they had been to me as a child and how dear they are to me now.

Mama would cook green beans with new potatoes and there would be a plate of fresh tomatoes just out of the garden. The juice from the tomatoes inevitably mixed with the green beans and even got into your corn bread. The mix was indescribably wonderful.

Of course there are other ways to eat homegrown tomatoes. I took one of my friends' offerings last week and sat down and ate it like an apple. Some of the abundant juice ran down my chin onto my shirt like it did with the tomatoes of my youth. I can still hear Mama: "Look at your shirt, and I just took it off the line."

I get my shirts dry-cleaned now. Oh, for one more of her gentle scoldings. I also use the tomatoes to make sandwiches. Behold, the fresh home-grown tomato sandwich. First, you need white bread. Never use any sort of bread other than soft, fresh, white bread—hang the nutritional value—when constructing a tomato sandwich. To use any sort of other bread is a transgression equal to putting lights in Wrigley Field and putting mushrooms on cheeseburgers.

Cover both slices of bread with mayonnaise. Salt and pepper the slices of tomatoes and then put them between the bread. Eat quickly. The juice of the tomato slices will quickly turn the white bread into mush and you will be wearing some of your tomato sandwich.

My grandfather, Bun Word, sold some of his tomatoes on the side of the road at the little fruit and vegetable stands he ran summers in my hometown of Moreland. One day he ran out of his own tomatoes and bought some to sell off a produce truck. A couple of Atlanta tourists stopped by. The lady picked up a basket of tomatoes and asked my grandfather, "Are these home-grown?"

"Yes, ma'am," he said.

She bought a basket of the tomatoes. I said to my grandfather, "You didn't grow those tomatoes at home."

"Well," he replied, "they were grown at somebody's home."

My grandfather was a God-fearing, foot-washing Baptist, but I later learned it was not considered sinful nor unethical to put the shuck on tourists. In bigger cities they allowed liquor and strippers in various dens of iniquity. The folks in the hinterlands were just getting even.

My boyhood friend and idol, Weyman C. Wan-namaker Jr., a great American, for instance, once sold cantaloupes to city folk as Exotic Moreland Yellow-meated Midget Watermelons for an obscene profit.

This is just to say be careful if you go out and try to buy home-grown tomatoes. Folks in the country still don't give the rest of us much credit for being very smart. Otherwise, we wouldn't lived crammed together like we do and spend half our day fighting traffic and eating, as some do, raw fish.

I've eaten all my tomatoes now and face a rather extensive dry-cleaning bill for the damage they did to my shirts. But it will be a pittance when I consider the ecstasy and memories they provided me.

And to think, it wasn't that long ago I felt the same way about sex.

Lewis Grizzard

Real Home Cooking Doesn't Fit in a Box

For weeks I had been seeing a television commercial for this certain chain of restaurants. The commercial claimed the restaurant served home cooking, "The kind mom used to do." I'm not going to name the restaurant chain. I've already got one libel suit pending. But I will say I've spent the nearly three decades since I left the cooking mama used to do looking for something, anything, that came close to it.

I grew up at a fried chicken, pork chops, pot roast and fresh vegetable table, with corn bread or mama's homemade biscuits on the side. I must have this sort of food at least once a week or be struck by the dreaded bland-food poisoning. That's because I have to eat a lot of airline food, as well as hotel food. The airlines and hotels get together each year and plan their menus. Steak au gristle and chicken a la belch.

So I gave this chain a try. I walked into one of its restaurants and looked over the menu. There was no fried chicken or pork chops. But there was country fried steak and pot roast. I decided to go for the pot roast.

"Can I get mashed potatoes and gravy with the pot roast?" I asked the waitress.

"Sure," she answered.

The pot roast was so-so. The gravy was suspect. One bite of the mashed potatoes, and I knew. I called the waitress back over.

"I would take it as a personal favor if you would be perfectly honest with me," I said. "These mashed potatoes came out of a box, didn't they?" The waitress dropped her eyes for a brief second. Then she looked up and said apologetically, "Yes, they are."

I hate mashed potatoes that come out of a box. When God created the mashed potato (I am certain the Bible points this out somewhere), he had no intention of anybody goofing around and coming up with mashed potatoes from a box.

He meant for real potatoes to be used. You peel them, you cut them into little pieces and put them in a pot of boiling water. You put in some salt and pepper, and then you add some butter and maybe even a little sour cream and then you beat them and stir them and you've got biblically correct mashed potatoes.

I realized the waitress didn't have anything to do with the fact that the restaurant served mashed potatoes from a box in a place that advertised mama's cooking, an affront to mothers everywhere. That was upper management's doing.

So when I paid my bill—reluctantly, due to the fact there should have been a warning on the menu that the mashed potatoes weren't really mashed potatoes—I did have a word with the assistant manager, who took my money anyway. "May the Lord forgive you, for ye know not what you do, you potato ruiner."

I think he thought I was some sort of religious nut. He was still waiting for me to hand him a pamphlet and ask him for money as I walked out the door.

Mashed potatoes from a box. That's what's wrong with this country. That, and non-alcoholic beer, instant grits, canned biscuits, soybean anything, frozen french fries, fake flowers, staged photo opportunities for politicians running for re-election, tanning salons, and I bought some Häagen Dazs vanilla ice cream at the grocery store recently, but when I went to eat it, I realized I had gotten yogurt instead.

What's real anymore? Computerized voices talk to me at the airport. I phone a friend and I talk to a machine. Musical stars are lip-syncing.

Did somebody mention silicone implants? As soon as I make the world safe from boxed mashed potatoes, I'll get around to that. It's a matter of priorities, you know.

Here's the Book on
Fried Green Tomatoes

A lot of people who saw the movie *Fried Green Tomatoes* probably asked themselves, "What's a fried green tomato?" There wasn't any dialogue that I recall concerning fried green tomatoes in the movie—just a sign outside the Whistle Stop Cafe that advertised they were on sale inside.

The type of food the movie dealt with mostly was barbecue, and if I go any further, I'd be giving away some of the plot for those who still haven't seen this "must-see" movie.

Truthfully, I hadn't thought about fried green tomatoes in a long time till I saw the movie.

My grandmother used to serve them when I was growing up, but after I left home, I don't recall eating another one.

So I set out a month or so ago trying to find some place that still served fried green tomatoes so I could reacquaint myself with their taste.

I was in a restaurant in Jackson, Mississippi, that served fried dill pickle slices. For the record, they're a perfect munchy with a cold longneck bottle of beer.

Fried eggplant is easily located in the South. Fried okra, of course, is served in just about every place that features the meat and three.

But fried green tomatoes? I searched and searched. Nothing.

But then I had business this week in the hamlet of Social Circle, 35 miles east of Atlanta, off I-20. When lunchtime came I asked a local, "Where's the best place in town to eat lunch?"

"Try the Blue Willow Inn," I was told.

The Blue Willow Inn, on the main drag in Social Circle (do they still say "main drag"?), was inside an old plantation-style home that obviously had been renovated recently.

The deal was $6.50 for all you could eat of any and everything sitting out on a couple of large tables.

I started with the sweet potato souffle. I went to the baby lima beans from there. Then to the squash casserole, the green beans, the rice, and on to the turnip greens. My plate runneth over and I wasn't to the meats and breads yet.

I piled three pieces of fried chicken on top of that and added a piece of hot, buttered corn bread. Next to the corn bread was something I didn't recognize right away.

"This wouldn't be . . ." I said to a waitress.

"Yessir," she replied. "They're fried green tomatoes."

I wound up eating 10 slices. The sweet sourness of the green tomato—quite different from the taste of red tomatoes, with the crust on the outside—was incredibly pleasing.

I talked to the proprietor, Louis Van Dyke, who said he had been in the restaurant business nearly all his life. I asked him about the fried green tomatoes.

"I was serving them a long time before the movie came out," he said. He even brought me out a green tomato and told me he bought it in a farmers market in Forest Park. You slice 'em, batter 'em, and throw 'em in the grease. Sounds easy in case somebody wants to try it.

I am a connoisseur of authentic Southern cooking,

which is getting more and more difficult to locate. If I gave ratings for Southern cooking, I'd have to give the Blue Willow my absolute highest mark—five bowls of turnip greens.

Every dish was authentic and delicious.

Lewis Grizzard

It's Southern Pride, Battered and Fried

My hero and professional role model, Chicago *Tribune's* Mike Royko, had an astounding piece recently. According to Royko, at an auto plant in Normal, Illinois, an executive asked the company that ran the plant's cafeteria to offer some more variety.

"Man cannot live by tuna patty melts alone," wrote Royko.

So the cafeteria people decided to offer some Southern cooking one day. They picked the wrong day.

The Friday before the Monday that was the holiday honoring Dr. Martin Luther King Jr.'s birthday, the cafeteria was to serve barbecue ribs, black-eyed peas, grits, and collards.

Two black employees at the plant, Royko further explained, went to see the executive and complained such a meal, just two days before Dr. King's birthday, was a stereotyping of black dining habits. They threatened a boycott of the meal. The executive, who was also black, ordered the Southern dishes be stricken from the Friday menu. Meatloaf and egg rolls were served instead.

What is astounding to me is, in our search to become politically correct and more sensitive, in this one instance at least, food became an issue. Southern food. What has come to be known as soul food. And my food, too.

I think it is very important to point out barbecue ribs, black-eyed peas, grits, and collards may, in fact, be a choice dish to many black Americans. But it also sounds pretty darn good to me, a white man.

I grew up on soul food. We just called it country cooking. My grandmother cooked it. My mother cooked it.

Friends cooked it. Still do. I might not have made it through my second heart operation if it hadn't been for the country cooking of one of the world's kindest ladies, Jackie Walburn, who delivered to me in the hospital.

And my friend Carol Dunn in Orlando has served me many an enchanting spread featuring her wonderful roast pork. My Aunt Una cooked me fried chicken, speckled-heart butterbeans, turnip greens, mashed potatoes, and creamed corn as recently as Thanksgiving eve. The creamed corn, the best I ever ate, was provided by my Aunt Jessie.

Don't tell me serving food like that is an affront to the memory of Dr. Martin Luther King Jr. What it would have been in Normal is a celebration of the sort of cooking that has been prevalent in the South, both for blacks and whites, for 200 years.

Royko asked, "Next Columbus Day would it be an insult to serve spaghetti and meatballs?" What a plate of hogwash, and I can get by with that. I have a pig valve in my own heart, and I can eat my share of barbecue ribs with anybody, black or white or whatever.

To charge stereotyping over food trivialized the King holiday. The man didn't give his life for something like that. It's silly and it's stupid and it makes me want to throw up. Had I eaten meatloaf and egg rolls for lunch, I might.

SOUTHERN ROOTS
GROW DEEP

Georgian by Birth

IF I HAD said to my mother, "I don't think I'll go to college," at some point during the years I lived at her house, she would have killed me.

Maybe she wouldn't have killed me, but she would have inflicted severe neck and head injuries upon me.

My mother was like a lot of baby boom parents. As soon as I reached the age where I could understand the basics of the English language, she began saying to me, "I want you to have it better than I did." Translated that meant, "If you ever say, 'I don't think I'll go to college,' I'm going to inflict serious neck and head injuries upon you."

My mother grew up red-clay poor, on her father's precious-few acres in Heard County, Georgia, the only one of 139 Georgia counties that didn't have one inch of railroad tracks.

My mother—and I have my grandmother's word on this—actually did walk three miles to school barefoot. It rarely snowed in Heard County, Georgia, which is the only thing that saved me from a complete guilt trip when my mother put the "I walked three miles, etc." line on me when I complained I didn't have a Thunderbird.

There were five children in my mother's family. The eldest, Uncle Johnny, also walked three miles to school barefoot and later became a doctor. I wish I could say he became a podiatrist but I can't. Well, I could, but I'd be lying. My mother, the third child, was the only other member of the family to get a degree.

My mother graduated from Martha Berry College in Rome, Georgia. Berry offered students from poor backgrounds one choice: Come here and wash dishes, clean toilets, work on our farm, and we'll give you an education. My mother, in other words, was never a member of a college sorority.

She finished Martha Berry in the '30s with a degree in education. Then she married my father, then World War II broke out, I was born in '46, Daddy went to Korea in 1950, came back from his second war a complete mess, and left my mother when I was six and she was forty-one.

We left Fort Benning, Georgia, my father's last station, and moved in with my mother's parents in a tiny little house in Moreland. My grandparents moved there from Heard County in the '40s when the few red-clay acres could no longer provide. My grandmother went to work in a local hospital as a maternity nurse. My grandfather got a job as janitor at the Moreland Elementary School.

Mother had never used her degree. Marriage and a child and life as a military wife had stripped her of an opportunity to do so. But it's 1953, she doesn't have a dime, her husband has just split, and no child of hers is going to walk to school barefoot. So my mother got a job teaching first grade in Senoia, Georgia, another small town near Moreland.

Her first year of teaching, she was paid $120 a month. A month.

And one day I would blow the opportunity to make as much as $125 a week selling encyclopedias for Howard (Dipstick) Barnes.

Senoia was six miles from Moreland. Mother needed a car. She bought a 1948 Chevrolet. Its body was the color of an orange Dreamsicle. The top was blue. The stuffing was coming out of the front seat upholstery. It was hard to crank on cold mornings, and it burned oil.

Mother taught one year at Senoia, and then she got a break, which she certainly deserved at that point in her life. The first-grade job came open at Moreland Elementary. Mother got the job.

The Moreland School was maybe a quarter of a mile from my grandparents' house. Most mornings I walked to school. When I asked mother if I could go barefoot, she said, "No. You might step on a rusty nail and get lockjaw."

Ever think about all the warnings your parents gave you growing up? Could stepping on a rusty nail really give you lockjaw and cause you to die a horrible death because you couldn't open your mouth to eat?

Remember, "Never drink milk with fish, it will make you sick?" How about, "No you can't have a BB gun. It will put your eye out?"

Today parents are worried about their children joining a religious cult or becoming drug dealers. When I was growing up they were worried about us putting an eye out.

My mother would teach first grade at Moreland School for twenty years before the illness that killed her forced her to take an early retirement with a pittance of a pension for her disability.

My mother's background taught her frugality. I'm convinced my mother could have solved the federal deficit problem. She simply would have said to the government, "OK, turn all your money over to me and give me the list of what you owe." She would have had us out of the hole shortly.

I cannot remember my mother ever spending a dime on herself for something she didn't desperately need. When the old Chevy finally gave out in 1955, she did buy a new car, a green Chevrolet. When the salesman said, "I can put a radio in for another twenty dollars," my mother said, "We already have a radio at home."

I can never remember her buying more than five dollars' worth of gas at a time, either. She would pull up to the pump and say each time, "Five, please." I think she was afraid if she filled up the tank and died, she would have wasted money on whatever gas remained in her car.

Mother began saving for my college education with the first paycheck she ever earned. She bought bonds. She put cash in shoe boxes and hid them in the back of her closet.

Having enough money to send me to college when the time came consumed my mother. Besides the bonds and the shoe-box cash, she kept a coin bank, bought day-old bread, sat in the dark to save on the electric bill, never had her hair done, quit smoking, and never put more than a dollar in the collection plate at church. She used simple logic for not tithing the biblical tenth: "If the Lord wanted me to tithe that much, he wouldn't have made college so expensive."

As a matter of fact my mother did have something to do with my interest in putting words on paper. My mother was on constant grammar patrol when I was growing up.

Going to school with children from poor, rural backgrounds, as I did, I often fell in with a bad grammar crowd. What follows is a glossary of the way a lot of words were mispronounced around me constantly:

"His'n" (his).

"Her'n" (hers).

"Their'n" (theirs).

"That there'n" (that one).

"You got air asack?" (Do you have a sack?).

"I ain't got nairn." (No, I'm afraid I don't).

Mother also disliked another common grammatical error of the times. Many of my friends would say, in referring to parents, "Daddy, he went to town last night," and, "Mamma, she went with him and they didn't bring us air a thang."

"There is no reason to say, 'Daddy, he,'" my mother would say. "'Daddy' is identification enough."

"Ain't," of course, was a hanging offense. You

never got away with double negatives or the popular answer to, "Have you done your homework?" "Yes, I done done it."

My mother did allow, however, certain words and phrases common to Southern speech that might not be able to stand a harsh review in the strickest sense, of whether or not they were proper.

My mother had no problem with the use of the word "fixing" in place of "going to" or "it is my intention to," as in, "I'm fixing to do my homework." I still say "fixing" and anybody who doesn't like it can stay in Boston and freeze.

My mother had no problem with certain Southern expletives, such as

"Hot-aw-mighty!"

"Dang-nab-it!"

"Dad-gum-it!"

"Shut yo' mouth!" (It's not "hush yo' mouth" as some up North think).

"Lawd have mercy."

"I'll be a suck-egg mule."

My mother would not abide, however, any form of swearing.

I never would have used the following words and phrases in this book if my mother were still alive, because it might have broken her heart. But she's gone now, and I suppose I can offer up such examples of common Southern curse words:

"Shee-yet far": Southerners can probaby say "shit" better than anybody else. We give it the ol' two syllable treatment, which brings out the ambience and adds the fire to string it out even more.

"Sumbitch": Southern, of course, for "son of a

bitch." However when people from the North try to say "sumbitch" it doesn't come out exactly right. I don't think Southerners actually say "sumbitch." I think it's more "suhbitch," as in, "That suhbitch can flat play a cello."

"Got-damn": You know.

"Ice": We don't say "ass" like other people do. I can't decide exactly how we say "ass," but "ice" comes close, as in, "Shee-yet far, Randy, if that got-damn suhbitch don't watch his ice, somebody's goin' to break that cello right over his got-damn head."

I remember the day the letter came. It said on the front of the envelope, "This is your official University of Georgia acceptance."

Mama paid for my first quarter. It was perhaps a two-hundred-dollar lick, counting books. She also gave me two hundred dollars cash from some hidden shoe box. She hugged me when I left home and said, "I've looked forward to this day for a long time. I know you will do well and don't drink."

I would do well.

One out of two's not bad.

Southern by the Grace of God

My mother was the third child of Charles Bunyon and Willie Word of Carroll County, Georgia. They named her Christine. Her two sisters, Una and Jessie, called her "Cricket." Her two brothers, Johnny and Dorsey, called her "Teenie." Nearly three decades of first-graders she taught knew her as "Miss Christine." I always called her Mama.

Mama had that thing some teachers develop, the idea that her students were her children, too. Often when I visited her in the hospital, a nurse would come into her room and introduce herself to me and say, "Your Mama taught me in the first grade."

Reading and writing are the basis of all learning. First-grade teachers teach that. Imagine being able to take a 6-year-old mind and teach it to write words and sentences and give it the precious ability to read.

As for me, Mama taught me that an education was necessary for a fuller life. She taught me an appreciation of the language. She taught a love of words, of how they should be used and how they can fill a creative soul with a passion and lead it to a life's work.

I'm proud of my Mama the teacher.

We put Mama next to her mother and father in the plot where her younger brother, Dorsey, was buried. Each headstone was etched with the name that the dead had been called by the rest of the family.

My grandmother was "Mama Willie." My grandfather was "Daddy Bun."

Uncle Dorsey's children had called him "Pop." We

had decided to put "Miss Christine" on Mama's headstone. That's what her legion of first-graders called her.

It was over so quickly at the grave site. A few words. Another prayer. Then the funeral people ushered the family away. To spare them from the covering of the grave, I suppose.

I greeted friends. My first ex-wife came up. We embraced. I recalled the feel of her in an instant.

We went back to the house. I wasn't planning to stay that night, either. Home was where Mama was, and she wasn't there anymore. I said my goodbyes. My girlfriend and I got into my car. I said, "Let's ride over to the cemetery before we start home."

There were still a lot of flowers. The red clay over Mama's grave was moist. A man I didn't know drove up in a truck. He was an older man. He wore overalls.

"I'm the one what dug the grave," he said to me. "I had to figure out a way not to dig up any of your boxwoods in your plot. I just came back to see the pretty flowers."

The gravedigger. I was talking to Mama's gravedigger, and the man had gone to extra trouble for a family he really didn't know. I thanked him. Only in a small town.

We drove away. Moreland was behind us in a matter of minutes. I began to hum "It Is No Secret."

My girlfriend touched my shoulder. Mama had touched my soul.

Lewis Grizzard

A Farewell Salute to
Sergeant Dews

Several years ago, I wrote a book about my father, a veteran of World War II and Korea, who died in 1970.

Captain Lewis M. Grizzard Sr. was a highly decorated soldier, but after he returned from Korea—where he had survived a bloody rout of his company by the Chinese and had survived only because a young Chinese soldier, attempting to surrender to the Americans, had hidden him from the enemy in a cave for six weeks—he was a changed man.

He began to bender-drink heavily. He couldn't handle the family finances and borrowed large sums of money. He eventually left the army, or the army left him.

My mother could no longer cope with my father's problems and had a 6-year-old on her hands. She moved us to her parents' home and eventually divorced my father.

I wasn't certain I could write the book. I didn't know if there was enough there. And there was so much about my father I didn't know.

He roamed the country from 1954 until his death. He taught school, sold shirts, ran restaurants, and the drinking just got worse. It was a stroke that killed him.

In order to write the book, I felt I needed to know more about Korea, the forgotten war. So I bought an oral history of Korea as told by those Americans who were there.

It was a huge volume. I took it off a shelf at the bookstore and opened it to the middle.

The first name I saw was that of Sergeant Robert Dews. Bobby Dews had been my father's first sergeant when he returned from Korea and was stationed at Fort Benning.

My dad's new assignment after Korea had been to run the athletic program at Benning. Bobby Dews also played baseball for him.

I would hear daddy speak of his talent and friendship on many occasions.

The sergeant noticed a byline of mine when I was with the Atlanta *Journal* sports department 20 years ago. I went by Lewis Grizzard Jr. back then. He wrote me a letter. He told me of his connection to Daddy and that he knew of his recent death.

He also wrote, "No matter what happened to the captain after Korea, never judge him too harshly. He had been through two wars and had seen so much blood, gore and death. It haunted him and the only way he could forget for a time, was by drinking.

"I sat by him at his desk at Benning and saw his hands shake. Many times, I'd say 'Captain, let's go for a ride and get you out of here.' But he'd always go back to the bottle. I wish I could have done more for him."

I knew there was something providential about opening that huge book to a page where Sergeant Dews' name appeared, so I began my own book.

During the writing I said a lot of things and felt a lot of things I needed to say and feel.

They buried Robert P. Dews the other day in Americus. He was 77.

He had a minor league baseball career after he left the army. His son, Bobby, followed. He later was the Braves' minor league field coordinator.

I learned of the sergeant's death too late to make the funeral. But I did want to write something in his honor. Something that could never square my father's debt to him but something that would say a little boy who used to sit on the bench next to his Daddy during Ft. Benning baseball games is thankful for what he tried to do for his Daddy.

I guess Sergeant Dews was Captain Grizzard's best friend. The preachers say we'll all be reunited.

Oh, let it be so.

First Cousins Made Lasting Impression

I've written quite a lot about my parents, grandparents and aunts and uncles. But I've never had much to say about my cousins, and I'll limit this to first cousins for brevity's sake.

I'm not certain how many living first cousins I have. My parents divorced when I was young, and you lose touch. But I can still come up with enough to fill a twin-engine charter flight, and I thought I would offer a list and describe a bit about each one. Some had a profound impact on my life.

Gwen: Once lined me up with a couple of her lovely friends. I didn't marry either of them, however. Nor did I marry any of my cousins. Cousin-marrying went out in the South after the birth of whoever it was who invented instant grits.

Albert: He and I are left to carry on the Grizzard name. He has daughters. I have no children, but plenty of time left on my biological clock. Right?

Melba: She's the only one of my cousins who is younger than me. We grew up together in our hometown of Moreland. One day when we were barely out of diapers, a bull got out of its pen and began to chase us.

"Run for it, Melba!" I screamed.

Melba picked up a rock and hit the bull between the eyes with it and it ran away. Melba saved my life. As far as I know, however, Melba never made it to Pamplona. Good news for the bulls there.

Mary Ann: Melba's sister. She was very smart and

399

married the smartest boy in Moreland. They had lots of smart children. Now they also have lots of smart grandchildren. We're getting old, Mary Ann. Seems like only yesterday you were quashing the Santa Claus myth for us younger kids.

Lynn: She's where my looks went.

Jim: Lynn's handsome brother. A nearby women's college named Jim the best looking man at the University of Georgia when he was a student there and invited him to a banquet in his honor. Legend has it, he wore white socks with his tuxedo to the banquet. Jim never married until he was in his late 40s. He's another one of my smart cousins.

Gerry: She babysat me when I was a child. If sweet and kind had faces, they would have hers. She taught me to play Monopoly, but where was she when I invested in all those limited partnerships?

Glenda: Gerry's sister. We were inside Cureton and Cole's store in Moreland one day when I was 8. Glenda was 12. There were some grapes sitting on a counter. "Like grapes?" Glenda asked me. "Love 'em," I answered.

"Why don't you take one?" she suggested. "They won't mind."

I pulled off one and ate it.

"You know you're going to hell for stealing that grape," Glenda said. That was the last thing I ever stole.

Scooter: Gerry and Glenda's brother. Great fisherman, great hunter and former county drag racing champion. He taught me to throw a curve ball. They hated the dreaded hook in Region 2-AA in '63 and '64.

Mickey: She also babysat me as a child and is why

I've always had a thing for redheads, which, incidentally, has cost me about as much as those limited partnerships.

Mary Jean: The classiest lady I've ever known. She wouldn't serve instant grits to a liberal Yankee Democrat.

It should be obvious I've been blessed with some great cousins. And if we had a family business, I wouldn't hesitate to put a single one of them in charge of it.

Lewis Grizzard

Great Memories of a Grandfather Go Pedaling Past

I was thinking about my bicycle. It was red. When I rode it, down a thousand dirt roads with no names and even five miles to Raymond Lake, I was the wind. Or at least a large Greyhound bus.

A couple of things prompted such thoughts. One is that bicycling has become an adult thing now. Grown people pedal by my house on a regular basis. They have bicycles that appear to be very expensive.

They also wear helmets and tight-fitting cyclists' outfits. A uniform wasn't necessary during my bicycle period.

I got my red bicycle when I was 9, thanks to my grandfather, Bun Word. My grandfather was a janitor at my elementary school. A kid today probably would be embarrassed if his grandfather was the janitor at his school. I wasn't. My grandfather was in his 60s when I was 9 and in the fourth grade. But he was still a tall, muscular man that dogs followed.

He told silly jokes to my classmates and passed out an occasional stick of gum with the warning, "Don't chew it until school's out."

Some heeded the warning; most didn't. My grandfather also farmed 12 acres and helped out over at the Atlanta and West Point railroad depot, and his days were full, up to an April afternoon 30 years ago when we found him slumped behind his tractor, holding his chest. He died a week later.

My grandfather got up at 5:00 each morning and walked in the cold and dark to school. Each room was heated by a coal-burning stove.

He would go down in the coal bin under the school and haul up the coal for the fires in a wheelbarrow. When we arrived three hours later, our rooms would be toasty and comfortable.

In the afternoon, he would return to the school and clean the wooden floors and throw out the trash. That's how I got my bicycle. We all used Blue Horse paper and notebooks. Each Blue Horse product had a label with a point value on it. The more expensive the product, the more points the label was worth.

You could save Blue Horse labels and when you got enough points you could send them in and Blue Horse would send you back a prize. If you saved 25,000 points, you got the grand prize, a bicycle.

Most of my classmates didn't save Blue Horse points. They threw their labels into the trash and my grandfather would go through each wastebasket and pick out the labels.

He started saving Blue Horse points when I was 7. Two years later, he counted one day, and he had 25,000 points.

We bundled the labels together with rubber bands and mailed them to Atlanta. Two weeks later my red bicycle came.

My grandfather held on to the back of the bicycle until I learned to ride it without adult assistance. It was a big day in my life.

I rode my bicycle until I was 14. Then it wasn't cool to ride a bicycle anymore, so one day I climbed down off it for good, counting the days until I could get my driver's license.

It is very unlikely I will take up adult cycling.

But as they pedal by my house, the memory of a

precious old man comes back and touches me at midlife when I find myself looking back more often than I look ahead.

Landing in Maturity's Speed Trap

Dudley Stamps and I have been friends since the second grade in Moreland.

In baseball, Dudley caught and I pitched. If there had been anybody around to scream, "You da man!" in baseball games back then, that person would have screamed it when Dudley launched another home run. He hit five in one game.

Dudley was a legend by the time he was 12. He started shaving when he was 9, and in the eighth grade he fought the school bully, Frankie Garfield—who was two years his elder—to a draw. It was a moral victory for us wimps that Frankie had had many a field day picking on.

As Dudley got older, he developed a great interest in seeing how fast he could drive a motorized vehicle. When he turned 16, his parents lost their minds and gave him an earlier model Thunderbird. The rest is speeding-ticket history. Parents warned their children: Don't get in a car with Dudley Stamps.

After a high school baseball game one evening in the county seat of Newnan, I didn't have a ride home so Dudley gave me one back to Moreland, six miles away. Dudley could do Newnan to Moreland in about 200 telephone poles an hour.

The road curved for the first four miles, so Dudley had to keep it in the high double digits. Then, however, came the Moreland Straight, a flat stretch of two miles that was Dudley's Bonneville Salt Flats.

When we hit the Straight, Dudley floored it. The state patrolman who pulled him over just outside the Moreland city limit sign said, "Son, did you know you were going 108 miles an hour?"

"No I wasn't," protested Dudley. "I top-ended at 127."

A charge of merely going 108 in a 60 mph speed zone was an affront to the streak of lightning we knew as Dudley.

I begged Dudley to slow down that night. I equated speed, and still do, with death. But Dudley just laughed at me and stepped down even harder on the accelerator.

So I'll keep this short: I played golf with Dudley recently at Orchard Hills Golf Club (a.k.a. Moreland National), which sits a wedge shot from the Moreland Straight. We hit our shots on a downhill par 3. I was driving the golf cart.

There was a sign near the cart path that read: Slow, steep grade. But I'm a bat-out-of-hell's-bunker in a golf cart. Full bore, we tooled down the steep grade.

Dudley screamed, "Slow down! You're going to turn this thing over!" I hit the brakes and savored the moment. I had tugged on Superman's cape. I had taken the mask off the Lone Ranger.

I had frightened Dudley Stamps in a motorized vehicle. Thirty years later I had my revenge.

I am a blur my very own self. I am the wind.

"You're a damned fool driving a golf cart like this," Dudley, slowed by maturity, had said.

Now, come out, Frankie Garfield, wherever you are.

Me and My Guccis

All my adult life, I have attempted to rise above my humble beginnings. Take shoes, for example. Now that I have steady work and live in the city, I like to wear nice shoes.

In the boondocks, we didn't wear shoes unless it was an absolute necessity. Like your feet would freeze if you didn't, or there was a funeral.

My boyhood friend and idol, Weyman C. Wannamaker Jr., a great American, didn't wear shoes even on those occasions, but he did wash his feet twice a week whether they needed it or not.

The first time I saw Weyman in a pair of shoes, they were forced upon him. We were in the sixth grade, and the teacher organized a field trip to Atlanta to hear a performance by the symphony orchestra. As the bus pulled away from the school, she noticed Weyman was barefooted.

Horrified, she ordered the bus driver to stop at the nearest shoe store, where she bought Weyman a pair of shoes. He protested, but the teacher hit him in the mouth, and Weyman didn't mention the shoes again.

During the performance of the symphony orchestra, however, Weyman's feet began hurting him, so he took off his shoes and hung his bare feet over the railing of the balcony. Unfortunately, he was between washes.

The entire percussion section and two flute players stopped in the middle of Chopin's Movement No. 5 to search for what had obviously passed away days earlier.

I always think of Weyman when I pull on a new pair of shoes. Lately, some of the fellows down at the lodge have been giving me the business because I now own a pair of stylish loafers by Gucci, the famous Italian leatherperson.

I prefer to think their boorish, catty remarks stem from ignorance, sprinkled with at least a tad of jealousy.

The other day, I called Weyman C. Wannamaker Jr. back home and told him I am now wearing Guccis. I knew he would be proud.

"You wearing them shoes," he said, "is like putting perfume on a hog."

FAITH IN THE BIBLE BELT

Gimmee That Old Time Religion

I GREW UP hearing that good things come to those who love the Lord; the Moreland, Georgia, Methodist Church was deeply and comfortably seated in the traditional interpretation of the Word. But religion, like so many other things, isn't as simple as it used to be. Nowadays the good guys sometimes wear black and white striped hats instead of just one or the other.

Almost every day in the mail I receive a letter from some television evangelist asking me for a donation to help buy a new truck for his television equipment or to pay off the debt for the new gym at New Testament University. The implication is that if I don't send them cash, I'm on the express train for hell.

Will I end up down there with Hitler and Attila the

Hun and Bonnie and Clyde just because I didn't send them five bucks for a new wrestling mat? Then again, is hell actually *down* there?

"Can you dig your way to hell?" I asked the preacher when I was a kid.

"Guess you can," he said, "but I can tell you how to get there a lot quicker."

My grandfather wouldn't have cared much for today's bigtime television preachers. In his oft-stated opinion, preachers were supposed to marry folks, preach funerals, mow the grass around the church and administer to the needs of his flock, which meant consoling the poor soul who lost his job, whose wife ran off, and whose trailer burned to the ground . . . all in the same week.

Our preacher even used to knock down the dirt dobbers' nests in the windows of the sanctuary so the inhabitants wouldn't bother the worshippers while we was trying to run the devil out of town on Sunday morning.

Do you suppose Oral Roberts or Jerry Falwell ever knocked down dirt dobbers' nests?

My grandfather also didn't like it when younger preachers used note cards to deliver their sermons. "They ought to get it straight from the Lord," he said many a time. "Politicians use notes."

The preacher at Moreland Methodist when I was growing up suited my grandfather just fine. He drove an old car. He had only one suit. He did the yard work, didn't use note cards and always attempted to answer the questions of a twelve-year-old boy when things didn't add up. Once he even preached a funeral for a dog because that little boy, who loved the dog very much, asked him to.

410

What would Pat Robertson say over a dog?

What bothers me today is that for every glamour boy of the pulpit, there are thousands out there who tackle the devil daily, one on one, with little or no audience, against long odds, and, occasionally, on an empty stomach.

God bless them. And God, please don't let my grandfather—I know he's around there some-where—find out that we've got preachers down here today who use cue cards and hang out with politicians.

"Jesus of Pasta" Is Just a Little Hard to Swallow

Jesus in the spaghetti. It was all over the news.

There's a billboard in suburban Atlanta with a picture of spaghetti on it, and people drove by and swore they saw Jesus in there amongst the noodles.

"I still don't see it, Harold," a wife said to her husband who brought her to see the Shroud of Pasta.

"Look right there in that big glob of sauce, Loreena. It's Hee-um."

No way. I'm not going for the Jesus in the spaghetti thing.

In the first place, who knows what Jesus really looks like? Until Jesus shows up on "Donahue" or "Oprah," we won't have a clue concerning his actual appearance.

I saw the spaghetti billboard on television. I looked at it, but I didn't see Jesus, unless Jesus looks a lot like Bjorn Borg, who I thought I saw in the spaghetti.

In the second place, if Jesus decided to come back for a little visit, I just can't see God dispatching him to appear on a picture of spaghetti located outside Atlanta, Georgia. Can you?

GOD: "Son, I have a little assignment for you."

JESUS: "What's that, Dad?"

GOD: "I want you to go down just outside Atlanta, Georgia, and hide in a picture on some spaghetti on a billboard."

JESUS: "Is this the Big One? Am I supposed to judge the quick and the dead?"

GOD: "No, that's later, son. Just go down and hide in the spaghetti and see if anybody notices you."

The thing about visions is that they can be misinterpreted. My grandfather used to tell of an old farmer from his boyhood days.

One morning in church the farmer got up and said, "I've been called to preach, and I'd like to deliver the sermon this morning."

That's serious stuff, being called to preach. So the pastor invited the farmer up to the pulpit to give the message.

My grandfather recalled the farmer was the worst preacher he'd ever heard. After the service somebody went up to the farmer and asked, "How'd you get the call?"

"I walked outside the other morning and there were words written in the sky that said, 'Go preach the gospel,'" he answered.

"I saw the same thing," said the man, "but you didn't read it right. It said, 'Go plow your corn.'"

Another thing about visions and the like is if you really want to see one, you can. I was staying at a beachfront condo once and a buddy and I played a trick on another friend one evening.

He said to me, "Do you see that red light way out in the distance? Wonder if it's a boat?" There was no red light, but I went along with the story.

"I've never seen anything quite that bright a red in the ocean at night. I'm not sure what it is." Our friend said, "What are you looking at?" We answered, "That bright, red light off in the distance."

"I don't see any light," said our buddy. "I see it," I said to my co-conspirator. "So do I," he answered.

After staring out to sea for a few moments our buddy finally said, "OK, now I see it. That bright, red light. Probably a fishing boat or the Coast Guard."

The same thing has happened with the spaghetti billboard, I am certain. Harold saw Jesus in the spaghetti and was able to convince his wife, Loreena, she saw the same thing. The fact that Harold earlier had stopped off for a six-pack may have helped him see it, too.

There was a great letter to the editor in the papers about all this. I paraphrase it: "Jesus might be a lot of places," said the writer, "but he's not in spaghetti." Verily.

It Pays to Listen to Voice from Above

The *Herald-Journal* of Greene County, an hour-and-a-half drive out Interstate 20 from Atlanta, recently carried what I consider to be one of the all-time news stories. Maybe THE all-time news story.

Keep in mind, the *Herald-Journal* is no *National Enquirer*. It doesn't carry stories about Hitler being alive and well on Neptune or stories about a woman giving birth to a duck, although the story I referred to earlier, to me, is even a bigger eye-popper.

I'll give the article's headline first: "The Lord Speaks to Pep Stone Warning Him Not to Go to Hay Field Where Over $30,000 in Machinery Was Stolen in the Early Morning."

Long headline, I realize, but the reader got all the facts in a hurry.

Local citizen Pep Stone, the article stated, has been in the hay business in Greene County since 1948.

He awakened one recent morning at two o'clock. It was raining. Pep Stone had a hayfield he hadn't covered the day before.

He decided he'd better go to the field and cover it. The article quoted Pep: "I was still in bed, fixing to put on my overalls, when a voice came to me and said, 'Don't go, you will get hurt.'" Pep went back to bed. When he awakened again, he and a friend drove to the hayfield 10 miles away.

At the gate they found the lock had been shot away.

415

"My eyes got big and my heart skipped fast when I realized that someone had stolen my tractor and hay baler. I had paid $30,000 for this equipment," Pep was quoted further.

Tough break, but Pep put it all in perspective.

"I am living today," he said, "because of my religious belief. It was a voice that spoke loud and clear. I honestly believe if I had gone down to the hayfield, I would have been killed. I can buy some more equipment," he went on, "but I can't replace my life."

A friend who knows Pep well told me, "Pep's in church every time the door opens. If he says the Lord spoke to him, I'm not going to doubt it one bit."

Obviously the *Herald-Journal* didn't, either. Refer to the headline and realize it didn't say, "Pep Stone says the Lord Spoke to Him. . . ."

It said, "The Lord Speaks to Pep Stone. . . ."

There is a huge difference.

Most newspapers would have used the first headline, casting some degree of doubt of the Lord's personal warning. Did the Lord actually speak to Pep or did Pep just say the Lord did? Not the *Herald-Journal*. It took Pep's word and told us in something close to 36-point type that the Lord did indeed get in touch with a Greene County man and save the man from harm's way, and that's what I call a major league news story.

Do you realize the news of the Lord speaking to a mortal is bigger than news that Hitler is alive and well, a woman has given birth to a duck or that Elvis is running a car wash on the outskirts of Little Rock? Of course it is. It says to atheists they'd better make an immediate turnaround. It says maybe

Jimmy Swaggart wasn't just making all that stuff up about his conversation with the Lord.

It says a marquee in front of a local church I rode past was absolutely correct: "Draw nigh with God and God will draw nigh with you." It also says there's a small town out there with a newspaper that has cast away the cynical nature of most other newspapers so that if a God-fearing local citizen says the Lord spoke to him, who is the local newspaper to cast any doubt as to the veracity of his words? Most other newspapers could use a little of that, too. Verily, verily, double-verily.

Old-Time Religion Is Good
Enough for Me

I'm looking for the Rev. Floyd Tenney. He's the pastor of a Methodist church somewhere in the Atlanta
area. Somebody told me that recently, but they
didn't have a name or address of the church.

I knew Floyd Tenney when I was a boy. He was a
young preacher at my home church, Moreland
Methodist. He was the first preacher with whom I
really identified. He wasn't a somber old man in a
blue suit, preaching out of Revelation, scaring me
about the moon turning to blood and the seas boiling over.

The Rev. Tenney kept it simple, kept it where a
young boy could get some idea of what the Methodist
gospel was all about, kept it where you didn't doze
off. I recall he always asked us to stand when he
read from the Bible. I'd never known a preacher to
ask that before.

Floyd Tenney married me for the first time in 1966
at the Moreland Methodist Church. She and I had
loved each other since the sixth grade, and it was
supposed to be forever.

When it turned out to be for four years, I tried to
find the Rev. Tenney to help me figure out a way to
get her back. But he was no longer at Moreland
Methodist Church. I found out he'd gone into the
used-car business. My barber died the same week I
got the news about the Rev. Tenney.

My preacher goes into used cars and my barber
dies in the same week. I was a lost soul. But youth
gets over setbacks as it gets over almost any malady.

I found myself, moved on, and except for the mention that the Rev. Tenney was back in the pulpit somewhere, he hadn't crossed my mind in years until I attended a fancy, big-city Methodist service Sunday.

The people were nice. The minister gave a thought-provoking sermon on repentance. But they spent at least ten minutes lighting candles. The choir was in fancy robes and sang something that could have been opera. And there were all sorts of associate ministers involved, and I never heard any of the four or five hymns we used to sing.

We were asked to sing the first and third verses of some ponderous Christmas hymn with which I was not familiar. And across from it in the hymn book was "Away in a Manger." I still know all the words to "Away in a Manger," but we didn't sing that.

Concerned about this, I turned to the hymnal's index. I did find "The Old Rugged Cross" but "Precious Memories" wasn't in there.

Yes, give me that old-time religion. Give it to me as I had it when I was a boy.

The choir in Moreland Methodist occasionally was off-key, and it didn't have any fancy robes, but when they rendered "What a Friend We Have in Jesus," it was a thing of beauty and a joy forever.

When they asked Fox Covin or Western Tidwell or Clyde Elrod to pray, there were no fancy words, no quoting of big-name theologians. It just came from the heart and said, "Lord, help us to do what's right."

I've just got the feeling Floyd Tenney's church, wherever it might be in this city, is still like that.

Floyd, I want to come hear you again. I want to sing the old songs.

"Would that you stand as we read God's word," you used to say.

I'll stand again as I did when I was 14, next to my mother as you read the Scriptures.

I want to sing "Precious Memories" and "When the Roll is Called Up Yonder" from that old brown Cokesbury hymnal.

It took a visit to a big-city church to make me remember how good it used to feel on the square at Moreland Methodist, where I married the first time, where I said goodbye to my mother and where they will say goodbye to me one day.

POSSUMS, COONS, GNATS AND TICKS—A SOUTHERN BESTIARY

And Other Creatures, Great and Small

THE FOURTH ANNUAL Gnat Days are under way in the hamlet of Camilla located about as far south as you can go in Georgia and still not be in the bordering state of Florida, where the Northern tourist ("That's not the way we did it back in Buffalo") is the leading pest.

Camilla is inhabited by 5,400 citizens and about 8 zillion gnats, known locally as the town birds. The loose sandy soil down there is given as the reason for the abundance of the creatures.

Gnats don't bite but they get in your eyes and your ears and in your mouth if you open it to say more than three words.

Gnats also get all over your food if you try to eat out of doors. I once played in a tennis tournament known as the "Thrilla in Camilla," back before my right arm fell off and I had to give up tennis.

After my match, I was hungry. Somebody was grilling hamburgers. I got one.

Before I could take a bite, a Camillian asked me, "Why is your forehand so atrocious?" I answered, "Who wants to know, Gnatface?" which is more than three words. Seventeen hundred or so gnats flew into my mouth, and when I looked down at my hamburger, it was alive with the little black boogers.

"Go ahead and eat it," said another Camillian. "Gnatburgers are a local delicacy."

I spit out the 1,700 or so gnats already in my mouth and gave my gnatburger to a dog who carried it off somewhere either to eat it, bury it, or have it sprayed by Orkin.

Gnat Days in Camilla is an effort to do something positive about a negative situation.

Gnat Days also include the Gnat 5K Run, an art show, and a cruise down the Flint River with the Gnat Patrol. You can buy a T-shirt with the picture of a gnat on it for $11.

What Gnat Days doesn't include is an answer to the annoying gnat question of all times: Why does "gnat" start with a "g"? I know why "gnawing" starts with a "g." If it didn't, people would get "gnawing" confused with "nawing," which is Southern for spending a leisurely afternoon saying "naw," the Southern pronunciation of the word "no."

But "nat" couldn't be confused with anything else. The Southern version of the word "evening" is pronounced "e'nin," as in, "Good e'nin, ladies."

So why did "nat" come out "g-nat"? I went to the history books to find out.

Spanish explorer Bubba DeJesus discovered South Georgia in the 1500s. While near the very spot where Camilla now stands, he became the first visitor from the Old World to encounter the gnat.

He opened his mouth to say, "Jesus! Lookito, los negros bugisimos," Spanish for "Help! I'm being attacked by 'nats,'" the Spanish word for "little bitty black bugs."

Seventeen hundred or so flew into his mouth and another covey got into his eyes. When he tried to write of his experiences in his journal, he was choking on the nats in his mouth and he couldn't see for the nats in his eyes, so he mistakenly put a "g" in front of "nats."

Unfortunately, Bubba DeJesus was run over and killed by an elderly Northern tourist driving a Cadillac soon after subsequently discovering PepsiCola, Florida, which he also misspelled in his journal as Pensacola.

He was not around, therefore, to explain why he had put the "g" in front of "nat," and the spelling stuck.

I wish Camilla great success with Gnat Days. Will I attend? Naw. Too many nats.

The Life You Save May Be a Possum's

You walk around in San Francisco and on every corner of every street, it seems, there is somebody with a hand out asking for money to save something.

They're big on saving the rain forests out here.

"Give to save the rain forest," a guy, who looked a little like the spotted owl somebody else is trying to save, asked.

"I gave at the last corner," I said.

"I don't give a hoot," he replied, "You should give at my corner, too. If we don't save the rain forest, there won't be any more oxygen to breathe."

"Well," I said, walking away by that time, "the hole in the ozone layer will have gotten a lot bigger and we'll all be french-fried anyway."

So I saved a little on that corner, but I got hit on the next one from somebody trying to save the whales.

They're trying to save the rain forests, the spotted owl, the whales, the manatees in Florida, and whatever happened to the snail darter? After experiencing this all day, I began to wonder if I were active enough in this area and was there anything I should get behind and try to save.

Just like that, it came to me: I think I ought to get busy and try to save the possum.

What, you might be asking, do I want to save the possum from? From getting run over by some sort of motorized vehicle every time one tries to cross the road, that's what.

I don't have any research statistics to back this up, but I will be willing to bet at least eight out of every ten possums that try to get from one side of the road to the other get smushed by a car, a Greyhound bus, or a pulpwood truck.

I'm not certain how many dead possums I have seen lying smushed in the road in my lifetime's travels around the South, but I'm certain I've seen more possums than dogs or chickens, legendary road-crossers themselves.

When I was a child, in order to keep me quiet in the car, my family would count dead dogs and dead possums on the road. My grandfather would take dead dogs and I would take dead possums and every time we arrived at our destination I had always counted more dead possums than my grandfather had counted dead dogs.

Chickens and dogs, of course, cross the road to get to the other side. Why possums cross the road remains a mystery. Perhaps they are looking for other possums; I'm not Marlin Perkins here.

Whatever, it is up to us to try to save as many possums crossing the road as possible. Some may be saying, "Isn't it supposed to be 'O' - possum?" That is correct, and the way possums got that 'O' in front of their names is from crossing the road and seeing headlights and thinking, " 'O' hell, I'm a goner now."

How to save the possum: Put up signs on roads that read, "Watch out for crossing possums."

Increase possum awareness so that motorists will be more sensitive and brake when they see one crossing the road.

In places where there is a high concentration of

possums trying to cross the road, possum patrol persons would stop traffic in order to allow the possum to cross in safety.

Save the possum. The 'O' stands for " 'O'nly You Can Stop the Road Killings."

And watch for me with my hand out at a street corner near you.

Eternally Grateful for Pigs' Sacrifice

I read an article not long ago about police in St. Petersburg, Florida, using a pig to sniff out drugs and other contraband.

The pig did terrifically, the article said, but that didn't save the pig's job. It was dismissed from duty because it emitted an odor unpleasant to some at the station house. I ask you a question: Didn't they know ahead of time that pigs just naturally come with a pungent aroma? I've been around a few pigs in my day and, although I also found their smell less than pleasing, I understood and accepted the fact that pigs aren't supposed to smell like petunias.

Pigs rarely get a break. When one person wants to insult another, that person often mentions the pig in a disparaging way. There are many examples: "Clean up your room, Ramona. It looks like a pig sty in here."

"Harold you're disgusting. You've gotten fat as a pig."

"Who was the sweathog I saw you with last night at the Moose Club?"

I recall telling a friend that my wife had given me my first pair of Gucci shoes. "What?" he asked. "That's like putting earrings on a hog."

Well, let me say this: Since March of 1982 I've been part pig. That's when I received my first porcine aortic valve. In 1985 I got my second pig valve. That's 11 years and two pigs, both of whom gave the supreme sacrifice to help me stay alive, and I want to take this opportunity to salute them and all pigs.

Pigs are smarter than most people might think.

My grandfather had three pigs named Hilda, Margaret and Big Boy. All three of them knew their names and would run to my grandfather whenever he called them.

My grandfather grew so close to his three pigs that when hog-killing time came, he didn't want to part with any of his pigs.

My grandmother said, "How can a grown man become attached to three hogs?" A compromise was made and only Hilda wound up in the freezer locker. She was older than both Margaret and Big Boy. My grandfather figured she had had about all the enjoyment a hog could have and wanted Margaret and Big Boy to get that chance, too.

My mother said when she was growing up there was a boy in her class who rode a pig to school every day.

"That pig stood out in the schoolyard and waited for him all day," she explained. "And when school was over, the boy would come out and ride his pig home again."

"One day," mother went on, "the boy showed up at school and his pig had a wooden leg."

Somebody asked, "Why has your pig got a wooden leg?"

The boy replied, "You don't eat a pig like this all at once."

(I realize there are those who know this is a stolen punch line from another pig story, but don't spoil everybody else's fun.) For my upcoming heart surgery I'm getting a new valve. This time it will be of a mechanical sort. It's too complicated to explain why I'm not getting another pig valve; just know I'm frankly happy no other pigs will have to give up their hearts to save mine.

I want to say it's been an honor and a privilege to be part pig these last 11 years, and my eyes will always tear when I pass a barbecue joint.

I also want to thank my Nashville friend and songwriter Dick Feller for writing and dedicating a pig song to me. It's titled "Pig Polo." I think I sniff a hit.

MAN'S BEST FRIEND—NO IFS, ANDS, OR BUTS

What Evil Lurks? Catfish Knows

IT WAS A night of terror I shall not soon forget.

I was sitting on my living room sofa around half past eleven eating a bowl of ice cream and searching for a movie on the cable.

My dog, Catfish, the black Lab, was lying at my feet. Suddenly he arose and broke into a series of yelps.

Catfish's yelps are capable of awakening the dead.

"Timmy's not in the well again, is he, boy?" I asked.

By this time Catfish had bolted to the back door. He was clawing at it in a fever I'd never seen before in this normally placid animal.

My God, what was out there? Had Charles Manson escaped? Was it a group of liberal Democrats

431

coming to set fire to my house? The dog was bonkers.

I certainly wasn't going to go out in the darkness of my back yard to see what lurked there and had Catfish in a frenzy.

I opened the back door and Catfish made the fastest move I'd ever seen him make.

The only other time I'd seen him leap with anywhere near the same resolve was at a pork chop that fell off my plate during a barbecuing exercise one evening.

It began a heartbeat later.

Catfish bellowed even louder. My first thought was if it's Charles Manson, he had it coming. My second thought was, if it's liberal Democrats, I've got my own personal pit bull here and didn't need Pat Buchanan.

My third thought was, Catfish has now awakened the entire neighborhood, but what could I do? Next, there came out of the dark pit that was my back yard a blood-curdling shriek. "WAAAAAACK!" cried whatever Catfish had or had him. There were more yelps and more waaaacks, not to mention hissing sounds.

It wasn't Charles Manson or liberal Democrats.

It was a lion that had escaped from the circus.

Either that or some alien thing with big claws and eyes.

Later I would recall the Jerry Clower story where a fellow climbed up a tree and met some sort of alien thing with big eyes and claws during a hunting trip.

"Shoot this thang!" the fellow cried to his friends.

"We're afraid we might shoot you," somebody said from the ground.

"Well," replied the man in the tree, "just shoot up

here amongst us, 'cause one of us has got to have some relief."

I was frightened.

I have no children. Catfish is my child, my boy, my most loyal friend.

Then a silence fell over my back-yard battlefield.

A few moments later, Catfish came loping up the steps and ran back inside. I could see blood on his mouth, but I didn't know if it was his or that of whatever it was with which he had tangled.

The next morning, I went to my back yard expecting God knows what.

I found a dead raccoon—a large dead raccoon.

It apparently had been trying to eat out of Catfish's food plate on the back porch when it was pounced upon by the rightful owner of the food plate.

So I'm looking for a dead-raccoon-in-the-yard removal service, and I apologize to any of my neighbors who might have been disturbed.

Stephen King probably could write an entire novel based on such an experience. As for me, I'll just end it here and hope for a good night's sleep after the Night of the Killer Lab.

An Exchange of Brief Remarks

There was a letter concerning me on the editorial page of the Atlanta *Constitution* recently. It didn't take me long to figure out that the letter writer wasn't digging the viewpoints I often express.

She called me a redneck, a backward Southerner, a racist, a homophobe, a sexist, and I got the idea she didn't like it when I occasionally point out "yankees" (her quote marks, not mine) aren't always correct, especially when they tell us how they used to do it back in Buffalo.

I can take all that, but what got to me about this letter was the part where she said I was the "equivalent of dirty underwear dragged out to the living room by the family dog in front of company."

This is my fifteenth year writing a column and never before has anybody ever compared me to dirty underwear, the kind the dog drags out in front of company or otherwise.

And, just for the record, my dog Catfish, the black Lab, has never dragged out any dirty underwear in front of company in my house.

He has dragged out shoes, the scraps of last night's dinner from the garbage, and once he came into the living room—where I was listening to two women who wanted to talk to me about becoming a Jehovah's Witness—with an empty beer can in his mouth.

"Dog's got a serious drinking problem," I said to the two women.

"And about half drunk, he tends to get mean. Last

434

week he got hammered and bit two guys trying to convince me to become a Mormon."

The two women were out the door a heartbeat later. Catfish just can't stand door-to-door religious soliciting. He also growls whenever he sees evangelists on television.

The reason it bothers me to be compared to dirty underwear is because my mother's greatest fear in life was that I would be in some sort of accident and I would be wearing dirty underwear and the doctors in the emergency room would see it.

"What kind of mother would they think I am if you were in a wreck and were wearing dirty underwear?" she often asked.

She never mentioned a word about my getting multiple head injuries or a broken neck in a wreck. As long as my underwear was clean, I suppose she figured I eventually would heal, and she would be off the hook as a lousy mother.

But as a result of that upbringing I would like to point out a couple of things here:

1. I never wear dirty underwear. If I get out of the shower and find I have no clean underwear, I get in my car, go to the store and buy a new pair. Rather than put on a pair of dirty underwear to go to the store, I don't wear any at all, and I drive very carefully. I don't want those emergency room doctors to think I'm some sort of sicko-kinko.

2. I don't put my dirty underwear where my dog can get to it and drag it into the living room in front of company. I throw it in the closet and close the door, and even if I left it in a pile on the floor, Catfish is a class act who has a lot more things to do than

drag out a pair of dirty underwear in front of company.

Like keeping me safe from religious fanatics and transplanted Yankees who occasionally knock on my door and ask if I know where they can get a good bargain on a grits tree.

Catfish the Lab Has Up and Died

My dog Catfish, the black Lab, died Thanksgiving night.

The vet said his heart gave out.

Down in the country, they would have said, "Lewis's dog up and died."

He would have been 12 had he lived until January.

Catfish had a good life. He slept indoors. Mostly he ate what I ate. We shared our last meal Tuesday evening in our living room in front of the television.

We had a Wendy's double cheeseburger and some chili.

Catfish was a gift from my friends Barbara and Vince Dooley. Vince, of course, is the athletic director at the University of Georgia. Barbara is a noted speaker and author.

I named him driving back to Atlanta from Athens where I had picked him up at the Dooleys' home. I don't know why I named him what I named him. He was all curled up in a blanket on my back seat. And I looked at him and it just came out. I called him, "Catfish."

I swear he raised up from the blanket and acknowledged. Then he severely fouled the blanket and my back seat.

He was a most destructive animal the first three years of his life. He chewed things. He chewed books. He chewed shoes.

"When I said to Catfish, 'Heel,'" I used to offer from behind the dais, "he went to my closet and chewed up my best pair of Guccis."

437

Catfish chewed television remote control devices. Batteries and all. He chewed my glasses. Five pairs of them.

One day, when he was still a puppy, he got out of the house without my knowledge. The doorbell rang. It was a young man who said, "I hit your dog with my car, but I think he's OK."

He was. He had a small cut on his head and he was frightened, but he was otherwise unhurt.

"I came around the corner," the young man explained, "and he was in the road chewing on something. I hit my brakes the second I saw him."

"Could you tell what he was chewing on?" I asked.

"I know this sounds crazy," the young man answered, "but I think it was a beer bottle."

Catfish stopped chewing while I still had a house. Barely.

He was a celebrity, Catfish. I spoke recently in Michigan. Afterward a lady came up to me and said, "I was real disappointed with your speech. You didn't mention Catfish."

Catfish used to get his own mail. Just the other day the manufacturer of a new brand of dog food called "Country Gold," with none other than George Jones's picture on the package, sent Catfish a sample of its new product. For the record, he still preferred cheeseburgers and chili.

Catfish was once grand marshall of the Scottsboro, Alabama, "Annual Catfish Festival." He was on television and got to ride in the front seat of a police car with its siren on.

Oh, that face and those eyes. What he could do to me with that face and those eyes. He would perch himself next to me on the sofa in the living room and look at me.

And love and loyalty would pour out with that look, and as long as I had that, there was very little the human race could do to harm my self-esteem.

Good dogs don't love bad people.

He was smart. He was fun. And he loved to ride in cars. There were times he was all that I had.

And now he has up and died. My own heart, or what is left of it, is breaking.

COLLEGE FOOTBALL—THE OTHER SOUTHERN RELIGION

Georgia on My Mind

THERE ARE THOSE who would like to see all this come to an end. All this is 90,000 people showing up to see a football game between the University of Georgia and some other less prestigious institution of higher education on a beautiful fall Saturday afternoon.

Those who believe as I do will come in droves of red, down from the hills of Habersham, the valleys of Hall and up from the marshes of Glynn. They will be with friends and family. They will renew old acquaintances and return to the campus from which they sprang into real life.

But there are the naysayers. They see all this as detrimental to the lofty purpose of education. They are the pointy-heads, the nabobs, the ones who look

441

Lewis Grizzard

at such an exercise as Neanderthal. They see only a game involving brawn and controlled violence. They don't see the real meaning, human beings living and loving a tradition that, in Georgia's case, is 100 years old.

So, I will tell them what my day will be like Saturday, and if they can still find something wrong with it, then they are hopeless.

I've been staying with the same friends on Athens football weekends long enough to know I'm always welcome in their home. After a slow morning of anticipation, we'll be in our parking place near the stadium at least a couple of hours before kickoff. Friends will come by. Football season is the only time we see some of them. It is what we have in common. It is what brings us together. We'll drink a beer and munch a bunch of wonderful chicken fingers.

I'll look at the bridge behind the stadium that separates the Old Campus from the New Campus. I walked a thousand miles crossing that bridge, starting in 1964. I was better on the Old Campus, incidentally. That's where they taught English and history and journalism. I could deal with those.

The New Campus, however, is where they tried to teach me botany. I made one C in college. It was in botany. I figured God was why trees grow, so I didn't take botany very seriously. When I think of all that, I'll be 21 again for a few precious moments. I'll still be basically innocent, and I'll still be married to a pretty blonde I fell in love with in grade school.

The arthritis in my right hand, the slightly balding spot on the back of my head and my schedule for the next week will jar me back to reality and the present. Then the game. We will bask in the glory of a Georgia

442

touchdown. We will sink into our seats at any opponent's advantage.

It will be five hours of love and caring and dedication, and we will do it from September until November, and anybody who doesn't like it can go sit in the library and read about the Punic Wars. Just let me have this time. It is the best time that I live.

Lewis Grizzard

Another Kind of Hunting Season

It was all over the Sunday paper about the recruiting of young athletes to play football at large universities in the region. It's that season. Children are snatched away from their mothers' arms back home in Twobit County, and the next thing you know, the Head Coach is saying, "Ol' Dram Bowie from down in Twobit County is the finest prospect I've ever seen."

Recruiting is important. "You gotta have the horses," a coach once told me, "before you can pull the wagon." Coaches talk like that. Translated, it means if he doesn't get off his tail and sign some talent, he'll be selling tires at Kmart the next time toe meets leather.

What I hear is that Tennessee is making a big move into Georgia in search of recruits to rebuild the once-mighty Volunteers program. You don't sign to go to Knoxville. You are sentenced there. Clemson is also usually heavy into seeking Georgia material. A Clemson raid makes Georgia Tech people especially mad.

"You know that tractorcade this weekend?" one asked me.

"They weren't farmers," he said. "They were Clemson fans on their way to Sears to buy clothes for the Gator Bowl."

From various sources around the Southeast, I have come into possession of the list of the most-wanted high school athletes in the state. None has signed yet. They are known as "blue-chippers" to the alumni. Coaches call them "job-savers." Here's the list.

444

ARDELL GROVER—Linebacker from Atlanta. Missed half his senior season with terminal acne. "He'll hit you," say the recruiters. Especially if you call him "Zit Head," which a tenthgrader did shortly before Ardell rendered him unconscious during fifth-period study hall.

MARVIN PALAFOX—Marvin is a tight end. He's from Macon. Wears No. 82. Scored same number on his college boards. "Great hands," say the coaches. So do the cheerleaders.

SCOOTER T. WASHINGTON—Halfback from Savannah. Olympic speed. Expensive tastes. Wants two Cadillacs and a mink coat like Reggie Jackson's to sign. Answers the telephone, "You need the loot to get the Scoot." Contact through his agent, Sam the Fly, at the Wise Owl Pool and Recreation Hall, Savannah.

BILLY BOB WALTON—Offensive tackle from Moultrie. Extremely offensive. Friends call him "Dump Truck" because that's how big he is, and he could eat all the pork chops and mashed potatoes out of the back of one. Made *Tifton Gazette* All-Area team. Makes Junior Samples look like David Niven. Loves buttermilk but can't spell it.

LAVONNE "The Rolling Stone" LARUE—Led Columbus high school in interceptions. Also led burglary ring to back entrance of Harry's One-Stop Stereo Shop. Got one to five, but sentence suspended when entire student body turned out as character witnesses after suggestion they do so by several of The Stone's "acquaintances." "Can start for any college team in the country," says his coach, who didn't start him once and still carries the scars.

IRVING BOATRIGHT III—Quarterback for a fashionable northside Atlanta private school. Father prominent Atlanta attorney with homes on Hilton Head and Sea Island. Can't play a lick, but the head coach gets free legal advice and either house three weeks each summer. Started every game during high school career. Bed-wetter.

BARTHANATOMAY RIMJOB—Place-kicker. Son of Pakistani professor of Eastern philosophy at Clayton Junior College. Kicks soccer style. Made 110 straight extra points during prep career. Does not speak English and goes through 15-minute ancient ritual before every kick. Weighs 90 pounds soaking wet. Once scored winning touchdown on fake field goal by hiding ball in his turban.

ALBERT WARTZ JR.—From South Georgia. 6'4", 250. Plays quarterback. Questionable student. Thinks Henry Cabot Lodge is a motel in Bainbridge. Filled out recruiting questionnaire. By "sex," wrote: "Not since Mavis Wilson moved out of Hahira." "This kid," says his high school coach, "doesn't know the meaning of 'quit.'" Doesn't know the meaning of third-grade arithmetic either. Leaning toward Alabama.

A Bear of a Man

I spent the afternoon drinking with Paul Bryant once.

I had been to Athens with him for an autographing session for the book he did with John Underwood of *Sports Illustrated.*

We returned to the old Atlanta Airport. There were still a couple of hours before his plane back home to Tuscaloosa.

"Let's get a drink," he said.

The weather was awful. Rain. High winds. Lightning and thunder. Bad flying weather. Good drinking weather.

He took me into the Eastern Ionosphere Lounge.

He ordered Double Black Jack and Coke. He ordered two at a time. I drank beer.

I probably got the best interview of my life. But I don't remember any of it. You can drink a lot of double Black Jack and Coke and beer in two hours.

I do remember leaving the lounge and walking to the Southern gate where his flight awaited, however.

At the gate, the Bear ran into a doctor from Tuscaloosa who was also booked on the flight. The doctor was also a part-time pilot.

"Coach," said the doctor. "I don't like this weather."

"You a drinking man, son?" Bryant asked him.

"Yes, sir," said the doctor.

"Well, let's go get a couple of motel rooms and have a drink and fly home tomorrow."

There were 50 or so other would-be passengers awaiting the same flight to Tuscaloosa. When they noticed Bryant turning in his ticket, all but a handful did the same.

"If Bear Bryant's afraid to fly in this weather," a man said, "I ain't about to."

When the word came that Paul "Bear" Bryant, had died, I immediately thought of a friend of mine. She first met Bear Bryant several years ago. At first their relationship was purely professional. But it grew past that. I'm not talking about hanky-panky here, however. Grandfather-granddaughter comes the closest to describing how they felt about each other.

They were an unlikely pair. He the gruff, growling, old coot of a football coach. She a bright, young, attractive woman with both a husband and a career and with a degree from the University of Texas, of all places.

He would call her even in the middle of football season, and they would talk, and he would do her any favor. Once, a friend of hers, a newspaper columnist, was having heart surgery.

She called the Bear and had him send the columnist a scowling picture with the autograph, "I hope you get well soon—Bear Bryant."

The picture still hangs in the columnist's home.

I called her the minute I heard the news. I didn't want her to get it on the radio.

She cried.

"I loved him," she said. "And he loved my baby."

My friend had a baby a few years back. Had it been a boy she would have named him for the Bear. David Bryant. But it was a girl, and she was called Marissa.

"I had no problems with naming my son 'David

448

Bryant,' but I wasn't about to name a little girl 'Beara,' " said my friend.

Of course, a busy big-time college football coach like Bear Bryant didn't give it a second thought that somebody else's little girl wasn't named for him.

He still sent her gifts. Gifts like a child's Alabama cheerleader uniform, and then an adult-size uniform for use later. He sent her footballs, dolls and probably a dozen or so letters that her mama read to her.

It's funny, though. When he sent his packages and letters, he always addressed them not to Marissa, but "To Paula."

Jealous Losers Name Them "Bubba Games"

So it has begun. Writers in other parts of the country have targeted Atlanta as Spartanburg with skyscrapers and are referring to the 1996 Olympics here as the Bubba Games. The ignorant dolts.

All this reminds me of the time in Chicago I met a young woman sitting on a bar stool next to mine. "Where are you all from?" she honked, mockingly, after I spoke.

"Atlanta," I said.

"I've always wondered," she went on, "if there were any nice restaurants out there?" Realizing at this point I was speaking to a Midwestern bimbo who had never been past Gary, Indiana, and realizing that if she were the last woman on earth, I'd rather change the spark plugs on my pickup than involve myself with her in any way, I corrected her on a few things.

"First of all, Thunderthighs," I began, "in the South we never use "you all" in the singular sense. When referring to one as you did with your snippy little remark about my origins, you should have used a simple 'you.' When we refer to more than one person, we don't say 'you all' either. We say 'y'all.' Is that clear, Snowbrain?" She seemed startled. She had stopped chewing her gum.

"As to your question about there being any nice restaurants 'out there' in Atlanta, it is apparent you know as much about geography as you know about fashion. Nice sweatshirt. New York is 'over there,' Milwaukee 'up there,' Los Angeles 'out there.' Atlanta is 'down there.' As far as nice restaurants are concerned, you'd be amazed how many there are in Atlanta.

"It is a cosmopolitan, modern city, with paved roads and indoor plumbing, and we don't have to put up with gray snow and Arctic temperatures six months out of the year. Now, if you'll excuse me," I ended, "I'm going back to my apartment and call somebody in Atlanta so I can say I've had at least one intelligent conversation today."

Atlanta has a world-class airport, and world-class hotels and restaurants, and it will offer the 1996 Olympians world-class facilities. What it won't offer is an opportunity for journalists around the country to travel 5,000 miles on expense accounts to some foreign site where they can impress their friends and colleagues with a dateline from somewhere their friends and colleagues have never been.

Instead of flying to someplace that sounds great until you get there and find it crowded, overpriced and rude, they'll be flying on expense accounts to Atlanta, a model city for race relations, a vibrant city that can flat get it done when it has to and a friendly city that very few visitors leave without some measure of regret that their time here is over.

Someone said Barcelona has cathedrals and Atlanta has strip joints.

How many sports writers have ever been to a cathedral? Whoever it was who wrote that a dried cow pie might be used in Atlanta as a discus is full of the undried version. Will the heathens ever learn the

451

worn out Bubba stereotype is not applicable to Atlanta and to much of the rest of the South? Probably not.

Boldly Standing Tall

I got hooked on baseball standings about the same time I learned to tie my shoes. I would have been about 8. It's embarrassing to admit I didn't learn to tie my shoes until I was 8, but manual dexterity has never been my long suit and as soon as I got out on my own, I never bought another pair of lace-up shoes.

I'm a loafer man, and what this has to do with baseball standings I don't know, but the Braves just beat the Dodgers 10-3 and today is another great standings morning.

When I was 8, I was a great fan of the Atlanta Crackers, this city's entry into the AA Southern Association. When my aunt and uncle came home from the Moreland Knitting Mill for lunch during baseball season, they would bring along the morning paper and I would take it into my hands as something precious—like a puppy or a pork chop. I would turn immediately to the sports page and the baseball standings.

We couldn't get the Cracker radio broadcast in Moreland, 40 miles from Atlanta, so this is how I got my baseball news. There were no superstations, no all-sports cable networks. I miss those days when the tension would build in me all morning, and the newspaper, not a talking head, would give me the good or bad news about my beloved Crackers.

I got away from staring at baseball standings in the late 1960s. The Crackers had ridden the last train out and had been replaced by the Milwaukee Braves. The Braves landed in Atlanta as a mediocre

453

team and just got worse. Who wants to look at the standings when your team is at rock bottom? When the Crackers were here, the newspaper would put ATLANTA in bold type in the standings. When the Braves came, the practice continued. That is, until I became executive sports editor of the Atlanta *Journal* in the 1970s.

Who wanted to draw even more attention to the fact that the city's baseball team was in the deep cellar? I nixed the bold ATLANTA. But that was then and this is now, and I've gone back to staring at the standings. How neat they are. How mathematically precise. What a story they have to tell.

The baseball season has been going on for almost five months, and everything that has happened is reflected to the last decimal point in the standings. Sunday morning, Atlanta was still on top of the National League West, and I looked at the name and the corresponding numbers next to it.

It was like looking upon a great painting, a beautiful woman or where an ocean meets a mountain range. The standings said Atlanta was 3 $1/2$ up on Cincinnati, with the best winning percentage in Major League Baseball. I slipped on my loafers and walked on air the rest of the day.

THE HEART, THE SOUL AND COUNTRY GOLD

Pardon Me, Are You in the Mood?

I GOT OLD the other day. I ordered a Glenn Miller tape off television. That's a sure sign the aging process has settled in for good. First of all, if you're not old, why are you still up at the hour they advertise musical tapes from the '40s while you're watching a black and white movie with Stewart Granger or a young Richard Widmark? It's either because you're not sleeping like you used to, or you can't run with the big dogs anymore out there in the neon arena.

And instead of listening to current musical offerings, you've gone and ordered a tape from your parents' generation because it's nostalgic, because you can understand the words when somebody sings, because Glenn Miller music never suggested killing anybody or anything, and because it reminds you of a time you actually knew what was going on in the world.

I wasn't born when Glenn Miller died, but I listened to his music as a child on the radio and I saw my late parents jitterbug to "In the Mood" once.

And I've seen "The Glenn Miller Story" about a thousand times on that same late-night television.

Jimmy Stewart was magnificent as Glenn Miller, and aren't all we lost males of divorce, now in the summer of our years, still looking for June Allyson in the Madonna era? So my Glenn Miller tape came in from Time-Life music.

The TV offer wasn't good in Nebraska, or was it New Jersey? I'm not certain why there's usually one state left out when they advertise things you can order on late-night television, but thankfully, they never seem to leave out Georgia.

I had to make a two-hour drive alone, and I decided that would be a perfect time to enjoy my tape for the first time.

There wouldn't be anybody younger than me in the car to ask "What on earth is that?" and to demand that I remove the tape and listen to a rock station, a practice that always makes me nervous and irritable.

I pulled onto the interstate. It was raining. Large trucks roared past me, leaving walls of water upon my windshield, something else that always makes me nervous and irritable.

Then my tape began.

The first selection was the immortal "In the Mood." It made me want to jitterbug like my mother and father, and I relaxed and forgot about the trucks.

Next was "Pennsylvania 6-5000." That was June

Allyson's New York telephone number in "The Glenn Miller Story" and Glenn was so smitten by her he wrote a musical piece about her telephone number.

Love was like that in the '40s. Today, there's too many digits in a phone number to write a love song about one. "Pennsylvania 1-800-485-6234."

The hits kept coming.

"Moonlight Becomes You." What a lovely thought.

"Sunrise Serenade." Soft and sweet.

"Don't Sit Under the Apple Tree." Lovers asking each other to be true until the war is over.

"Chattanooga Choo-Choo." I enjoyed the piece, but I cringed at the political incorrectness of "Pardon me, boy."

All the greats were there, including "Little Brown Jug," which set me to bouncing around in my seat.

A kid with an earring and his hat on backward passed me. He probably thought I was in rhythm with rapper "Booger Nose" and his recent hit, "I'm Gonna Kill Your Dog."

So, I'm old.

There are benefits, including being able to listen to non-violent music, being satisfied with a living room couch instead of a bar stool, and realizing I can make it on four or five hours sleep instead of the eight or nine of my youth.

And the young women will be calling me "mister." But I still believe I'll run into June Allyson one of these days, and she'll invite me to go sit under an apple tree.

Yo, June. I'm in the mood.

Cool as Country Gets?

Las Vegas. This town once belonged to Sinatra. To Sammy Davis Jr. To Dean Martin. To Hollywood.

But look what's happening now: Conway Twitty and George Jones have just left Bally's and Randy Travis has taken their place.

Others who've either just closed or who are just opening are Reba McIntyre, Lorrie Morgan, Doug Kershaw, Charlie Daniels and Dolly Parton.

It's Nashville West. Vegas entertainment is in boots and jeans and out of tuxedos.

The primary reason country plays so well here, and everywhere else, is that it is no longer a stepchild of American music.

Country is now the No. 1 selling music in this country, and it isn't just crossover stars like Garth Brooks who have done it.

Conway Twitty, who can plead to get a lost love back with the best of them, has been here, and George (Possum) Jones, whose voice even sounds like a steel guitar, was with him.

And Randy Travis. He brought back the traditional sound of country music when it was headed Lord-knows-where with too many rock-sounding licks and not enough twin-fiddle intros.

I'm playing a rather minor role in all this. Randy Travis is giving me a half hour to tell jokes at Bally's before he brings them to their feet with "On the Other Hand."

A couple of my boyhood friends, Danny Thompson and Dudley Stamps, were here with me for a couple of days and it was Dudley who surveyed this scene and asked, "What was that song about being country a long time ago?"

" 'I was Country When Country Wasn't Cool,' by Barbara Mandrell," I, quite the country music expert, answered.

"You know something?" Dudley went on, "That's us. We were country when they would laugh at you for listening to it."

We were. I gave up on rock 'n' roll when the Beatles arrived, adopted country and have never looked back.

"Steve Smith had the best country jukebox I've ever heard," Dudley added.

Steve Smith's truck stop in Moreland was our gathering place as boys. You could get a great cheeseburger for a quarter, and I can still hear that jukebox filling the night with Ernest Tubb and Faron Young and Patsy Cline as we sat on the hoods of our cars in Steve's parking lot dreaming our dreams.

"I never thought back then," said Danny, "that three of us would be in Las Vegas one day with all these country acts and you would be on stage telling jokes."

Neither did I. But country music and three ol' boys from Moreland, Georgia, have come a long ways. Keep us humble and grateful.

Conway Left Them Begging for More

My friend Ron Hudspeth, who gave up sports writing to write about how to have a good time, probably has seen more live country music acts than anybody else who doesn't promote them for a living.

He also has met Willie Nelson, has been on Waylon Jennings's bus, and once had a beer in a booth with Tom T. Hall, one of my country music heroes, in Tootsie's Orchid Lounge in Nashville.

For that reason, I always have valued his opinions on country music and he has often said of Conway Twitty, "Nobody can get down there and beg like Ol' Conway."

And country music has a lot of getting down there and begging in it, even the modern variety. Doesn't Billy Ray Cyrus do a great deal of pleading in "Achy Breaky Heart"? Country songs beg for forgiveness, beg for departed lovers to come back, beg for peace of mind.

It's why country touches a lot of us.

"Honey, just forgive me and come on back home so I don't have to toss and turn and stare at this ceiling no more."

A thousand country songs have been written on that one sentence.

But Conway. The very sound of his voice was a cry for relief. It exuded agony. It broke and cracked at just the right time.

Nobody could put forth two simple words—"Hello, darlin' "—and imply more pain than Conway Twitty.

Willie Nelson can get close with, "Well, hello, there," but it's still not Conway running upon his lost love and greeting her as pitifully and as humbly with "Hello, darlin' " before launching into that plea to return that hits the bottom of the belly of anybody who has ever been in that sorrowful place.

We lost Conway over the weekend. He was 59.

I've already mentioned one reason for his success, that ability of his to find our own pain. But there was something else Conway did late in his career that gave him tremendous appeal to female country music fans, especially those we'll say who were over 30. Those whose husbands were on the couch with a beer wondering why the Braves can't hit.

Conway appealed to their sexuality. He went after their sexual frustrations, forged by the Creator's little joke of making the male's sexual peak at 19 and the female's at 35. (I read that somewhere.) Do you think I'm kidding? OK, what about this Conway line: "Even with your hair up in curlers, I'd still love to lay you down." He wasn't talking about sprawling on the living room carpet for a rousing game of Monopoly.

How about, "There's a tiger in these tight fittin' jeans," and, "You can't call him a cowboy until you've seen him ride?"

And didn't Conway record "Slow Hands?" Never was there a more suggestive song on a country label.

I was at a live Conway concert myself once. The over-30 female set flocked to the stage with flowers for Conway. I saw the over-50 set do the same once at a Frank Sinatra gig in New York in the '70s.

Conway had all that permed hair and that Elvis-like stare and snarl, having sprung from the same era, and he made his female fans feel he would, in

461

fact, swim the Mississippi to satisfy their longings. Billy Ray or Garth can't touch that.

Conway Twitty was a sex symbol, perhaps country music's first, and I've got to believe the tears are flowing like—if this were a country song—warm, red wine as the man groans one last time: "Hello, dar-lin.'"

Medallions' Music Is a Gift That Endures

We had the Swingin' Medallions for a pre–Georgia–Florida football game party on lovely Sea Island, Georgia, home of the five-star retreat, The Cloister.

They come to the Georgia coast by the thousands annually for the game, played in nearby Jacksonville.

The Swingin' Medallions. I have asked often what, if anything, endures? Well, the Swingin' Medallions and their kind of music—my generation's music—has.

I first heard them sing and play in the parking lot of a fraternity house at the University of Georgia in 1965. They had the land's No. 1 rock 'n' roll hit at the time, the celebrated, "Double Shot of My Baby's Love."

That was so long ago. I'd never been married and my father was living with me. He had appeared at my apartment one day after one of his long absences, hat in hand.

I gave him a bed. He got a job running a local cafeteria. He paid his part of the rent out of what he would bring home to eat each night from the cafeteria. I never had a better eating year.

We were strolling along the campus together and heard the music. We went to the fraternity parking lot from whence it came and listened for a half an hour.

Daddy said, "Marvelous music. Simply marvelous."

463

My daddy said the same thing about World War II. "Marvelous war. Simply marvelous."

The major thought practically everything was marvelous, simply marvelous, except women who smoked. I'm not sure why he thought more of world wars than women who smoked. I never got to know the man that well.

The Swingin' Medallions at the party were one original and the sons of originals. How nice to see one generation pass down its music to another. That rarely happens.

What clean-cut, personable young men they were. They let the more celebratory join for a few numbers behind their microphones. There is something about a microphone and an amplifying system and a little see-through whiskey to bring out imagined musical talent.

They did "Double Shot" twice. And they played all the other great shagging sounds from the '50s and '60s.

Sure, I'll list a few of them: "Stand By Me." Haunting melody if you listen to it very closely. Will you just hang around, darling, even through the bad times?

"My Girl." The Temptations' finest, in my mind.

"Be Young, Be Foolish, Be Happy." The Tams's greatest hit. I know a lady who wants it sung at her funeral.

"It's funny about this kind of music," one of the younger Medallions was saying. "We play for people your age [high side of 40 and up] and we play a lot of high school proms. The kids like it as much as you do, and they think it's something brand new."

Compared to what rock 'n' roll became in the '70s,

it's tame music, soft music. It is music to which there are actually discernable words.

And, perhaps the best thing about it is, you can actually talk above it.

My generation hasn't given what others have been asked to give. We've been through no depressions or world wars, for instance. We've given you Bill and Hillary.

But we have left our music, the kind the South Carolina-based Swingin' Medallions still plays with great feeling and just the right amount of showmanship for a group that didn't riot when it was announced the bar was closing down at 10:30.

It was a nice party and nobody is young enough to jump in the pool anymore. Marvelous. Simply marvelous.

Lewis Grizzard

Country Willie Has Forsaken
His Heritage

I was a Willie Nelson fan before most of today's Willie Nelson fans ever heard of Willie Nelson.

If you still haven't heard of Willie Nelson, you are seriously out of touch, but I will explain anyway. He currently is one of country music's most celebrated artists, whose appeal crosses over to almost every sort of audience.

He even made a successful album of songs your parents snuggled to when they were kids. "All of Me" and "Springtime in Vermont," for example, were songs Willie sang on his album, "Stardust."

Yeah, I go way back with Willie. Back to when people would throw rocks at you and not invite you to their parties if you confessed to a musical leaning toward anything or anybody out of Nashville.

I first heard of him as a writer of music. Some terrific old songs: "Funny How Time Slips Away," "Crazy," "The Night Life."

But then Willie started singing, too, and listening to that rather odd style of his—he almost talks songs at times—became one of my steady habits.

Willie sang songs like "Bloody Mary Morning" and "Mountain Dew," but he was just another Nashville hayseed until something about him suddenly began to appeal to the masses. The rest is millions of dollars' worth of history.

I have seen Willie perform live on any number of occasions. Once, in the back yard of the White House. It was a Southern sort of occasion. They served corn bread and cold beer, and as Willie did "Georgia On My Mind," a friend of mine, a true son of the South, turned and whispered to me: "My great-great-grandfather was wounded at Gettysburg and had to walk all the way back home to Fayette County, Georgia, after the war. If he were here to-night, he'd think we by-God won it."

Another friend and I were into deep fascination with Willie late one evening in my friends's living room. The womenfolk had gone to bed.

We were listening to Willie's incredible rendition of the hymn, "Precious Memories." My friend, quite se-riously, said to me: "Promise me something. Promise if I die before you do, you'll make sure somebody plays Willie Nelson singing 'Precious Memories' at my funeral."

I promised. And he promised to do the same for me.

"Thinking about Willie singing," said my friend, "sort of makes you look forward to it, don't it?" I need to go on with the point here, and this is it: When Willie left Nashville for Texas and proclaimed himself an "outlaw," that was OK by me.

When I went to a Willie Nelson concert in a big hall and the smell of smoke was deeper than the smell of beer, I figured: The times, they are a-changin'.

When I listened to hard rock creep into some of Willie's used-to-be-classic country arrangements, I stood for that, too.

And when Willie grew a beard ("just to see what the rednecks would do"), tied on a headband and started wearing an earring, I accepted all that as well. If Willie Nelson wants to put odd things in his ears, or in his nose, that is his business.

But enough is enough, and designer blue jeans with Willie Nelson's name sewn onto a back pocket is enough. They are available—"Willie" jeans—I read the other day.

Think about it. Calvin Klein. Gloria Vanderbilt. Vidal Sassoon. And now, Willie Nelson, forever yours in designer denim. For the record, they used to call Willie Nelson "Country Willie."

Precious memories. How they linger.

EDITOR'S NOTE: "Precious Memories" was sung at Lewis Grizzard's funeral, not by Willie Nelson but by hundreds of friends, fans and family members.